TOUCH 'EM ALL

Short Stories and Observations from America and its Pastime

TRAVIS PARKER SMITH

Touch 'Em All
Short Stories and Observations from America and its Pastime

ISBN for Print Edition: 978-1-7335837-0-1
ISBN for eBook: 978-1-7335837-2-5

Cover art and map by Jennifer Smart

Based on the true story of the 2011 Seattle Ballpark Boys.

———————————————

To Kendal Young, Kellan Larson, Jack Wilson,
and Ruben Palmer, for the obvious;

To our parents, for their eternal assistance and being crazy
enough to let their kids be crazy;

To Oma and Opa, for accurately reminding
me that this book was a must;

To the many people who helped us along the way;

And to Edgar Martinez, for his wonderful charity,
for a well-deserved Hall of Fame selection,
and for saving baseball in Seattle.

Oh, and to the Mariners…may you someday
make the playoffs again.

LINEUP CARD

Comerica Park 11
Progressive Field 19
Great American Ballpark 21

Miller Park 7
Wrigley Field 6
U.S. Cellular Field 8

Fenway Park 17
Citi Field 16
Yankee Stadium 14
Citizens Bank Park 15
Camden Yards 20
Nationals Park 18

SunLife Stadium

Rogers Centre 13
PNC Park 12
19
11
21
Turner Field 22
Tropicana Field 23
26

7
6 8
9
Busch Stadium

5
Target Field
10
Kauffman Stadium

Minute Maid Park
24

Coors Field 4
Rangers Ballpark
25

Chase Field 3

Safeco Field 30
Oakland Coliseum
28
29
AT&T Park
2 1
27

Dodger Stadium 2
Angel Stadium 1
Petco Park 27

PRE-GAME ANNOUNCEMENT

Travel is a drug. Once you've experienced your first trip, the effects of it soon kindle a serious addiction—suddenly, you find yourself obsessing over memories of what you saw and the emotions you felt, all fueled by a subtle uncertainty of whether or not those things were real. Did that actually happen? Of course it did.

. . . Right?

As is the case with any drug, the highs of travel are easy to spot: postcard images of far off places are always attainable, wild experiences the likes of which you could rarely have at home certainly abound, and, if you're open to them, novel interactions with people you never thought you'd meet seem to pop up around every corner. But travel addicts, like drug addicts, often get blinded by the highs. Craving a return to this nomadic ecstasy, they revel only in such images, experiences, and interactions, and frequently overlook what you have to trudge through to attain these wonderful moments. For alongside the highs, travel brings with it plenty of lows—lows can be utterly devastating. Time away from home, living out of a suitcase, and quarantined exposure to a small assortment of individuals can weigh heavy on your spirit and quickly trigger an onset of depression. We've all had moments where we were struck by homesickness, longed for something other than a meal out, and grew tired of the people we were on the road with. Travel isn't just happiness and bliss.

The 2011 baseball trip that Andrew, Michael, Frazier, and I completed wasn't just happiness and bliss. Instead, it stood at the intersection of well organized and utterly chaotic. It was always hot outside and we were always cold toward each other. It was wonderful and it was awful. Ah to hell with it: it was the best of times, it was the worst of times. (Damn it, Dickens). The journey's mercurial nature meant that its memoir—this book—isn't all happiness and bliss, either. Such a narrative mood would be a disservice to what the four of us went through that summer, and misrepresent the realities of travel overall; you'd close this book thinking that our journey was nothing but comical moments on the road, fun facts about baseball, and quirky anecdotes about a faulty vehicle. These enjoyable memories of course took place, but like any journey with your friends, there were plenty of negative ones as well. And I feel that in any travel story, fact or fiction, it's necessary to elaborate on the punishing moments just as much as the positive moments. Not only does this paint a more realistic picture of life on the road, but it also gives stronger validation to the highs of travel; such euphoria is even more appreciated once you come to grips with its darker side and understand that you have to persevere through the ugly times if you are to celebrate the beautiful ones.

As you read this book, I'll bet your mood goes up and down and up and down and up and down. If so, good! That's what travel's *really* like. But even with that, I'll also bet you still emerge with a desire to travel nonetheless . . . because in the end, the highs are so worth the lows. Despite fully recognizing its many drudgeries and depressions, I'm still a proud advocate for the drug of travel. I use it all the time.

PLAYER INTRODUCTIONS

A Few Days after Returning

The cleanup process that was necessary to revive our old camper took far longer than expected. Or rather, our idiocy proved far less capable of *estimating* the time required as we stood outside The Van and looked in at its utterly ravaged interior. I mean, that thing was a mess. Clothes, food wrappers, baseball tickets, and everything in between lay strewn about the vehicle; it looked like a page from an *I Spy* book. I had forgotten that the car's floor was carpeted. Frazier folded his arms, staring at a cheap cowboy hat that poked out from behind the driver's seat. It had a large maroon *TC* stamped on the front.

"Where did that thing come from?" he asked.

"What?" Michael replied, his eyes also lost in the mess that had accrued within the walls of that 1999 Volkswagen Eurovan after the thing had somehow rolled over fourteen thousand miles in only fifty-three days.

"The cowboy hat."

"Oh." It took him ten seconds to locate it. "Minnesota, I think."

"How's it you've always got such a good memory?"

"The TC is the Twins' logo. So I'm assuming we got it at Target."

"Target?"

"Target Field."

"Oh. Yeah, OK. That was a cool ballpark."

"Wasn't it raining that night?"

"I dunno. How would *I* remember that? Hey, Andy—was it raining in Minnesota?"

"Uh," Andrew said from the other side of car, where I'm pretty sure he was taking a piss onto the curb. "Was that the night I punched you?"

"No, that was New York."

"Right."

"I'm still gonna hit you back for that someday, by the way."

"Whatever," Michael said, restoring order as always and returning everyone's attention to The Van's entropic contents. "How long do we think it's going to take to clean this thing up?"

I poked my head through the car's sliding door and looked around.

"Looks like a few hours to me."

"Yeah," Andrew replied, zipping up his pants and joining the rest of us. He quickly glanced inside and shrugged. "I say we do it tomorrow afternoon. All those in favor?"

"Yep."

"Yep."

"Yep."

Three weeks later, we finally removed the last thing from the innards of that vehicle. As I said: far longer than expected—or at least what the teenage brain expects. Any sane person would have taken a look at The Van and said, with the utmost seriousness: "I'll shave my head if you four idiots can get this thing clean in a week," and surely seven days would pass and they would walk away with just as much hair as before.

We weren't idiots. But my god did we try hard to be at times. I can barely look back on that summer odyssey without shaking my head critically—yet at the same time still emitting a smirk of appreciation for the beautiful thing that is juvenile naiveté. From ignoring a clear burgeoning issue with our car until the point when it practically exploded and left us at the hands of a coked-out tow truck driver in Florida, to the time when Andrew became petrified of getting eaten by a big black dog, to letting a total stranger simply hop in and join us for a few days, that journey provided endless examples of innocent ignorance. Juvenile naiveté. Most would just call it stupidity.

Not that the whole thing had sprung out of stupidity, though. A journey of that nature doesn't just emerge from nothing. But I do have to give us credit where credit is due: we etched that thing out of nothing. A year before we departed, such a trip wasn't even on our radar.

One Year Earlier

Andrew's basement was the de facto location for our collective friendship. A dingy, light-challenged room equipped with a television, a computer, two couches, and a beanbag chair, it provided a natural home for regular teenage activity: watching sports, eating junk food, and actively doing nothing. It was also the site of the inspiration for this trip. We had all been watching a Mariners game down there when Frazier, examining a map of the United States on the wall, wondered aloud: "Where's the next closest ballpark to us?"

"Oakland," Michael replied from behind the computer. "Lemme look it up." He typed in a few letters before replying. "Yeah, Oakland."

"Whoa. How far away is that?"

"Hang on." More typing. "Eight hundred miles."

"*Eight hundred?*" Frazier responded, his eyes now staring at the ceiling. "Wow, we've gotta be the most isolated stadium in the MLB."

"Hang on," Michael said again, punching more key words into Google before waiting a few seconds. This was 2010; the internet wasn't all that fast in those days, and I think that the last time the old Dell in Andrew's basement had gone through a software update, America was still counting Bush vs. Gore votes. "Yep, we are. By a long shot."

"Huh. Maybe that explains why I've never been to a game at a ballpark that isn't Safeco Field."

"Neither have I," Michael replied, and I voiced a third in accordance.

"Me neither," Andrew said, rounding out the group.

And like that, it began. Furious planning, projecting mileage, and estimating costs to get a better idea of the logistics it would require to pull off seeing not just one other but *all* other Major League Baseball stadiums that following summer, after we would graduate from high school. Kitchen tables sat covered with papers for weeks, the product of the dozens of mock trips we made, using the MLB schedules of the past few years to get a feel for what was possible and what was not within the time frame of early July and mid-August.

A note: juvenile naiveté assumes most things are possible.

"Think we can do that drive in a day?" I asked, my eyes widening slightly as I clicked *zoom out* six times to get Seattle and Los Angeles in the same image on MapQuest (MapQuest!). It was now early September 2010, and the MLB schedules for the upcoming year had just been released. The best route we could determine was totally nonsensical: a plummet straight down to Los Angeles followed by a slow curve up to the Midwest, a few loop the loops in the Northeast, a trickle down to the South, a long jaunt west on Interstate 10, and then a retracing of our original descent on Interstate 5 to return home to Seattle.

It was a confusing route, but it had to be like this. We wanted to see a game in every single Major League Baseball stadium, and baseball teams don't play in their own ballparks every night. So we had to find a date when the team in question played at home. And then we would often have to move that date because of when the home team in the closest city *after* that played next—but then the team in the *next* closest city was on the road for two and a half weeks and we'd have to redraw our route, erasing the penciled-in date next to the original city and yada, yada, yada. Where were we? Boston? No. Denver. As I said: confusing. Seattle to Los Angeles in a day was our first step, and Andrew's answer to my question set the tone for our highly optimistic estimations when it came to time and what our bodies (and car) could handle.

"Huh?"

"Think we could do here to LA in a day?" I restated.

"Oh. How long is it?"

"Almost twelve hundred miles."

"Oh for *sure* we could."

Thus, our schedule developed as a product of inexperienced confidence over anything else. If we thought we could do Seattle to Los Angeles in twenty-four hours, then we could definitely cover Tampa to Houston in two-thirds of that time and Kansas City to Detroit in even less. By the time December 2010 rolled around, we had etched out a route that fit with the following season's schedule. Andrew and Frazier were set to graduate from high school on June 10; we would leave immediately the next morning and spend the following fifty-three days on the road.

Thirteen Days before Departing

That trip was a kitchen table dream that quickly became a reality beyond what we had ever originally planned. We had each saved a few thousand dollars through working high school jobs, but our collective sums wouldn't cover all the costs. So, blinded by youthful confidence, we partnered with a local charity and ran a campaign to raise money, pledging to donate all funds we did not use on the trip's necessities: gas, tickets, and food. Our Mariners affection led us to the Martinez Foundation, a nonprofit started by Seattle baseball legend—and Hall of Fame inductee—Edgar Martinez that goes to support teachers in underserved communities in the Pacific Northwest.[i] We printed out hundreds of brochures, launched a website that hosted a continuous pledge drive, and canvassed at each ballpark—and are incredibly proud (and at times amazed) to say that we raised over $10,000 for Edgar's foundation by the time all was said and done.

Pause.

For the purpose of reader enjoyment, the majority of this book strays from our fund-raising and instead focuses on our encounters with baseball stadiums and life on the road. Our efforts for the Martinez Foundation were ongoing throughout—and indeed appear in this collection at times—but their exposure is minimized in hopes of avoiding narrative repetition.

Resume.

The elephant in the room was, of course, how we would actually travel between the stadiums. We tinkered with the idea of taking trains, but this was quickly eliminated as the cost estimates began to skyrocket. A car it would have to be—but what type of car? True to the prone-to-overlook mind-set of eighteen-year-olds, we planned everything out *before* fitting this key piece of the puzzle into place and were thirteen days away from

---

[i] The Martinez Foundation has now entrusted its mission to the Technology Access Foundation.

departing in Andrew's 2008 Honda when what seemed like the perfect option flashed across Craigslist.

"1999 Volkswagen Eurovan," Michael said, as we crowded around the Dell to take a look. "Automatic. Pop-top."

"Ooh, so we can sleep on the road?" I asked.

"Looks like it."

"That'll probably be necessary, huh? I think four dudes sleeping in Andy's CRV would get old after a while." I still shudder when I think about what that would've been like.

"How much?" Frazier asked.

"Sixteen."

"Sixteen thousand?"

"No, sixteen dollars," Andrew replied.

"Wha—"

"*Yes,* sixteen thousand, you idiot. What'd you think we were buying, a *toy* camper?"

"I don't know . . . you said sixteen—"

"Shut up."

We bought that vehicle after barely even looking at it, taking out a decent loan and vowing to sell it upon returning home—a feat that we somehow pulled off, selling the old camper to some travel fanatic for the exact price we had originally purchased it for. To whoever that was: I'm sorry.

. . .

Andrew Clement, Frazier Moore, Michael Gonzalez, and I had grown up within ten blocks of each other in the Queen Anne area of Seattle, Washington. While our childhood bonds were forged out of proximity and drifted between local athletic fields, home basements, and cheap burger joints, one place in particular solidified our friendships: Safeco Field, the home of Seattle

Mariners baseball.[ii] Living within walking distance of the ball-park, we attended over forty games a year, often deciding to go just thirty minutes before first pitch. I can remember my home phone ringing on Tuesday nights in early May 2009 and picking up to hear Michael's voice on the other line.

"You done with homework?"

"Yeah."

"Cool. M's?"

"Sure. Meet up in five?"

"Sounds good."

We grew up on seven-dollar bleacher tickets, ballpark hot dogs, and jingles from the PA system. We knew the walkup songs of every player and were often singing them before that batter was even announced. Even when we were not at the ballpark, we were in Andrew's basement watching the games on television, living and breathing the life of a die-hard Seattle Mariners fan.

And when you consider yourself a die-hard Seattle Mariners fan, you die a lot.

Our always-abysmal baseball team regularly flunked and was sure to fail all expectations every season, despite the optimistic spoonfuls of "hope" that were given to us every spring training by similarly upbeat Seattle sports writers. Here's a touch of perspective: Since becoming a team in 1977, the Mariners have made the playoffs four times. The New York Yankees, meanwhile, have made it twenty-four times in that same duration—including winning ten pennants and seven World Series. Now, there are a handful of teams that have never won it at all, but Seattle is one of only two that have never even *made* it to the World Series. And just to toss some salt into an already deep

---

[ii] The Mariners' ballpark has since had its name changed to T-Mobile Park. However, it will be referenced as Safeco Field throughout this book, as that is how it was in 2011 and continues to be in our hearts.

wound: the Mariners currently hold the longest postseason drought of any team—not only in baseball but also in the major five sports leagues in North America—at seventeen years and (quickly) counting.

Misery loves misery, the old adage goes. And when your favorite sports team constantly produces such misery as just listed, you need companions to cry with. Cue: our friend group. We celebrated manically during the team's occasional winning stretches and communally bemoaned the many, many losing streaks. We still do.

Andrew Clement was the rowdiest of the group, despite his initial appearance. His small physique and curly baby-blond hair always acted as a false front for those who met him and who soon discovered his personality to be one that enjoyed command and a verbal argument or two, which always had the uneasy potential to escalate into something physical. The best example of this came during his sophomore year in high school, when he punched the senior catcher on the baseball team for calling him short—an action that resulted in Andrew getting both a black eye and, through a strange series of consequential events, his first girlfriend. Andrew's attitude was never one of conscious anger or a yearning to fight; no, it was out of intense passion and protection. He was always the first to step up for "his boys" when something controversial arose. Nobody screamed more frustrated insults than Andrew did; nobody patted his buddy's back harder than Andrew did.

Frazier Moore was the foil to Andrew's energy. His long hair, laid-back mentality, and all-around "chill" vibe created a persona that was the relaxed yin to Andrew's intense yang. Always hesitant to react immediately, Frazier would often watch as Andy threw the proverbial first punch, to which he would most certainly have a critique or two to make—and would never hesitate to do so. It was always in good fun; Frazier's wit and love of the arts gave him a slightly different perspective on the world—a perspective that kept throwing us curveballs on the trip. He would often wander off to take hipster photos of things like brick walls, or sit and wait to be transcendentally inspired by something like an abandoned billboard. Sometimes he would simply disappear completely for a while.

Michael Gonzalez was the organized one. The son of an accountant, he inherited an appreciation for punctuality and meticulous analytics that showed through in every endeavor he undertook. His spreadsheets were the most detailed, his pitches for the Martinez Foundation were the most professional, and his thinking ahead saved us numerous times on the road. Michael monitored our spending, decided which roads to take, and declared departure times. He was the businessman of the trip, and we never doubted him for a second. Honestly, we hadn't doubted him since eighth grade, when he corrected the teacher on the proper way to solve a math problem. (We hadn't forgiven him for that either.)

I was very much the nervous one of the group. Having grown up as the most timid and thus most hesitant to do anything that might be illegal or audacious, I often took to the sidelines to observe events before cautiously stepping into them. Sometimes I didn't step into them at all. For example, early in high school, I received an invite to see one of my favorite bands, the Pogues, perform a rare show at the Showbox Theater in Seattle's Pike Place Market. But the concert was marketed at eighteen-plus and, fearful of breaking the law, I balked and never showed up. The Pogues have since stopped touring, and I've never forgiven myself for those cold feet. It was this trip—a moment in Detroit, to be precise—that completely wiped away my youthful apprehensiveness but not before placing me into a comfortable pattern of observing and recording, a combination of traits that understandably made me the documenter of our 2011 summer baseball peregrination.

Were you to find the four of us at a Mariners game, Andrew would be screaming at the umpire, complaining that the call was "bullshit" and that the runner was safe, even though replay showed that he was clearly out. Frazier would be calmly trying to convince us of any morsel of hope, resulting in pointless utterances, such as "Come on, guys. We can score seven in the ninth." Michael would be analyzing every move the manager made, potentially knowing the stats of the opposing players better than our current skipper. I would be keeping score.

So here is the scorecard of that summer. Instead of dragging you through one long and boring account, I have broken up our adventure into twenty-eight anecdotes that can be digested separately but that can also join together to tell the overarching narrative of us. As the book's subtitle suggests, this work is a collection of short stories and observations from America's roads and of America's pastime. Nearly each starts at one of the thirty major league ballparks, describing unique characteristics or perhaps going deeper into the histories behind the national cathedrals that are baseball stadiums. Some stories focus purely on baseball, perhaps offering a new perspective on that beautiful, beautiful sport through observations we made. Some stories do not mention baseball at all but instead recount an event that occurred along the way, perhaps offering a new perspective on this beautiful, beautiful country and its many different cultures. This book is not an expository work that evaluates each stadium, bringing you factoids, food suggestions, and price estimates—nor is it a guidebook for the country, offering you descriptions of customs that explain why things are the way they are. Nope: it's a chopped-up young adult travel story that is built around baseball.

And baseball has the uncanny ability to be wonderfully romantic. Yeah, that's a botched quote from *Moneyball*—but I'll echo it with the utmost sincerity. The nation's pastime is written in the annals of the nation's history, telling the story of this country alongside its athletic heroes. Baseball's origins date back over one hundred years, and the sport has woven itself into all of us, whether you recognize it or not. And best of all, baseball has a strange power to generate memorable, if not life-changing, stories for those who throw themselves into its welcoming arms.

This is ours.

TAKING THE FIELD

THE VAN

4:03 a.m. | Saturday, June 11

That first drive was a total disaster. It all started with our overly optimistic departure time: we set out at 4:00 a.m. from Seattle on the morning of Saturday, June 11, sticking to the prior assumption of *sure, we could definitely cover the twelve hundred miles to Los Angeles in a day*. We tossed our duffel bags into the back of the idling Volkswagen camper van, said a quick goodbye to our families, and pulled out of the driveway, resetting the odometer to zero before rolling the first few yards of the 14,171 miles we were about to cover in a little under two months. I was driving, Andrew was in the front seat, and Michael and Frazier were in the back.

"Who's that?" Frazier asked, looking out the rear window.

"Who?" Andrew replied.

"The girl next to your mom."

"Oh—that's Brigd, my family's Moldovan exchange student."

"You have a Moldovan exchange student?"

"Yeah, man."

"Why didn't you tell us?"

"I mean, she's the girl who's been staying at my house the past few months. You've met her like twenty times."

"Huh."

"Seriously, you don't remember?" Andrew twisted from the shotgun seat and stared back at Frazier. "She's, like, madly in love with me?"

"Why?"

Andrew turned back around and stared out the front. "Shut up, Frazier."

"I'm serio—"

"I said shut up."

This was the first discussion of the trip: small banter between Andrew and Frazier that would pave the way for plenty more arguments to come. It was, however, enough to distract us from the intimidation we each felt. We descended off Queen Anne Hill and moved toward the Interstate 5 junction, with Los Angeles programmed as our destination.

Ten seconds later, the sliding door of The Van popped open.

"Jesus!" Frazier yelled, springing up from his seat to try to push the heavy door shut. I slowed the camper down to a crawling ten miles per hour so that he could get enough leverage to do so as cars honked from behind us.

"How the hell'd that happen?" Andrew asked from the front, after hearing the click that indicated Frazier's success in latching the door back to its secure position.

"I dunno," I replied. "I took the on-ramp a little too fast, I guess."

"What were you going?"

"Thirty."

"Woof. What'd the caution sign say?"

"It said twenty-five," Michael answered from the back, referencing the yellow sign that accompanied the fairly sharp turn.

"Yikes," I said, "are we actually gonna have to abide by those things?" I had always looked at those signs more like super conservative suggestions than actual rules.

"I guess so," Michael replied, as The Van increased back to normal speed. "I guess . . . god, I guess we really don't know anything about how this car functions."

Truer words had never been spoken. The red 1999 Volkswagen Eurovan that we now found ourselves driving was completely and utterly foreign to us at this moment in time. As previously mentioned, we had found the vehicle fewer than two weeks ago on Craigslist—thirteen days, to be exact. A pooling of money and the extraction of a loan had allowed us to feel OK purchasing the car, under the assumption that we would try to sell it again when we returned in August later that summer. At eighteen years old, none of us really knew what we were supposed to be looking for in a vehicle, so we each pretended as if we knew a lot about cars while speaking with the seller. The guy was a dead ringer for Jerry Garcia, and he watched us lazily as we "inspected" the camper. Ten minutes later, we each nodded slowly and put on our best serious faces.

"Looks good to me," Frazier said.

"Yep," I replied. Andrew remained silent. Of the four of us, he had been the only one who hesitated on the idea of buying the camper, but he realized he was outnumbered as Michael spoke up next.

"Me too," Michael said, then turned toward the owner. "How many miles?"

"Uh," the old bearded man uttered, leaning his head inside the open driver's window and glancing at the odometer. "A little under 160,000."

Now 160,000 is simply a ton of miles for any vehicle to have rolled—but even *more* for something as delicate as an old camper. But hey, we were eighteen. One hundred sixty thousand miles sounded fine. The man could have said 260,000 and we most likely would have replied with the same answer:

"Cool. You guys good with it?"

"Yep."

"Yep."

"I guess."

"Sold."

Almost immediately, we brought the vehicle to a local mechanic to get it a basic tune-up before demanding its poor old engine to tack on 14,171 miles in a mere fifty-three days. Yet this meant that the car was in a mechanic's shop for well over a week, and we didn't actually see it again until Thursday, June 9—two days before our scheduled departure date. Therefore, returning to Michael's earlier statement, we had absolutely *zero* experience driving the thing, save to and from the auto shop. Mere residential commutes were barely under our belt: no highways, no speeds above fifty, no long drives through hot weather. In other words, everything we were about to encounter that summer was going to be a first and would probably lead to some mistakes—like taking the first freeway on-ramp just a bit too fast.

It was exactly what it sounds like: four high school graduates thinking they're hot stuff and in control of everything as they begin the culminating trip of their childhood but in reality are setting off on a round-the-country road trip without a clue as to the actual status or function of the large automobile that they merely assumed would carry them over fourteen thousand miles in the approaching two months.

Eh, we'll figure it out was the unfortunate mentality that developed among us, the product of groupthink whenever someone would bring up the highly likely possibility of a malfunction of some sort happening along the way. *We'll deal with that when it comes.* Optimism. Ignorant optimism.

Incident number two happened only ten minutes later. We had just recovered from the episode on the on-ramp when I began to descend a small hill somewhere past Renton and soon noticed we were humming along at eighty-two miles per hour in a sixty-five zone. Unfortunately at that same moment, a Washington State trooper also noticed us to be humming along at eighty-two miles per hour in a sixty-five zone.

"Oh god!" Andrew yelled from beside me, seeing the flashing lights in the rearview mirror. His voice cracked a bit as he then yelled: "Slow your tits down!" I followed with a chorus of similarly obscure curse words and pulled over onto the median that divided the freeway's north- and southbound lanes.

"License and registration, please," came the regular demand from the officer. His mustache was intimidatingly well groomed. "And please pull over to the right side of the road next time."

"Sorry," I said, stuttering and hoping there would not be a *next time*. The mustached man wasn't having any of it, however, and instead slapped a ticket into my hands in what felt like record time, informing me that it had to be postmarked within ten days.

"How much?" Frazier asked from the back, after snapping a few photos of the cop car through the rear window. He had purchased a nice Nikon DSLR for the journey, in hopes of capturing the places we saw, people we met, and roads we traveled—what he preferred to refer to as *visions of Americana*. Frazier had always loved photography, but it had not always loved him. A little over a year ago, he had quit his high school's photography club because it "took up too much of his time," but we each secretly suspected that it was actually because the club rarely published his images, which often leaned heavily toward experimental rather than traditional. "Your lines are off," the club's leader would say. "That's the point," Frazier would respond. I think part of his decision to purchase that Nikon was out of spite and to prove his ability. And even though I rarely understood the intended meaning behind his photos, I could appreciate that he had an eye for aesthetics and was a darn good photographer.

"One seventy-five," I grunted, replying to his initial question.

"Wow," Andrew replied, "that didn't take long. What's the odometer say?"

"Twenty point four miles."

"And what time is it?"

"Four twenty-five."

To my surprise, Andrew began laughing. "Holy hell," he said between chuckles. "Twenty point four miles, twenty-five minutes in, and we've already got a ticket. At this rate we're gonna get like three thousand."

"Oh shut up," I said, a slight grin now appearing on my face as well, forced there by seeing the ridiculousness of what had just happened. I flipped on the blinker and cautiously reentered traffic from the left. "But, I mean, we've never driven this thing on the highway," I continued. "I had no idea how top-heavy it was. Looks like we should just chill in the right lane from now on."

"Yo," Frazier interrupted, "did you actually say 'slow your tits down,' Andy?"

"I did," Andrew confirmed, patting The Van's dashboard like one would pat the head of a dog. "And you didn't listen, did you?"

We would often find ourselves speaking to The Van like this, referencing it as if it were another companion on the trip—because in all honesty, it was. That car had a personality, and it did not want to go unrecognized. The Van reacted to our angry exclamations, threw its own tantrums, and regularly acted in a manner that solidified it as being anthropomorphic. Vanthropomorphic, if you will.

Yet even with its seemingly archaic status as a functioning automobile, the old Eurovan had been a necessary investment for that trip. There were many gray areas regarding where we would be passing the upcoming evenings, and a bed on the road was necessary. The Van provided one. The interior of the vehicle consisted of two traditional seats up front, one backward-facing jump seat behind the driver, and a collapsible bench seat in the back that flipped down to morph into a horizontal pad that we generously called a mattress. Two could sleep here while the other two could pop the top of the camper and climb up to a similarly uncomfortable sleeping platform above. A screw-on table could be attached in front of the jump seat, but this was rarely used. I think we actually lost that table at one point. We lost a lot of things to The Van.

Each of us had packed one large duffel bag, in which we stored all our clothes and various things that would be necessary for two months on the road, such as contacts, sunglasses, and lots and lots of deodorant. While driving, we would toss these bags behind the upright bench seat that, when not flipped down, created an accessible trunk area like that of a station wagon. With us we also brought two light sleeping bags, two blankets, some pillows, one red lawn chair, one yellow lawn chair, a white Igloo cooler, a few baseball mitts, a few balls, a two-burner Coleman stove, a small pot, a tiny frying pan, and a minimal assortment of cups, plates, bowls, and cutlery. It sounded like a lot, but The Van could handle it.

Beneath the shotgun seat was a hidden compartment where we stored valuables, such as cash, our passports (because the Blue Jays exist), tickets to ballgames—you name it. Meanwhile, the jump seat sat above a small sliding container that we used as a food cupboard. It was always stocked with pasta, marinara sauce, chips, and a constantly rotating assortment of flavored sunflower seeds. The white, flat-topped Igloo cooler would regularly sit beside the jump seat and hold bags of ice, drinks, cold foods, and this soft plastic water jug thing that we simply called "the Jelly."

There were two other objects in The Van that, despite not originally being included in our list of things to bring, proved to be invaluable and pertinent to our success, enjoyment, and relief. The first was a Garmin GPS machine that Michael had discovered in his basement only two days before we took off. (This was 2011, when many teenagers—like us—still held flip phones, not the latest smartphones equipped with maps.) Suction-cupped to our dashboard for nearly every minute we were in motion, we named the GPS "Tina," an acronym of the first names of girls we had crushes on at the time. (This was 2011, when teenage romanticism was still as sappy as it is today.) This name actually felt appropriate, however, as we each quickly developed quite the relationship with the feminine-voiced Garmin; arguments and professions of love became common iterations among the four of us and our dashboard girlfriend.

The other item was a translucent plastic carton that was mainly rectangular in shape, apart from a circular hole three inches in diameter that protruded from the top at a forty-five-degree angle. Near the middle of it was a small handle that allowed us to hold the carton up to our waist while we relieved ourselves into its depths—which, we were surprised to discover, could hold about a half liter of urine. This on-the-go piss bottle had actually been gifted to us by a friend as an ironic donation to the trip, but we used it with alarming frequency.

OK, away from the pee and back to our car.

As previously mentioned, the vehicle was a 1999 Volkswagen Eurovan. It was red—that is, before we got to it. One of the local organizations that had gotten wind of what we were doing was an advertising agency that approached us about four days before we took off and inquired about supporting the

Martinez Foundation. However, the representative had said that he wanted to do it in a way that didn't involve money.

"What if we wrap it for ya?" the longhaired man had asked Michael.

"Sorry?"

"Your car. I'm assuming you're driving, correct?"

"Yeah. We're driving a camper."

"Here's what we'll do." The guy leaned in, as if he was negotiating some drug deal. "We'll take your car in and put a wrap on it. That way, everyone'll know what you're up to and what the Martin Found—"

"The Martinez Foundation."

"—what the Martinez Foundation is all about. Sound good?"

"Uh." What else was he going to say? "Sure."

It sounded good, but it did not end up looking good. Before the wrap job, The Van had indeed been red. But after, it was . . . well, it was difficult to say. Logos, dates, and words about baseball and our trip were splattered on every part of the vehicle, all slapped on top of a gigantic, poorly pixelated image of a baseball diamond. We were not driving a car; we were driving a piece of expressionist art. And a bad one at that.

"Huh . . . where's The Van?" someone would inevitably ask in a joking manner as we returned to a parking lot after a game, only to see our camper stick out like a sore thumb, unavoidably noticeable, submerged in a sea of neutral-colored sedans and SUVs. "Oh yeah, there it is. The peacock among pigeons."

With its storage, sleeping compatibility, handheld urinal, and Jackson Pollock-inspired design, the car of course needed a proper name. We toyed around with this for a while and chewed on a couple of options—but while doing so, each of us began to naturally reference the vehicle simply as "the van." Repetition without resistance prevailed, and our steed officially adopted this simple, two-syllable title. It was a superlative name in the highest degree; among all other vans out there on the road, ours was *the* van. With capital letters necessary to honor its official status, the car was and shall continue to be referenced as The Van.

The rainbow coating of The Van did, of course, make us quite a spectacle on the road. One of the first things we noticed as we continued motoring down Interstate 5—at sixty-five miles per hour, not eighty-two—was the number of people who honked at us. Nearly blinded by its clash of colors, drivers would obviously recognize our car and, after somehow comprehending what we were up to through deciphering the papier-mâché design, often shoot a thumbs-up as they passed by or approached us at a rest stop to strike up a conversation. As we descended through Oregon, some guy even pulled up the sleeve of his shirt to flash a massive Mariners tattoo at us.

"Hey!" Andrew said, giving the guy a wave in return. "That's some fan right there."

"We're better ones," Frazier answered from the back, showing a rare rise.

"I'm not saying we're worse, you ass," Andrew replied, showing a normal rise. "I'm just saying that a Mariners tattoo on your bicep is pretty dope." He then turned to me. "Also, why're you going so slow? Did the ticket take away your gas pedal?"

"I'm not!" I retaliated, turning my eyes down to the speedometer, only to discover that we were indeed now rolling at forty miles per hour and slowly descending in velocity. "What the . . . I'm not sure what happened. I hit cruise control, and—" I repeated the motion, gunning the car back to sixty-five and hitting the *Set Cruise* button, only to find our speed begin to drop again. "Uh. Does cruise control not work?"

"It should," Michael said, leaning his head up between the driver and passenger seats and checking out the console for himself. "Try it again." I did. Same result. "That's weird . . ." He then cut himself off. "Actually, come to think of it, I don't know if we ever tested the cruise control."

"Huh?"

"I don't think we ever tried it. We only drove this thing a few miles before today, and it was just to and from the mechanic, pretty much. No freeways or long roads where we might've needed to use cruise control."

A beat of silence passed through the car as we each digested Michael's words.

"So," I said, trying to gauge what this meant moving forward. "We're about to drive over fourteen thousand miles—on nothing but long stretches of freeway—in a car that has to be manually monitored every foot it rolls in order to keep its speed?"

"It would appear so," Michael confirmed.

In a simple, sudden movement, Andrew leaned forward and banged his head against the dashboard. "You're already proving your uselessness!" he yelled at The Van. "What *else* do you have in store?" The Van muttered something in response to this, but I couldn't make out what it was.

"Hey, don't talk to The Van like that," Frazier countered, defending the car. "It's still new to the group." Andrew whipped around immediately.

"Frazier," he said, taking care to pronounce each syllable diligently. "When you are departing on a road trip that demands that you cover long distances for extended periods of time, something like cruise control is *extremely* ideal to monitor your speed." Andrew had a tendency to turn to this technical, almost legal tone when arguing. It was annoying. "It's a heavy vehicle, and it's extremely easy to lose track of how fast it's going. I mean, we've already seen that happen once, haven't we?" I elected not to respond. Andrew sat back in his chair and turned his head toward the passenger window. "I knew we shouldn't have bought this thing," I heard him mutter.

"What?" I asked.

"Nothing." He then leaned forward and began messing with the dashboard console. "I'm hot—let's turn on the AC." Yet after a few seconds, he turned to me. "Where is it?"

"Where is what?"

"The air-conditioning button."

"Oh, I think it's . . ." I twisted my head to look at the buttons. "It's . . . actually, I have no idea where it is."

"Do we even have AC?"

"We may not, come to think of it."

I could feel him about to explode next to me. But whatever angry exclamation he was about to erupt into was quickly swallowed up, and he then began speaking in a manner that was far too calm and upbeat for his current mood. I could read right through the happy-go-lucky tone.

"Oh look at us. Nothing but fifteen-hour drives ahead! Yes, sir. Fifteen-hour drives on looonnng interstates that will take us through places like, oh I don't know, Arizona, Florida, and Texas, in the middle of summer! I wonder what the weather is gonna be like in *those* states. What'ya think—ninety-nine? A hundred and nine? No cruise control, no air-conditioning . . . swell. Yeah, this car's totally ready for this journey."

I tuned him out by rolling down the window and letting the wind whip through The Van. It was uncomfortable, it was loud—but it was looking like the way it would have to be for the following fifty-three days.

As The Van trickled its way down past the Oregon-California border and into the northern part of the Golden State, we began to install a series of driver rotations. By 7:00 p.m., I was sitting in the jump seat facing backward and looking out over the rolling hills that caressed the horizon of the town of Los Banos when the group determined it was time to stop for food. And where do teenagers decide sounds like a good place to have their inaugural dinner?

"Ah, *Lay Dennay*," Frazier mumbled, pronouncing the name with a French accent in mockery of its utter American-ness. We were already turning into a billboard for US roadside cuisine, having adjourned at a rest stop Starbucks for breakfast, a McDonald's for lunch, and now a Denny's for dinner. "Yum."

The dull yellow glow of the restaurant's sign barely illuminated the parking lot as we locked up The Van and walked in. Despite the thirty or so tables in the establishment, we were the only ones in there. As we made our way to a corner booth, a Shakira song played loudly over the speakers, starkly contrasting the rest of the atmosphere in the plain diner. The waitress didn't even say anything when she came over to take our orders. She just stood there with a small pad of paper.

"Uh," I said, interpreting her gesture correctly. "I'll have the chicken sandwich."

"Spaghetti," Andrew replied tartly.

"Me too," Michael said, beginning to collect the menus for the waitress.

"I'll try the *Bacon Slamburger*," Frazier uttered, nodding his head in interest at the menu like one does when selecting a bottle of wine. The girl nodded and walked away, silent to the bone.

"The what, Frazier?" Andrew asked, disgusted.

"I dunno. It's something that looks like breakfast food in a burger."

"Ugh, man."

"Hey, when at *Lay Dennay* . . ."

The background music soon shifted to Usher, and our food came out far too quickly for anyone's comfort. Whatever—we were hungry. Frazier bit into his *Slamburger* and contorted his face into a confusing expression. It looked like he was in pain—but enjoying it.

"This is the nastiest thing I've ever eaten," he said, "but also disturbingly good. I have to finish it." He took another bite, only to have a little bit of egg squirt out the back and fly across the table into Andrew's eye.

"Yuck!" Andrew yelled, the exclamation flying around the empty Denny's. "What the hell was that?"

"Egg," Frazier replied between mouthfuls of *Slamburger*. "Sorry 'bout that."

The rest of the dinner passed without much conversation as Michael, Frazier, and I awkwardly listened to Andrew swear under his breath while attempting to rub the soggy bit of egg out of his pupil. By the time we got up to leave, a Ricky Martin tune had overtaken the restaurant's speakers. We exited and returned to The Van, grateful to be leaving the place.

"Hey, did we leave the brake lights on?" Frazier asked as we approached the colorful car. It took the rest of us a couple of seconds to comprehend what he was saying—but sure enough, The Van's brake lights were fully illuminated, despite Michael holding the keys in his hand.

"Huh," Andrew said, his eye now egg-free. "Is there even a way *to* leave them lit without the car being on?"

"I don't think so," Michael replied, opening the driver's door. "Here. I'll try starting it and let's see what happens." He did, but the brake lights remained lit.

"Try hitting the brakes," I yelled over the chugging engine. No change.

It was only after a couple of restarts and some messing around with the wiring beneath the steering wheel that we realized that The Van's brake lights had *never* turned off. Not once. We had driven it the whole way down from Seattle with them constantly illuminated, never showing cars behind us when we were slowing down. But this was yet another product of our lack of knowledge of the vehicle we were driving: we had never taken it out at night. The few times we had driven it in Seattle *before* leaving earlier that morning had been during the day, and we must have simply overlooked the constantly illuminated brake lights because it was light outside.

"Oh god," Frazier said, as we each comprehended this bit of idiocy. "That ain't good."

"No, it's not," Michael confirmed. "It's illegal to drive without working brake lights—whether they're on or off. Nobody can tell when you're slowing down. We might've been driving this way since we bought The Van."

Andrew turned away, and once more I heard him mutter something about regretting the purchase of the vehicle. I chose to ignore it. Frazier, who apparently hadn't noticed this, began speaking again.

"Another problem is that the brake lights always being on will definitely drain our battery. It's like leaving the cabin light on, right? Slowly it'll trickle the battery's level down . . ." His eyes then widened as he turned to me. "God, the engine might be dead right now!"

"Michael just started it, man."

"Oh . . . yeah. Well still, it could die at any moment when we kill it for a long period of time." This was true. Michael opened the driver's door again and leaned back in, fumbling with the wires beneath the steering wheel. After about a minute, he spoke.

"If I disconnect these wires, the lights should turn off." He did so, and the brake lights indeed cut out. "But the problem is, we can't start the engine this way." He twisted the key, but The Van made no response. Yet after he reconnected the wires and tried the ignition again, the car roared to life once more.

"All right," Frazier said, nodding his head in an encouraging manner. "This is good! We have a way to save our battery. Maybe this is simply how we'll have to do it for the rest of the trip."

"What, perform a gymnastics maneuver to fit beneath the steering wheel in order to disconnect a cable every time we stop and then do the same process whenever we want to get going again?"

"Yeah . . ."

For a brief second, we actually considered it. Thank god for Andrew, who voiced the sanity we each needed to hear right then and there.

"Nope," he said. "No way in *hell* are we going to do that. First off, it's a stupid thing to have to do—did you see the way Michael bent to reach those wires? Nuh-uh. Second, you guys forgot that plugging them back in means that they're *always* on. That means we'd be driving the next two months with no functioning brake lights while on the road. No, let's get this fixed."

"Oh yeah," I said, now recognizing the fault in that option. "Yeah, you're totally right. What do we propose?"

An awkward pause followed this statement, as none of us knew what on earth the first step toward fixing such a problem might be. The Van's light panting seemed to be the only noise in Los Banos as we each silently mulled over the problem while the lifeless yellow glow of the Denny's sign formed fuzzy silhouettes of our bodies on the cracked pavement of the parking lot.

"I say we figure this out when we get to Los Angeles." It didn't matter who said it—we were all thinking it. "All in favor?"

"Yep."

"Yep."

"Yep."

Eh, we'll figure it out later. Surely shoving this substantial issue under the rug was definitely the best way to deal with it right now. We each climbed back into The Van, feeling as if we had solved the problem. If we had made it fourteen hours without our brake light malfunction being noticed by a police officer, we could certainly make it to Los Angeles. It was only three hundred more miles through the middle of the night.

TOP OF THE FIRST
Angel Stadium

CARPOCALYPSE

2:15 p.m. | Sunday, June 12

Somewhere on the outskirts of Los Angeles, in a funky place called Anaheim, stands a ballpark that subtly masks its age. Believe it or not, Angel Stadium is the fourth oldest field in the majors, trailing only Fenway Park, Wrigley Field, and its crosstown rival, Dodger Stadium. Opened in 1966, the fifty-three-year-old yard sits in the middle of a concrete oasis of parking lots only a block off Interstate 5, the likes of which we had already seen enough of after driving on it for nearly twenty-four hours. The only thing outside the stadium that is not a parking lot or a freeway is a gigantic red *A* with a round wheel atop it that lights up whenever the Angels win. The structure is the team's logo (apparently the wheel is a halo), but really it looks more like a large sign advertising fast food—something you would see at an In-N-Out or a McDonald's along the highway.

I still don't know whether the Angels are the California Angels, the Los Angeles Angels, the Anaheim Angels, or the Los Angeles Angels of Anaheim—but their ballpark is officially called "Angel Stadium of Anaheim," and it has always been a sea of red. True to their home team's main color, fans flock to the stadium in their Angels T-shirts and jerseys, the majority of which are this classic primary hue. When the stands are packed, it makes for quite the impressive sight.

The ballpark's main feature is a rock collection in left center field that is topped with a trickling fountain. The ballpark's second main feature is a stuffed monkey. Yep. Angel fans simply love this thing (it's a small sock puppet that's shaped generously like a primate), and they bring it to the stadium and whirl it around whenever the team is down and in need of a few runs to make the game interesting. This tradition started back in 2000, when the ballpark's video board operators showed a clip of the monkey from *Ace Ventura* jumping about as the bottom of the ninth approached and the Angels were down by a run. The team scored two, won the game, and that was that.[1] Nineteen years later, the "rally monkey" is now not only a fan favorite but also has evolved into the unofficial mascot of the Anaheim/Los Angeles/California team, and it can be purchased at nearly every concession stand at the stadium. We bought one at a hot-dog joint almost immediately and made our way to the nosebleed seats somewhere in the upper deck above the right-field foul pole, giddy to take in the game as locals.

6:30 a.m. | The Following Morning

Twice on the trip, we awoke to someone tapping on the window of The Van. The first happened early the next morning, Monday the thirteenth, as the sunlight greeted the West Coast to find our polychromatic camper parked, with the top popped up, on a peaceful street in Beverley Hills in front of a house that might have been a resort.

Tap, tap, tap.

It took Frazier a minute to rustle himself awake. "Hello?" he said, sliding open the side door of The Van while rubbing the sleep out of his eyes and doing his best to calm down his shoulder-length locks. Frazier's hairstyle was a mercurial one. At times it was a work of art, up there with the best of male celebrities who could pull off the ponytail; at others it was a nesting place for insects and small birds. Regardless, it was normally enough to make people's eyes widen—but on this instance, it was Frazier's eyebrows that rose as he came face-to-face with an older woman in an all-pink jogging suit. She was out walking her dog, a large white poodle with a matching pink bow wrapped around its neck. The dog was urinating onto the sidewalk, completely ignoring the patch of grass that stood only two feet away.

"What are you doing?" the woman asked, one hand on her hip while the other held the dog's leash. She did not notice the puddle of pee that was growing closer and closer to her (also pink) Nike shoe. That, or she consciously chose to ignore it.

"Uh," Frazier replied, still trying to wipe the cobwebs of fatigue out of his mind. I couldn't help but smile as I took in the scene from the back of The Van: Frazier had lost the battle against his hair, which stuck up in the back and cascaded down his face in the front, covering his still-droopy eyes. He totally clashed against the ritzy-looking woman with her pink jogging suit and poodle. "We got in late last night and decided to sleep here."

"You can't sleep here," the woman said promptly. "This is a prestigious area, and we can't have vagabonds just sleeping on the side of the road." She pronounced *prestigious* with four syllables. From my perch behind Frazier, I vomited slightly into my mouth.

"Vagabonds?" Frazier blankly responded.

"Yes. Vagabonds." And without delay, she spun on her heel and walked away, leaving the puddle of pee for us to enjoy.

"All right," Frazier said, staring after her. "Welcome to Los Angeles, I guess."

"Where are we, even?" Andrew asked, sticking his head down from the upper area of The Van.

"Beverly Hills," Michael answered next to him. The two of them had slept up top while Frazier and I had crashed below.

"Why did we come here again?"

"Because we wanted somewhere quiet, unlike last night."

He was right. After departing the Denny's in Los Banos two nights ago, we didn't arrive in Los Angeles until roughly 3:30 a.m. the following morning. Unsure of our ability to merely camp on LA streets, we had instead pulled into the parking lot of an El Pollo Loco fast-food restaurant somewhere in the northern outskirts of the city and slept there. None of us were too keen on doing that again, however, as we had awoken to food wrappers tucked into our wheels and beneath our wiper blades.

"Ah," Andrew responded, the memory coming back to him. "Fair." He leaped down from the top and shifted into the driver's seat, eager to get out of Beverly Hills and away from further encounters with the *prestigious* pink woman. The rest of us were onboard with this sentiment, and Michael lowered the roof of The Van while Andrew twisted the keys in the ignition—but nothing happened.

"What?" he yelled, panic rising in his voice. "We aren't starting!"

"Brake lights, bro," Frazier said between yawns.

"Ah. Yeah."

After Andrew squeezed himself beneath the wheel and plugged the brake cables back in, we pulled out of Beverley Hills, hoping to never see it again. After the ball game the day before, we had been able to make an appointment at an auto electrician for later this morning in hopes of fixing our light problem. Traffic delayed us and we were a good thirty minutes late, but the mechanic agreed to take us anyway. We drove The

Van around back, entered the shop's brightly lit lobby, and waited, seated on black folding chairs.

"How many times do you think we'll be in one of these places this trip?" Andrew asked.

"What do you have against The Van?" Frazier replied sharply.

"Nothing! I was just merely postulating. C'mon—over or under three?"

"Stop it, Andrew."

"Over," Michael interjected, much to Frazier's disappointment. I could tell that he was also slightly uneasy at The Van's early signs of malfunctioning; two days into the journey and we were already at the mechanic. His cynicism wasn't quite at the level of Andrew's, but a touch of it was definitely there.

"Under," I said, trying to even out the group and show some optimism. (Frazier and I would go on to lose that bet.)

Yet this particular visit was quite easy, as only fifteen minutes passed before the technician reappeared and informed us that the car was ready. We paid, left a handful of Martinez Foundation brochures on the lobby's table, and reentered Los Angeles, now with fully functioning brake lights. It felt like a fresh start for our relationship with The Van. To celebrate, we sat in another hour and a half of LA traffic.

"This is absurd," Andrew voiced, looking at the endless rows of taillights that stretched out in front of us on whatever freeway we were now on. "Is it always like this?"

While our alien status to the city meant that none of *us* could answer this question, we soon met a man who apparently could. After the touristic urge got the best of us, we made our way to Venice Beach, where the afternoon sun soon found us sitting on a concrete median, watching a conveyor belt of oddballs walk by. After about thirty minutes, a man carrying a small briefcase soon approached us. He was fairly tall and pale skinned, with dark-brown dreadlocks that dangled across his face. His eyes were barely visible through yellow-tinted circular sunglasses that had golden frames, and his silver briefcase was untouched save for a single Bob Marley sticker slapped slightly off-center on one side. Although the guy might have been a fish out of water in most places, he swam with the rest of the school of quirky individuals we had been staring at for the past half hour. We didn't even notice him until he walked up and stood directly in front of us for a good ten seconds, during which nobody uttered a word.

"I'm a true Venetian," he then said, breaking the incredibly awkward silence.

"Sorry?" Frazier replied. His inquiry was apparently enough to engage the guy fully, for he walked over and sat beside Frazier on the median.

"Venice," he said, gesturing at the surf shops, taco stands, and people who continued to buzz, indifferent to us visitors and our new acquaintance. "Nobody is from here. They all come here to skate, shop, smoke a little pot, and stretch out before the waves." He spoke with a relaxed tone that barely fluctuated in volume but still had a weird, mysterious ring to it. Like a melodramatic wizard.

"Right."

"I'm *from* here." He pointed down the street at a small shop called the Venice Smoke Shack. "I was born there."

"You were born in the Smoke Shack?"

"Yes. Well, it wasn't that when I was born. Used to be a house."

"OK."

"Where are *you* from?" It was tough to see through the heavy yellow tint of the guy's sunglasses, but I don't think he had blinked yet.

"Uh, Seattle," Frazier responded.

"Ooh, the great Northwest." The man raised his head toward the sun, allowing his long spools of hair to drop down from his shoulders and hang freely, almost touching the concrete on which he sat. "I wandered up there once. Wonderful place. I'd go back if I could."

"Can you not?"

The man shook his head. "It's impossible to leave here. Once you get settled into the lifestyle, you can't get out. And even if you tried," he laughed slightly, "well, the traffic wouldn't let you anyway." Michael, Andrew, and I had been trying to isolate ourselves from the odd dude, but the mention of the impenetrable LA traffic was enough to reel us in.

"What's *with* the traffic in your city?" Andrew asked, sticking his head forward to get a better look at our new friend.

"Carpocalypse" was all the man said.

Andrew hesitated a few seconds, unsure if any explanation was to follow. When none came, he cleared his throat. "Uh, carpocalypse? That's what the locals call it?"

"Nah, man. Carpocalypse. With a capital *C*. It's a phenomenon. It's what's coming."

"I'm confused."

The guy drummed the tops of his thighs a few times before turning his head to look at Andrew. "The traffic is always bad here," he explained, keeping that smooth, calm tone, "but it's nothing compared to what's about to happen." He then began nodding his head rhythmically, listening to a song we could not hear.

"What's about to happen?" I soon asked, taking the bait.

"In a few months," he said, his head still bobbing along, "they're closing down a big road. Yeah, part of I-405, I think. One of the big thoroughfares here. It's gonna cause all sorts of chaos, man. Hundreds of thousands of cars are gonna be redirected to other freeways. It'll get bad, I'm telling you."

"Wow," Michael replied, "and you think it's *already* affecting the traffic here, even though it's not supposed to happen for a few months?"

"Oh yeah . . . yeah, you're already seeing the effects, man. They're closing down lanes one stripe at a time, and it's already getting clogged. I sold my car last week 'cause I got scared."

Andrew quickly jumped in: "Hang on. You sold your *car* last week just because there was traffic coming?"

"Mm-hmm."

"Interesting decision."

The man appeared not to recognize Andrew's criticism, continuing to speak in the same relaxed voice of his. "It feels like a natural disaster or something like that is about to happen. There are warning signs everywhere. Even the mayor of LA came out recently and advised everyone to *stay in your homes!* if possible." He then leaned his head back again, and screamed at the top of his voice: "STAY IN YOUR HOMES!" This made the four of us jump immediately—but nobody else on the boardwalk seemed to notice. Just another day at Venice Beach.

"That . . . he actually said that?" Frazier asked after a few seconds.

"Mm-hmm," the man muttered again, his voice now back to its normal volume. "I'm thinking about busting out my old signs, you know? *Repent, the end is near*—stuff like that."

"Wow."

"Yeah . . . traffic, man."

"I'll say."

"Carpocalypse, man."

"If you say so."

"Yeah." The man's head slowly tilted back down, until it stared directly at the concrete in front of his feet. The four of us made eye contact with one another in a *shall we go?* manner—but then the guy's demeanor suddenly changed. His head perked up, his voice dropped to a more professional sound, and he reached over and grabbed the silver briefcase with the Bob Marley sticker. "Well!" he said, tapping it enthusiastically. "You guys are here to buy some weed, I assume?"

MIDDLE OF THE FIRST
Dodger Stadium

THE RED LAWN CHAIR

6:55 p.m. | Monday, June 14

Dodger Stadium is the only field in Major League Baseball where the main entrance is located on the upper level. Nestled into the golden hillside of Chavez Ravine, the ballpark descends from this gate, sloping naturally with the hill. After entering, visitors pop out onto the top concourse and are treated to a magnificent view of the diamond below while straight ahead is a collection of large white letters à la the Hollywood sign spelling THINK BLUE on the hillside beyond the outfield bleachers and parking lots. And if you spin 180 degrees and stare in the opposite direction back *through* the gate, the entirety of Los Angeles spreads out before you. It's not a bad introduction to a ballpark.

Built in 1962, Dodger Stadium is the third oldest in baseball, and it still sports a few unique attributes that make it feel archaic compared to modern fields. For instance, while many stadiums nowadays have an impressive assortment of options when it comes to cuisine at the ballpark—perhaps too many, at times—Dodger Stadium's primary culinary focus harkens back to the traditional idea of dining at a baseball game: hot dogs. Nearly everywhere in the stadium you can find the *Dodger Dog,* a long, skinny, and average-tasting ballpark hot dog that comes wrapped in blue-and-white tinfoil. The park was projected to sell over three million of these things in 2018 (roughly one per attendee per game), earning Dodger fans the title of most hot dogs eaten in Major League Baseball.[2] Yes, there are plenty of other foods at the stadium, including churros, funnel cake, and elote, but most of these can be found at only one stand in the stadium, respectively. The Dodger Dog? "Every ten feet," the locals say.[3]

The layout of Dodger Stadium separates the outfield bleachers completely from the remaining ballpark seats. Those who hold tickets for this general admission section cannot visit the rest of the stadium—and vice versa. This type of division used to be popular with older ballparks (Wrigley Field functions in a similar way), for it forced the beer-guzzling bleacher bums to be isolated from the rest of the crowd. Yet I must say that even though we held decent tickets for an infield section, we dearly wished we could have hung out in the separate outfield area when we visited. It looked more fun.

"Where is everyone?" Frazier asked as we entered through the main entrance, pausing a few minutes to take in the view of the city behind us and the ballpark before us. His question was understandable: despite it being only ten minutes before first pitch, hardly any fans had arrived. The opening notes to the national anthem were just starting to play, and whoever was singing was about to perform to what felt like an empty stadium.

We had felt this sense of vacancy back in the parking lot as well, as The Van had pulled up to the backside of Dodger Stadium at 6:45 p.m. for the 7:05 game. We had been worried about the parking situation; would the lot be filled because we were cutting it pretty close? No. There were hardly any cars there when we arrived. And not only were there no cars but there weren't any *things* either—no food stands, no team stores, no people selling knockoff hats. Apparently it's illegal to vend beyond the gates of Dodger Stadium. Whereas most ballparks don't mind if ticket scalpers, T-shirt sellers, and hot-dog carts roam the immediate area surrounding their grounds, Dodger

Stadium has opted to keep everything *inside* the ballpark. This means that there isn't much in terms of pregame atmosphere that goes on in the lots beyond the stadium walls—and with no bars anywhere nearby, everyone heads straight for the gates.

Yet *everyone* is a relative term, for, as we were discovering, hardly anybody actually makes it to Dodger Stadium before first pitch. This is the legendary "late-arriving" LA fan base, which we had heard vaguely referenced before but did not recognize to be real until now, as we gazed out over thousands of empty seats as *"Let's play ball!"* rang out from the PA system.

"Where do you think they all are?" Frazier asked again.

"Gotta be the traffic," Andrew replied.

"Yeah," Michael said. "We left Venice Beach at four thirty and didn't make it here till six forty-five. I can only imagine the logjams that the regular-hour working crew has to fight if they hold tickets to a weeknight ballgame. My god, even if you were to leave immediately after a five o'clock shift ended, you would certainly still be pushing an on-time arrival for a seven oh five first pitch. Like tonight."

"True. So you think that more will come?"

"I would guess so, yeah. Probably in a couple innings."

"Man, and all because of traffic. Maybe Carpocalypse *is* coming."

Sure enough, thousands more fans filed in at the top of the third inning, delayed by traffic. Then the majority of them left in the seventh, trying to beat the traffic. I highly doubt they succeeded.

10:55 a.m. | The Following Morning

We departed from our curbside camping spot near Venice Beach the following morning, turning The Van east for the first time and taking off for an undecided destination somewhere near the California-Arizona state line. But as The Van made its way out of town on Interstate 10, the heat made its way into The Van. Only two hours passed before the amount of sweat began to rival the amount of air inside the vehicle, and a rest stop was determined necessary. A roadside sign soon told us that the next commercial exit would not be for another seventy-four miles—and not wanting to simply pull over in unprotected sun, we had to keep going. The Van grumbled, panting like a dog in the heat. I sympathized with it.

Civilization is scarce on this stretch of American freeway—but billboards are common, as I-10 is pretty much the only means of transport between these sections of California and Arizona. We were each struck by how outrageous a few of these advertisements were, namely because of the lengthy travel that was required to get to whatever was being advertised. Our rest stop wasn't for another seventy-four miles, and soon we passed another billboard with a sign for a McDonald's that was eighty-six miles away.

It took us well over an hour to cover those seventy-four miles, The Van barely able to go sixty-five in the sweltering heat. The exit dumped us into a large, apocalyptic-looking parking lot. Maybe it was the mirage of the heat, but it seemed to us that the concrete stretched on for a mile before ending in front of a SuperTarget at the far end. Completely ignoring any sort of lane indicators, The Van drove toward the building, crossing over white-painted parking spaces that looked as if they had not been occupied for years. We came to a halt in the one nearest the entrance to the department store, and the four of us filed out and walked to the sliding door, pausing only for Frazier to take a few pictures of the vacant lot before entering the building. We didn't really need anything in the Target; we just figured that they'd have air-conditioning. We were correct.

"Why don't we just . . . hang here for a while?" Frazier proposed. We each nodded in silent agreement. The cold air blasting from the overhead vents felt like heaven.

.   .   .

Of the two collapsible lawn chairs we brought with us, the red one was my favorite. For some subconscious reason, I always reached for it instead of the yellow one when deciding it was time to stop and take a moment to simply sit for a while. You get a different perspective from sitting; you're stopped while everything else is moving. Yet finding spots to just sit on that trip could be difficult at times: benches were great, the floor sometimes worked, maybe a large rock would do—but a lawn chair was always the best, as it was portable. So as Andrew, Michael, and Frazier went into that SuperTarget in search of drinks, I returned to The Van and grabbed the red lawn chair. Bringing it inside, I made my way to the electronics section at the far end of the gigantic store. Unfolding the plastic chair and plopping it down in the middle of the deserted aisle, I kicked my feet up onto a cardboard box and proceeded to watch the HD televisions for sale. Each was turned on to demo mode, which repeatedly showed highlights from the past winter's X Games in vivid color. It was a moment of true displacement, as I sat in the middle of the desert and watched skiers pop tricks on mountain half pipes. Snow on the TV, burning sun on the outside. A gigantic department store with nobody in it other than, it seemed, myself and my three friends. (I hadn't seen a single other attendant since wandering past the sole cashier at the checkout counter near the entrance of the store.) I chuckled, loving everything absurd about it.

I actually fell asleep in the lawn chair there, lulled into a cool doze by the Target's effective air-conditioning. It was not until I heard footsteps behind me that I startled awake and turned to see Andrew, Michael, and Frazier wandering down the aisle, pushing a cart that held a weird assortment of items.

"There you are," Andrew said. "Enjoy your nap?" I mumbled something in reply and stood up from my comfortable spot. Yawning and shaking myself awake, I bent over and folded up the chair, placing it into the cart alongside a whole watermelon, two boxes of pasta, some marinara sauce, a few sausages, and a small spray water bottle.

"Dinner?" I asked, looking at the food. Michael answered with a nod. "What's the water bottle for?" Instead of replying, Andrew simply picked up the plastic thing and pulled the trigger, squirting mist at me. Even in the comfort of the building's AC, I could still feel the relief of the cooling water. "Ah. Yes. Absolutely."

We made our way to the checkout lines and wandered all the way to register thirty-five, the only one with its sign illuminated to say it was open. Setting our objects onto the conveyor belt, the cashier began scanning items and placing them in plastic sacks. I wondered what was going through her mind as she looked at the four of us eighteen-year-olds, who were most likely the only customers she had dealt with in the past hour. Without smiling, the woman then nodded her head at the cart.

"The lawn chair?"

"Sorry?" I replied.

"The lawn chair," she repeated, gesturing to the red clump of plastic and vinyl that was still in the cart.

"Ah," I said haltingly, slightly embarrassed. "That's, well actually . . . uh, that's actually mine."

"You brought it in here?"

"Yeah . . ."

She stared at the chair for a few seconds before shrugging her shoulders and returning to the objects.

"Seventeen thirty-two, please."

Ten minutes later, we were back on the road. The squirting water bottle was passed around constantly, as we each cooled ourselves off for thirty seconds before reaching for it again thirty seconds later.

"Don't bogart that bottle," Frazier said from behind the wheel. It was pointless; we used up all the water in a matter of minutes. The squirting bottle was then placed somewhere in The Van and was not seen again until we cleaned the vehicle out after returning to Seattle.

6:00 p.m.

We decided to sleep at Joshua Tree National Park that evening. After a few more hours of driving, we took the appropriate exit and turned left, crossing over the freeway and then heading toward the massive rock facade that had lined the valley for the past hundred or so miles. It was now early evening, and the weather was only just beginning dip below one hundred. U2 appropriately played in the background as we drove toward the tall, imposing cliffs, stopping first at the WELCOME TO JOSHUA TREE sign for Frazier to take a few photos and for each of us to call our parents. My call home rang through to voice mail, and after leaving a brief message, I returned to The Van, pulled out the red chair again, and plopped it down in the shade of the Joshua Tree sign.

Michael, Andrew, and Frazier had each connected with their parents, it appeared. Subconsciously, the three of them had walked in polar opposite directions from The Van once their conversations had begun; a more perfect equilateral triangle could not have been drawn were I to have connected the points at which they now stood. It was like they were magnetically repelled from each other: faced with the prospect of talking with a mother or father, privacy was all that the young mind desired. When you're that age, you use a different tone of voice when speaking with a parent—a lighter tone, one that gives off an air of innocence and trustworthiness. It's a tone you don't want your friends to hear, even though they're using the same one as well.

From the center of the triangle, I watched as each of them went through a nearly identical set of motions. Flip phone in their right hands, they reached down and picked up rocks with their left. Pinning the phone between their shoulders and ears, they then transferred the rocks to their right hands. Grabbing the phone now with their left, they shifted the device to their left ears and proceeded to throw the rocks with their right hands. They weren't throwing at anything in particular, just tossing whatever they could find into the desert, using it as a means to pass the time as they punched their minutes with their parents. I couldn't hear the majority of the words that were being said, but I could discern numerous iterations of "I love you too!," sometimes with an exclamation point, sometimes without.

Like puppets on a string, the three boys returned to the center of their perfect triangle at the same time. We then resumed our positions in The Van and continued into the desert, eventually locating the campground and parking the car on a small bluff for the evening.

The heat cooled off significantly over the next hour, and we were soon able to relax outside without being covered in sweat. As the small Coleman stove cooked our pathetic servings of sausage, penne pasta, and marinara sauce, we debated how best to break the whole watermelon. We hadn't packed a sharp knife, and the dull ones we had brought proved completely worthless against the fruit's hard shell—as did a feeble attempt with a sharp stick. So we threw it at a rock. The watermelon exploded into small pieces, each of which landed on the ground and became covered in dirt.

"God damnit," Frazier said, summarizing our shared annoyance at our collective stupidity.

Yet soon the sun began to set, and our minds quickly forgot about our harebrained approach to the watermelon. A brief but powerful moment of silence passed as we gazed at the scene of natural beauty that was beginning to unfold around the bluff on which we now sat.

Ahead of us to the south, beyond the borders of the national park, sat the Salton Sea, shimmering silvery-gold in the last of the rapidly disappearing daylight. To our right was the sunset: yellow and orange against the sky, it caressed the endless horizon that we had somehow emerged from that day. To the left was the moonrise: a purple and blue combination shouldering a nearly full moon that rose bright above the endless horizon that we somehow still had yet to cover. No cell service, no human contact. Nothing but Andrew, Michael, Frazier, and myself.

From the red lawn chair, I smiled. This was the first moment since we had departed Seattle when we each had taken the time together to simply stop, be peaceful, and enjoy the moment. I hate to admit that it would soon prove to be one of the last.

BOTTOM OF THE FIRST
Chase Field

8:43 p.m. | Wednesday, June 15

Chase Field is just a whole bunch of air-conditioning. The ballpark sits in the middle of Phoenix, which sits in the middle of Arizona, which is as hot as hell: Between the months of May and September (baseball season), the average daily high here often touches triple digits. So in order to avoid melting at the hands of this nonsense, the Diamondbacks' stadium incorporates a few nifty methods to keep fans cool. A large retractable roof rolls over the field when the sun is out, providing necessary shade for day games. For night games, this roof remains shut during the hours leading up to first pitch while gigantic AC units blast cool air into the stadium all morning and afternoon. Then, when game time approaches, the roof rolls back and fans are left to enjoy the rest of the game in a peaceful, eighty-degree climate while still basking in the final rays of the desert sun. And if you get too hot? Well, theoretically, there's a pool in center field. Yeah, you must reserve it ahead of time (way ahead of time), but the pool still represents all that Chase stands for: cooling things down. It's easily the most unique element of the ballpark.

We of course tried to swim in the little pool, and we of course were denied. But the air-conditioning was still great; it was 108 degrees when The Van had initially pulled up to the stadium.

1:02 a.m.

In the beginning of this book I spoke about how I see travel as a drug, and that that every drug brings with it both a high and a low. I felt my first low of our trip that night.

The sweltering heat that had weighed us down in Phoenix followed The Van as it departed Chase Field after the game and immediately hit the road, trying to make a dent in the long drive between Arizona and Colorado that we had to cover by the following evening. I was behind the wheel as the camper turned right onto I-40, destined for somewhere in New Mexico.

By this point in the trip, I had already established myself as first to offer to cover graveyard shifts when needed. Driving at night had become addictive for me, and I sought it out whenever possible. It's peaceful and relaxing; the lack of traffic offers extended periods of silence that are ideal for thinking or listening to light music—and yet at the same time, night drives are uncomfortable and edgy. Covering America's freeways while surrounded by nothing but darkness can be unnerving, and it was not uncommon for us to plunge into the blackness of the countryside without another car in sight. At one point during this particular drive, The Van was the only light that could be seen in the Arizona midnight. There were no cars visible, no lights from buildings in the distance—nothing but our headlamps shining onto the two lanes that directed us east.

Andrew sat beside me in the passenger seat while Michael and Frazier rested in the back, having folded the bench seat down to try to catch a few hours of sleep before their shift took over when dawn hit. No music played; the only sound was the air whirring through the windows of The Van, which were wide open in an attempt to cut down a bit of the sweltering heat that, even at this hour, was still overwhelming. The dashboard clock and the dashboard thermometer both read 102.

Fifteen minutes later, Andrew suddenly perked his head up next to me. "What's that sound?" he asked.

"Huh?" I replied. His question had startled me slightly; my mind had a tendency to wander when nothing but night unfolded in front of The Van.

"What's that sound?" he asked again. "Do you hear that clicking?"

"That's the wind rattling through the window."

"No, this is different."

Confused, I listened intently for what he was hearing. When nothing became apparent, the two of us rolled up the windows to eliminate the whipping rhythm of air rushing into the car. Sure enough, a new noise was now audible: A faint clicking began to emerge from somewhere beneath The Van's hood—faint but repetitive. It sped up when The Van accelerated and slowed down when it coasted.

"Oof," I grunted. "There's no way that's good."

"Does the car feel different at all?"

"No. But any abnormal noise scares me." The Van muttered in uneasy agreement.

I glanced at the rearview mirror. Michael and Frazier had not moved from their horizontal positions on the pulled-out bench seat, so I assumed they were still asleep.

"Should we tell Michael?" I asked. Andrew shook his head vigorously, his curly blond hair bouncing along with the motion.

"Nah. Unless it gets worse, I say let it be. Let's not escalate something that isn't threatening yet. You know Michael will freak if he hears that."

"True."

The Van tried to object, but it was defeated two to one.

As if hearing our pleas for distraction from the clicking noise, a small glimmer suddenly appeared on the horizon. It was the first light that we had seen for the past twenty or so minutes; the first sign of life that had appeared for miles. Andrew and I did not speak as the brightness grew, soon proving to be a cluster of intense beams rising above the black horizon. As The Van drove closer, it became apparent that we were approaching some sort of industrial structure that was lit from all angles by fluorescent floodlights and emergency flashers. A green sign on the side of the road announced that the next exit was for Joseph City—which, upon later research, I learned is an enormous power plant that has been plopped into the middle of the Arizona desert. Juxtaposed against the otherwise prevailing darkness, driving by it at 1:10 a.m. was simply mesmerizing; a fireworks show of electricity presented against the still, silent backdrop of empty night.

Yet by the time Joseph City retreated in the rearview mirror and total blackness surrounded us once more, the repetitive clicking noise became audible again. Neither of us could ignore it any longer.

"Think it'll make it?" Andrew asked quietly.

Now this was an obvious unknown with the trip. When it came to stability, The Van was a wild card; none of us truly knew its current state. We knew we needed it to complete our journey, but in the back of our minds, we also knew that it could theoretically break down at any second. The clicks were only echoing this knowledge louder and louder with every turn of the car's wheels. I took a few seconds before replying.

"Yeah."

"Really?"

"Yeah." I took a breath. "I dunno, man. I'm optimistic about this stuff, you know that. If something happens, I'm confident we'll find a way to fix it."

Andrew digested my words silently before muttering another comment about regretting the purchase of The Van. His eyes were focused on the road ahead, watching as the white lane dividers appeared in the beam provided by our headlights and then disappeared quickly beneath our wheels. He rolled the window back down, but I couldn't tell if this was to cool off or to cover the noise of the clicking. It was another minute before he opened his mouth and spoke again.

"Think *we'll* make it?"

"Yeah," I replied again, this time quicker than before. "I mean, I think our status kind of depends on The Van as well. We need it to complete the trip, right? So if it makes it around the country, we will too." Andrew nodded his head slowly, his eyes still fixed on the pavement before us.

"But what about after this?" he then asked.

"Hmm?"

"You know, once this trip is done." He now turned in his seat and looked directly at me. "What do you think will happen *after* this?"

"What're you talking about?"

"When we're through with this trip, man. I mean, we're each going separate ways, right?"

"Like, in terms of college?"

"Yeah. You're heading off to Wisconsin, me to Oregon. Michael's going to California while Frazier's moving to Illinois. We're separating completely." Now it was his turn to take a breath. "I dunno, man. I haven't been able to shake the realization that the four of us became best friends . . . well, 'cause we lived within a few blocks of one another. We could wander out of our houses and see each other in a couple of minutes. Do you think that'll stay the same when we live *states* apart?"

I paused before responding. "I guess . . . I guess I've never thought of it that way. I mean, we *became* friends because of where we lived—but I think we've *stayed* friends for other reasons . . . so yes?"

Andrew continued as if he didn't hear me. "I don't mean to sound harsh or anything. But I was speaking with my mom before we took off from Seattle, and I realized . . . well, I realized that she pretty much never speaks to her friends from childhood. She's still in touch with a few from college, but most of the people she sees regularly are from work, or the gym, or something like that."

"What's your point?"

"My point is that her current friends are the ones who live close to her today. She's moved around a lot, and her friends have changed along with her location. Whenever she mentions the friends she had in childhood or high school, it's only in passing—'cause she never sees them. I don't even know where they are. Or *who* they are."

"Maybe your mom wasn't as close with her friends as the four of us are?" I asked, trying to keep my voice close to a whisper. In the rearview mirror, I had noticed Michael shift. I couldn't tell if he had woken up or was just rolling over in his sleep. Either way, he remained silent.

"Possibly," Andrew replied, his voice much louder than mine. "But I can't help but think about it. It scares me, man. I mean, do *your* parents still talk to their childhood friends?"

This question took my mind to a place that I did not want it to go. As I stared ahead at the oncoming lane stripes that continued to emerge magically from the darkness ahead, I reflected on my parents and their current friends. No, neither of them really spoke with, or even *about,* their friends from childhood. My father still stayed in touch with his best friend growing up, but they chatted only once or twice a year and always on the phone. The friend lived in San Diego now, and the two of them saw each other once every other year, if that. My mother, meanwhile, hardly ever mentioned such things. On rare occasions she might bring up a friend she had made in high school, but such conversations always ended in a statement somewhere along the lines of "I wonder where they are now." Hell, she couldn't remember the names of some of the kids she had grown up with. At times, my father couldn't either. They both had great friends today, yes, but those friends were people they had met recently—since they had relocated to Seattle.

Did the same eventual loss of contact await me with my friends? It certainly never *felt* that way. But then again, as a kid you know nothing other than the connections you have formed during your minimal years of life. You haven't yet encountered the many other things that life throws at you. You haven't lived independently, you haven't held a real occupation, you haven't met someone with whom you might spend the rest of your days. With nothing else to tell you otherwise, you automatically assume that the friendships you have made with those who grew up alongside you are unbreakable—because at that point in your life, they are. There has been nothing presented to you yet that would make you doubt their validity or durability. You haven't been pulled in a different direction yet by the various other life events just mentioned: relocation, job, spouse, and so on. And although such events are indeed great, they unfortunately carry the consequence of distracting you from these friendships—the friendships you, in your youthful and naive state, assumed were unbreakable. Had I simply not recognized this yet? Does *anybody* recognize this before it slips away? Was I just going to turn around one day in the future and realize that, distracted by the other requirements of life, I hadn't spoken to these guys in years?

"But don't you guys think that we've shared enough to overcome a change in location?" I asked, seeking something positive to wrench me out of those thoughts.

"Possibly," Andrew replied. "But what if they—our parents—also thought that that had been the case when *they* were in our position?"

"I suppose. I don't know. I don't really like thinking about it, to be honest." Within me, a sickening feeling had begun to grow. This seemed like far too intense a conversation to be having just a handful of days into our journey; it felt like one that would be more appropriate for a final leg, or the climax of such a saga. Yet it was happening now. Suddenly my mind started to wonder whether this trip was actually the beginning of the end of what I had long assumed were the best friendships I would ever have, and that was not something I wanted to think about in the slightest. "I think we'll be fine," I said, in a final attempt to salvage some optimism from the scenario.

Looking for a distraction, I flipped on the stereo system and switched my iPod to shuffle. The first song that came through the speakers was a tune by the Pogues, which I quickly skipped. I hadn't listened to the band since my eternal tentativeness forced me to miss their show a few years ago. Now certainly did not feel like the time to begin again.

The remainder of the drive that night seemed to drag on for eternity. The clicks of The Van soon blended into the background music and formed a monotonous lull unheard by my mind, which was now preoccupied with everything that was to come when I soon left home for good. By the time dawn hit, we had reached New Mexico. Frazier and Michael jumped up front while Andrew and I switched to the back seat, which remained folded down so that the two of us could sleep. But while Andrew snored through nearly the entire rest of the drive, I remained wide awake. The clicks of The Van quickly proved impossible to hide, and I made a brief mention of them to Frazier and Michael. They digested the information poorly.

Nobody said much at all that day, as The Van eventually turned left at Albuquerque and began ascending north in the direction of Denver. Frazier was driving as we crossed the Colorado state line while news radio played lightly in the background. The local reporters were discussing a series of forest fires that had erupted in the southern foothills of the Rocky Mountains—the area that, coincidentally, we found ourselves driving through at that very moment. With my back propped against the rear window of The Van, I sat with my legs spread in front of me, writing in a navy spiral-bound notebook that I had purchased in Phoenix the day before. Andrew continued to sleep as twilight began to descend on the scene. From my vantage point, I could just see the orange haze of the fires in the distance. The smoke rose from the foothills, gathering in pockets in the sky and wrapping itself around the full moon. The wisps played with the moon's appearance, shifting its shape and color completely and making it difficult to discern between what was reality and what was mirage.

TOP OF THE SECOND
Coors Field and Target Field

THE ONLY SPORT THIS WORKS FOR

7:55 p.m. | Friday, June 17

The upper deck of Coors Field is adorned with a single row of purple seats that wrap continuously around the top sections, forming a thin line of vivid color that clashes against the remaining sea of dark-green seats. This line stands to mark 5,280 feet above sea level, offering the fun ability for fans to claim that they were (physically) a mile high while watching the hometown Rockies play baseball. In right center, a small fountain and an impressive collection of evergreen trees ooze into the visitor's bullpen, mirroring forestry one would find in the nearby Rocky Mountains.

The four of us had randomly stumbled on "Free Taco Night" at Coors, a promotion at the ballpark where if the Rockies scored at least seven runs in that night's game, attendees could bring their tickets to a participating Taco Bell restaurant the following day for a complimentary assortment of tacos. Each sporting giveaway T-shirts that bluntly stated WE WANT TACOS on the front, we cheered as the Rockies went on to score seven runs in the first two innings, eventually besting the visiting Tigers 13–6. Yet seeing as we had to depart for Minneapolis immediately following the game, we never got to cash in our tickets for the free food (understandably, there were no Colorado Rockies-participating Taco Bell locations in the state of Minnesota). I still have my T-shirt, however, and I still maintain that Coors Field owes me tacos.

Outside of our cheers for free food, the four of us spent the majority of the evening being entertained by a large purple dinosaur that wandered between the various sections of the ballpark, interacting with fans and doing its best to get them to start chants throughout the game. This thing is "Dinger," the Rockies mascot.

Allow me to admit that baseball mascots are incredibly confusing at times. Some are easy to understand: the Pittsburgh Pirates' mascot is a patch-eyed buccaneer while the Milwaukee Brewers have "Bernie the Brewer," a yellow-haired man who used to slide into a vat of beer whenever a Milwaukee player hit a home run. Other mascots, however, don't quite make sense. In Seattle, for example, we have the "Mariner Moose" while in Philadelphia they have this strange green alien thing called the "Philly Phanatic." Then, just as you are thinking that some teams simply fell to alliteration to represent their ball club, the Oakland Athletics' mascot is a large white elephant.

And although I am still attempting to discern the reasoning behind the A's choice, the Rockies' purple dinosaur—which, yes, does look unfortunately like Barney—actually has a cool story behind it. When construction broke ground on Coors Field, the workers discovered a dinosaur egg buried deep beneath the earth on which they were preparing to build the stadium.[4] Figuring that they had to somehow incorporate this odd find into the ballpark, the team's front office decided that their mascot would now be a large dinosaur, which was introduced in 1994 by being ceremoniously hatched from the egg to the tune of "Wild Thing."[5] Its purple color is the alternative hue of the Rockies—the same color that fills the aforementioned seats that stand a mile high in Coors Field.

3:50 a.m.

The dreary mood from the very real conversation Andrew and I had on the way into Colorado was not helped by the equally dreary weather that met us on the way out of the state. A rainstorm pounded The Van as it entered Nebraska and shifted from I-76 to I-80, heading somewhat in the direction of Minnesota.

"Screw this," Andrew muttered, squinting to see through the downpour. I silently shared this sentiment from the back-bench seat, writing in my navy notebook and watching intently as he did his best to keep the wheel straight. Every fifteen seconds or so, he took a sip from a large energy drink that was perched precariously in the cupholder next to him. The drink was called "Chaos in a Can."

6:50 p.m. | Saturday, June 18

The stormed followed us all the way to Minneapolis, and although it eased up significantly as game time approached the following day, the rain still continued in a steady drizzle. Yet something about the cold and gloomy weather made Target Field feel warm and welcoming to us. It sounds oxymoronic, but it was true: the shower that had settled over Minnesota reminded the four of us of Seattle and allowed for the ballpark to provide a homey shelter.

"I feel like I'm about to watch a baseball game in a coffee shop," Frazier said.

I agreed with his statement. The design of Target Field creates an intimate, cozy atmosphere within its appealing confines. The majority of the ballpark is covered with sunbaked limestone that had been taken from a cliff only an hour or so away from the field's location.[6] This beige coating combines with the dark-blue hue of the seats to further amplify the—I'll say it again—*cozy* feel of Target Field. Symmetry is rejected almost everywhere here, as bleachers, landings, and billboards jut out at random angles. The buildings of Minneapolis loom over the stadium, which is well hidden in urban anonymity in the city's Warehouse District; you hardly notice the ballpark until you are standing across the street from it.

Staying true to Frazier's comment, I appropriately sipped a cup of coffee as the four of us sat midway up the third-base line roughly an hour before first pitch, keeping an eye on the weather. The pregame giveaway that evening had been cheap straw cowboy hats with the Twins' logo stamped on the front. Bizarre and out of place, they were also useful, as they provided excellent defense against the persisting drizzle. A fear of rainout spread through the relatively small crowd, as the weather showed little sign of letting up.

"Rainouts," a man in the row behind us grumbled to nobody in particular. "Rainouts! Just another thing I've got against this bullshit sport." That felt like a hot take, so I turned in my seat to look at him. He was overweight, with patchy black hair and a five o'clock shadow that looked as if it had not left in years. He wore a Minnesota Vikings football jersey and held a twenty-four-ounce can of Budweiser. Spotting me looking at him, he directed his anger toward me. "No damn sport should depend on the weather! The weather's just another element— you play rain or shine!" He tugged at his Vikings jersey. "That's what we do!"

"Don't you guys play indoors?" Andrew replied from next to me. Normally I hated his combative attitude. Sometimes I loved it.

"Well, yeah, but we're building a new stadium."

"Won't that be indoors too?"

"Doesn't matter," the man said quickly. Reason was quickly proving pointless. "Football ain't got no rainouts! Rain or shine, we play the game. Hell, football even plays in the snow! The *snow!* Now that's a real sport. Yeah, I'm not a baseball fan."

"Why are you here then?"

"Got free tickets—and food vouchers." He raised his beer can happily. "Well, food *and drink* vouchers, I guess I should say. But I didn't know I'd be drinkin' in a stupid *rainstorm!*" He shouted the last word toward the diamond, as if angry at Target Field. "This's dumb. Baseball's the only sport that gets rained out."

"You don't watch much tennis, do you?" I asked.

"Tennis? That ain't no sport."

"OK."

I turned back around in my seat, never wanting to talk to this man again. But he continued grumbling and then inquired about the four of us and *our* reason for being at the rainy ballgame. "What brought *you* guys to this unfortunate spot?" he asked. Andrew then politely informed him of our trip.

"Humph," he said, pulling on the front of his jersey once more. "You'd be better seeing all the NFL stadiums! They don't got rainouts!"

I soon tuned the guy out, but my mind stayed with that last comment. Yes, baseball games get rained out here and there. The delicate nature of the sport means that bad weather can affect gameplay in unfair ways at times, and an abundance of rain (or snow) can—and *should*—postpone contests. Yet while this may be case, baseball is the only sport that a trip like ours would work for.

I'll begin with logistics. If you are a sports fan and want to set out to see a game played in every venue of your favorite league, the only one that allows for this to be done in a timely manner is baseball. MLB teams play 162 games a year, half of which are at home. This means that you, the nomadic game watcher, have eighty-one chances for *each* stadium to try to catch a game in a roughly six-month span. As shown by our trip, we were able to see all thirty in fewer than two months.

Returning to the Viking fan's comment, football teams play only sixteen games a year, eight of which are at home. There are thirty-two teams in the NFL, which means that it would take at least two years for you to see a game played in every single stadium—and that's only if the schedules worked out perfectly (which, let me tell you, they never would). Teams do not play at home based on the demand of your ideal route.

Theoretically, it would be plausible to schedule a trip to see every basketball arena in a few months, for there are eighty-two games in an NBA team's season, forty-one of which are played at their home courts. Yet basketball normally takes two, three, if not four days off between each contest, which means that you may be waiting awhile to see a team play—and that's *if* they are on a home stand. It would most likely take you at least a full season to see every NBA arena, and even then it might be difficult to succeed in doing so.

But even if you were able to somehow perfectly wrangle up the basketball schedule into a logical road trip, seeing every NBA arena would simply not be as *interesting* as seeing every MLB ballpark. If I were to plop you onto an NBA court and remove all signs (logos, advertisements, etc.), I will bet that you wouldn't be able to name the arena in which you stood. Most bleacher levels look the same, most overhead scoreboards look the same, most benches look the same.

The reason for this? Every basketball arena must be built around a court that is the exact same as all others in the NBA. There are strict set dimensions in basketball: every court must be ninety-four feet long and fifty feet wide. The three-point arc is twenty-three feet nine inches away from the hoop, save for where it is twenty-two feet away near the baseline. The rim is always ten feet above the floor, and it is always surrounded by a backboard that is seventy-two inches wide and forty-two inches tall. Even the bench area on every court is restricted to twenty-eight feet of space.[7]

This required uniformity means that the majority of NBA arenas feel very similar on the inside; having to build around the same exact court as the other twenty-nine venues in the league leaves little room for contractors to get creative. The same goes for a hockey rink. And although the NFL has a dose of variety in its stadiums (primarily because most are outdoors), the field itself still must be the exact same dimensions as every other one in the league.

Baseball is different, for it is a sport with no set dimensions. The only things that must be the same in each ballpark are the ninety feet to every base and the sixty feet six inches from the pitcher's rubber to the home plate. After that, everything is up to the ballpark. This autonomy in design has the reverse effect for ballpark contractors as it does for those in charge of chalking out the layout of NBA arenas, NHL rinks, and NFL stadiums. Every baseball field is different, and this means gameplay varies depending on the location; a baseball game at one ballpark is very different at another.

Perhaps the most recognizable element of ballpark variety is the distance between home plate and the outfield walls. Some stadiums are symmetrical: it's 329 feet (100 meters) to left at Toronto's Rogers Centre, 329 feet to right, and 400 feet to straightaway center. Dodger Stadium is also symmetrical, checking in at 330 feet to both left and right and 395 feet to center.

Yet symmetry like this is a rarity when it comes to the cathedrals of America's pastime, for the majority of ballparks vary in their outfield distances. Some are deep, such as Chicago's Wrigley Field, where the distances exceed 350 feet to both left and right field. Pittsburgh's PNC Park is another good example: it has the deepest distance of all parks to the power alley in left-center at 410 feet while San Francisco's AT&T Park has the deepest right-center power alley at 421 feet. These are "pitchers' parks," as the deep fences allow for more fly balls to be tracked down by outfielders, resulting in outs instead of home runs.

But there are plenty of "hitters' parks" as well. The smallest stadium in all of Major League Baseball is Boston's Fenway Park, which stands proud at 310 feet to left, 390 feet to center, and 302 feet to right. (More on Fenway's wacky dimensions when we get to Boston.) Other shallow fields include Tampa Bay's Tropicana Field (315'/404'/322'), Baltimore's Camden Yards (333'/400'/318'), and New York's Yankee Stadium (319'/408'/314'). This particularly short porch to right field in New York has earned Yankee Stadium the comical title of "the Great Wiffle Ball Park in the Bronx" for the way that some balls, which should be routine fly outs, leave the yard instead. I've seen home runs hit in that place that feel more like accidents than accomplishments.

Fence *height* varies significantly as well. A few ballparks, such as Miller Park or our own Safeco Field, have a fence that maintains the same height throughout the ballpark, normally standing at eight or nine feet tall. Yet as was the case with fence *distances,* so, too, is this symmetry a rarity in fence *height.* The shortest wall in MLB is at Fenway, where it's three feet tall in right field. The corner sections of the outfield wall in Angel Stadium are also short, at four feet six inches next to both foul poles.

Many stadiums, however, have tall walls. The highest right field wall in all of baseball is the one at AT&T Park, which stands at twenty-five feet down the line—although Minnesota's Target Field (where we now sat) isn't too shabby either: its right field porch looms at twenty-three feet tall. The tallest center field wall can be found in Arizona's Chase Field, which is twenty-five feet tall and located 407 feet away from home plate. (Dingers rarely leave the yard over that thing.) And to left field—well, nothing tops Fenway's "Green Monster," which soars at thirty-seven feet high.

Some walls are padded, some are brick, and Wrigley Field's is covered in ivy.

Oh, but the variety in baseball stadiums does not stop there. The dimensions in fair territory have been for the most part just described, but baseball also takes place outside the lines—and ballpark uniqueness is not restricted here either. Ballparks with little foul territory, such as Wrigley Field or (again) Fenway Park, regularly see pop flies just to the side of first base drift into the stands, giving the batter another chance. Other fields, like Detroit's Comerica Park or Saint Louis's Busch Stadium, have a ton of foul territory—and my god, it seems that there's more grass growing *outside* the foul lines than within them at the Oakland Coliseum. The same foul pop that lands in the bleachers at Wrigley/Fenway is an easy out here.

And just when you thought that every bit of ballpark uniqueness comes in their dimensions, there's even more at play. The Rogers Centre and Tropicana Field are turf diamonds, which means that a ground ball hit in one of these stadiums has a far greater chance of skipping through the infield for a base hit than it would on a grass diamond. Comerica Park has a strip of dirt that leads from the pitching mound to home plate, the lip of which often keeps bunts directly in front of home plate if they are not sternly directed elsewhere. Tropicana Field also has catwalks that often obstruct the path of the ball—but they are considered in play, so the fielder must react to the ball's new direction if it hits one. And just up until 2016, there was a hill—yep, a hill—in center field in Houston.

Depending on which stadium a team is playing in (or you are watching a game in), the field has a real effect on how the game proceeds. Lazy fly balls to right in San Francisco are game-changing home runs in New York; a slow groundball back up the middle is an easy out in Seattle but is a base hit in Toronto; a ball off the Monster in Fenway is a single, but the same ball is a triple in Pittsburgh.

These ballpark-specific elements make home field advantage something more than just the crowd in baseball. The fans still, of course, play a role, but for players, playing in your home stadium brings with it a familiarity of your field's dimensions, terrain, and the like. And returning to the original point, all this makes viewing a baseball game in different stadiums *interesting*. The atmosphere in each park is different because the setup of each field is different. I've seen NBA games in different arenas, and I've seen NFL games in different stadiums. Although both are very enjoyable, for me, nothing compares to the intrigue of seeing a baseball game in a different ballpark. It is the only sport that makes a trip like ours logistically feasible—and genuinely interesting.

So yes, there are indeed rainouts in baseball. But none came to us that evening at Target Field. The umpires determined that the continuing drizzle was not enough to cancel the game, and first pitch happened as scheduled. Our challenger, the Vikings fan, departed before the third inning even finished, and we never saw him again.

MIDDLE OF THE SECOND
Wrigley Field

A DIFFERENT STORY FROM WRIGLEY

7:30 p.m. | Sunday, June 19

Wrigley Field is a pilgrimage site for those who practice the religion of baseball. It's old, so everyone wants to—and should—go see it. As we sat in four dingy seats in the upper rows of the third-base side, we were struck by how many fans in our section were from places *other* than Chicago. To our left was a woman who had flown in from Pittsburgh, to our right was a couple from Cincinnati, and directly in front of us was a family of fellow Pacific Northwesterners from Portland. Yet despite coming from such different locations, they all seemed to be cheering for the Cubs.

Since that trip, I have come to understand more about the geographical mélange that chooses to root for the Cubs. Chicago's Northside baseball team is and seems to have always been widely accepted as the most "lovable" across the country—not because of their winning ways but because of their *losing* ways. Up until 2016, the Cubbies had not won a World Series for over a century, with their last title coming in 1908, 108 years earlier. During this time span, an affection for these "Lovable Losers" spread across America; everybody enjoys rooting for the underdog, and the Cubs were certainly that: one hundred years is a long, long time. As the decades passed, more people grew attached. Rooting for Chicago slowly became a family tradition, as the fandom was passed down from parent to child to grandchild, permeating generations without regard to location; no matter how far away from Chicago you may be, the Cubs attachment never fades.

"I was born in Pittsburgh," the woman to our left explained, "and I like the Pirates, but my grandfather was a Cubs fan. So naturally, I love the Cubbies as well." She pulled down the zipper on her sweatshirt to reveal a black-and-yellow Pittsburgh tee, which clashed with the blue-and-red Cub hat she sported on her head.

"That sounds like us," the mother from the Portland family replied, gesturing to her two kids and husband. "We three are from the West Coast, but Todd here was born in southern Illinois—so we've got Cubs roots as well."

A local Chicagoan behind us appeared to scoff into his beer. "Been here my entire life," he muttered, just loud enough for me to hear, "and I've struggled through every losing season firsthand."

The Cubs' incredible World Series drought indeed came to an end in 2016—and with it came one massive party. Everyone, however they located their Chicago baseball allegiance, seemed to want in on the celebrations: over five million people showed up for the team's championship parade. The love for the losers spoke for itself, as the parade was recorded as the seventh largest gathering of humans in history.[8]

Even if you don't have "Cub roots," a visit to Wrigley Field is a must. Standing as the second-oldest venue in baseball (Fenway Park edges it by a few years), the ballpark cost only $250,000 to construct in 1914[9] and still maintains its early 1900s influence, housing some of the more distinct attributes of any park in Major League Baseball. The interior and exterior are fairly bare, as pole-heavy architecture left very few blank facades in and around the stadium—facades that that would normally be swept up by companies looking to slap an advertisement or two up there. Meanwhile, Wrigley's urban status allows for those living nearby to cater to alternative methods of viewing the games: warehouses and apartment buildings across the street have erected their own seats, each offering semidecent views from beyond the outfield walls. They're great spots for private events and parties. Within the actual confines of the ballpark, the outfield bleachers are separated from the rest of the venue—like those at Dodger Stadium. It is here that the famous Chicago "Bleacher Creature" exists, taking shape in the form of a fan who stumbles into this general admission section after spending hours at one of the many nearby pubs. They're more prepared than anyone to enter verbal jousting competitions with somebody who dares challenge their support of the Cubs. Andrew belonged here.

The entire outfield wall at Wrigley is made of brick. While most stadiums have a decent layer of padding on their fences—which minimizes the physical harm received by a player who might crash into it while attempting to snag a deep fly ball—at Wrigley, such a play results in the player smacking into the cold, hard brick. The wall is covered with draping ivy, but that's really just a false front for the solid material behind it. If a ball goes into the ivy and does not pop out immediately, the outfielder raises his hands in an "I give up!" sort of way, and the batter is awarded a ground-rule double. It's up there with when someone gets a hit off the catwalk in Tampa for the most peculiar moments that can happen in the sport.

Yet while Wrigley remains archaic in many ways, maintaining pace with the rest of baseball (and the twenty-first century) has required the stadium to make a few modern additions in recent decades. Stadium lighting was added in 1988 to allow for night games to take place at the ballpark,[10] and a large electric scoreboard was built in 2014 to complement the old-style hand-operated one that still stands above the center field bleachers.[11]

And although new training rooms, media centers, dugouts, and clubhouses have also made their way into the century-old ballpark, the tale behind its PA system is a good one that often goes unrecognized.

Up until the turn of the millennium, Wrigley Field had always been used as a venue for sports—and sports only. The Cubs baseball team was obviously the main tenant of the grounds, but on occasion various other athletic competitions crept in as well. The Bears football team played at Wrigley from 1921 to 1970 and actually chose their name to fit alongside that of the Cubs.[12] Here and there, soccer matches and hockey games took place within the old ballpark too—but that was it. Yet in the mid-1990s, American performing artist Jimmy Buffett approached the Wrigley Owners Group about the possibility of doing a concert at the historic stadium. True to their tradition as a sports venue, Cubs team president Andy MacPhail rejected the idea immediately.[13] Wrigley was a baseball stadium, not a music venue.

But the Cubs were bad, and Buffett was good. The Chicago ball club had made the playoffs only four times in the past sixty years, and MacPhail soon began to see the benefits that might come in shaking things up a little; Wrigley Field could do with a bit of life, and Buffett might be able to give it some. As the years passed, he began to ponder the idea, but the rest of the Wrigley Owners Group was not sold—nor were the purists in the stands. The stadium had been around for over eight decades at this point, and many complained that a concert would ruin the aura of the classic building.

"The acoustics would be terrible," they argued.

"The place would not be able to support a rock concert," they said.

"And no artist could *ever* properly live up to the history of the stadium."

They turned out to be wrong.

Jimmy Buffett was (is) a lifelong baseball fan—and not just that, he is a lifelong Cubs fan. Similar to the woman from Pittsburgh, the couple from Cincinnati, and the family from Portland who sat near us, Buffett had been hooked by a single Wrigley experience and had pledged allegiance to the Chicago baseball team ever since. (More on that soon.)

Ten years after his original inquiry about the possibility of playing at Wrigley, the "Margaritaville" star finally got his wish. The Wrigley Owners Group allowed him to do a two-day show on Labor Day weekend 2005, when the Cubs would be out of town. With things now in motion, the stadium assembled a planning committee, the sole purpose of which was to make sure that Wrigley's first-ever concert was a big success. The technical preparations began months before the show's dates were even finalized.

As the concert drew nearer, large hanging speakers were strategically installed in the old building to combat the stadium's poor acoustics. The extra boom in the new PA system provided a different feel to Cubs games: "Now batting, Derek Lee!" rang out not only through all of Wrigley but also through all of Wrigley*ville* in a loud, crisp, exciting manner. Residents weren't too pleased, but fans loved it. The atmosphere continued to build as early September rolled around, and the city felt that something big was about to happen. For the first time in decades, a baseball game was not the most important event that would take place at Wrigley Field.

The energy on the eve of the concert was foreign to the old stadium. At that point in time, the Cubs had never won a World Series since they began playing in Wrigley, ninety-one years prior. Its fan base was looking for a reason to party at their ballpark—and if the five million people who showed up to the 2016 Championship Parade tells you anything, it's that Chicago loves to party. If you have ever attended a Jimmy Buffett concert, you will know that his loyal *Parrotheads* love to party as well. The perfect combination.

An astounding eighty thousand people poured into the old stadium on the night of the first show. Some were dressed in Cubs jerseys and baseball caps, some were dressed in straw hats and coconut bras—but all were excited to witness the first concert at one of America's greatest venues. The concourses of the old ballpark creaked beneath the pressure as the lights went down, the new PA system was turned up to full, and the show began.

Buffett killed it. Not only did his shows produce over $8 million in revenue for Wrigley[14] but also he blew the skeptics out of the water and exceeded the hopes of even the planning committee. Alongside his classic numbers and a handful of deeper cuts, he took a few special moments to pay tribute to the team and the stadium throughout the show, including performing in a white Cubs jersey and leading the crowd in a singing of "Go Cubs Go" and "Take Me Out to the Ballgame" in classic Wrigley tradition. But it was Buffett's encore on that first night that truly struck home for the Wrigley Field faithful.

After he exited the stage, every light in the stadium went out and a hush fell over the audience, the majority of whom were standing on the field or sitting in the bleachers behind home plate (the stage was in center field). The eerie silence continued for a few minutes, until a single beam of light appeared out of the night and began scanning the empty outfield bleachers. It eventually located Buffett, who sat near the right field foul pole about five rows up. Joined by his lead guitarist, Mac McAnally, the two of them sat completely alone, strumming a basic chord pattern on acoustic guitars to the silent and watchful crowd.

Amplified by a small microphone, Buffett explained that the first Cubs game he had ever attended was right here at Wrigley, back in "Nineteen seventy . . . something." Smiling, he informed the eighty thousand before him that he had come with his longtime friend Steve Goodman, a fellow musician. The two of them had sat in the exact seats from which he and McAnally now played the guitar.

"This brings back a lot of memories to me," he said into the microphone. The phrase echoed through the stadium, finding agreement in many who experienced a similar sensation each time they visited Wrigley.

But it was the mention of Steve Goodman's name that triggered nostalgia in the crowd. The local musician was beloved in Chicago not only for his music but also for his die-hard allegiance to the Cubs: they've been playing "Go Cubs Go" and "A Dying Cubs Fan's Last Wish" at Wrigley for years—both of which were written by Goodman, who had passed away from leukemia in 1984. (His ashes were reportedly secretly scattered in Wrigley by his friends.)[15]

In a classy move, Buffett then took his own sentimental moment to play Goodman's "City of New Orleans." He officially declared it a nod to those devastated by Hurricane Katrina—but everyone in the crowd knew that it was also a nod to Goodman, the Cubs, and beautiful Wrigley Field.

It was that moment that solidified Wrigley's first-ever concert as a success. Greg Kot of the *Chicago Tribune* writes that, after the encore, "even [Andy] MacPhail was convinced that concerts weren't such a bad idea."[16] In every fan and every Parrothead in attendance, Buffett had found a way to declare that, despite the many places baseball is played across the country and around the world, Wrigley Field was and would always be the sport's *true* home. The concert was not just a concert; it was a tribute to America's pastime and to one of America's greatest monuments.

BOTTOM OF THE SECOND
Miller Park

HAVING A CATCH

5:45 p.m. | Monday, June 20

Miller Park feels like a fairground encircling a baseball diamond. The food, drink, and atmosphere you'd find at a carnival are happily offered during the game by the kiosks and vendors and even the PA broadcasters. To make it to your seats, you must wade through the large crowds that are most likely waiting in line at concession stands, some of which stand in the *middle* of the walkways. Would you like a Miller Lite? Yes, you would like a Miller Lite.

Nearly every half inning, some sort of funky in-game promotion takes place at the Brewers' ballpark. These acts range from the beer barrel polka, when everyone stretches their legs by shifting around to an old drinking song, to the running of the sausages, when participants dressed as tubular meats stretch their legs by running around the warning track. They were all fun, but our favorite in-game promotion on the evening of June 20 was easily the "Fan of the Game," which was quite simple: the camera panned to three fans, aired their images on the big screen, and asked the crowd of forty thousand to cheer loudest for which one they thought deserved the title of "Fan of the Game." There were no criteria for this judgment; everything was up to the Wisconsin fans' discretion. The choices that night were between a beautiful woman in a Packers jersey (mild applause), a marine sitting behind home plate (mild applause), and a man of absolutely gigantic proportions who sat isolated in the top row of the upper deck and sported a cheese-head, cargo shorts, and a very greasy gray T-shirt. A Twinkie shy of four hundred pounds, this simply huge individual noticed himself on the big screen and proceeded to engulf an entire hot dog before downing the rest of his Miller Lite and stacking the now-empty cup atop four others that were sitting discarded at his feet. (Enormous applause.) Voilà, your "Fan of the Game."

Although a crowd of forty thousand on a Monday night may seem outstanding for a small-market team like Milwaukee, the Brewers regularly draw an impressive attendance. Part of the reason for this is the loyal sports fan base that resides in Wisconsin: Packers, Brewers, Bucks, you name it—people who live there will show up for their teams. It's a wonderful sports environment—one of the most passionate in the United States.

Another reason for the impressive Brewers crowd is the Miller Park tailgate scene. In fact, none of us were all that surprised at the substantial number of people who had gathered for the Monday night game because we had seen nearly every single one of them in the parking lot hours before first pitch. Tired and yearning to escape the stuffy Chicago heat, we had left the Windy City around 2:00 p.m. that day, hoping to make it up to Milwaukee by four or five o'clock. "Maybe we can park The Van near the stadium and get some sleep," Michael had said, directing the group in a manner that we not only had grown used to but also had come to expect. His idea was a good one, but as we pulled into the Miller Park parking lot around five o'clock, we quickly realized that naps were out of the picture.

Beers, barbecues, and baseballs: these are the three Bs of the Brewers—or, at least, of the Brewers' fan base. We had arrived two hours before first pitch, but we still had to park a good half mile away from the stadium because all the other spots were already filled with tailgaters. For once, The Van didn't stand out too much here: our car's kaleidoscopic design actually mixed well with the eclectic colors of the lawn chairs and coolers that were spread out on the dark concrete.

"What on earth?" Andrew asked, looking out the window incredulously. I didn't blame him for his confusion. Tailgating is something normally associated with football, a pregame ritual that fans do a few times a year. But as we quickly found out, a "few" is too few in Milwaukee. Here anything goes: if you've got tickets to a baseball game and the weather's good, you're packing up the cooler, buying a new bag of charcoal, tossing the grill into the back of the station wagon, and heading to the ball-park hours before first pitch. Who cares what day of the week it is? Nothing should get in the way of spending time outside and partying a bit with family and friends. That's the Wisconsin Way.

The four of us tried to fit in, but our efforts were lame and utterly in vain. After being directed to an open spot on the fringes of the parking lot, Frazier wandered off to take pictures of a charcoal pit while Michael, Andrew, and I slid the door open and pulled out whatever we could that might make it look as if we belonged. Unfortunately, our Coleman stove and box of rotini pasta was nothing compared to the full-size grill and butcher's assortment of meats that the tailgaters adjacent to us had. (The guy unloaded a backyard barbecue from his pickup and then asked what cut of the pig his friends desired.) But Wisconsinites are welcoming; it was only a matter of minutes before our neighbors took pity on our plebian tailgate and invited us to join their own. The man at the grill handed each of us a Miller Lite.

"Screw yer age," he said with a gruff guffaw, his eyes wandering across The Van's outlandish coating. "Yer in Wisconsin! Now tell me about this journey you guys appear to be on."

What happened next unfolded all at once. As Michael and I began to describe our trip to the kind tailgater, Frazier returned to the scene, and Andrew felt something wet hit the top of his head. Reaching up to run his hand through his hair, his fingers returned covered in white liquid.

"Bird shit," he said, disgusted. "Yuck."

"Well, can't say you didn't have that coming," Frazier said with a chuckle, speaking far louder than was appropriate for the situation as he looked at the screen of his camera. Under his breath, he then mentioned something stupid about Andrew eating the last of his chicken nuggets the day before, Andrew replied by making fun of Frazier "quitting" the photography club, and before Michael and I knew it, the two were screaming at each other. The argument was a complete nothingburger, but its explosive nature was indicative of some pent-up tension that Andrew and Frazier clearly had toward each other—which was more a product of the stress from the past few days than anything else. We were in the middle of seeing nine baseball games in nine days, maneuvering through a heavy heat wave to do so. When you travel under such conditions and spend that much time together in a tight, enclosed space, even something as dumb as a thieved McDonald's lunch can mean a lot.

"All right, asshole!" Andrew yelled. "You want some food back—here, eat the shit that's in my hair!" I apologized to our tailgating neighbors while Michael did his best to calm Andrew down, but he was having none of it. "No," he said, pushing Michael away and jogging back toward The Van. "No, this is between the two of us." He pushed open the sliding door and threw up the bench seat, reaching under it to dig through our supplies that lay beneath. At first I was slightly worried he was going to grab a crowbar, or something with which he would then use to try to beat Frazier to a pulp. But instead he withdrew two baseball gloves and a ball. Slipping one of the mitts onto his left hand, he shoved the other into Frazier's stomach. It nearly knocked the wind out of him.

"You walk," Andrew said, nodding his head away from The Van. Frazier, smiling smugly, abided the order, placing his camera inside The Van and trotting about twenty steps farther down the lane of the parking lot before turning around. Then, without speaking, the two began to have a catch. I pulled out the red lawn chair, sat down, and observed.

It's a funny thing, baseball. This very plain action of "having a catch" has an oddly remedial effect embedded somewhere in its performance. As I watched the ball zip from Andrew's hand to Frazier's glove, and then from Frazier's hand back to Andrew's glove, and then back again, I came to recognize that I was watching a healing of sorts take place. With every *wssssh-pop!* of the baseball hitting the mitt, the two vented their anger at each other—not through words or fists but through the ball. It was like applying an antidote to a wound or stitching up a tear in a piece of cloth: every time the baseball was exchanged, the two of them breathed a little easier. Slowly, the argument they had just exploded into melted into rhythmic cooperation.

It makes sense that having a catch carries with it this therapeutic element. To successfully have a catch requires (at least) two people, both of whom must be able to capably throw the ball and then also receive it in their glove. You must work with the other person to successfully have a catch; none of it can be done alone. It's like a relationship.

The phrase *have a catch* has been ingrained in our heads to automatically reference America's pastime. When I say, "Want to have a catch?," you undoubtedly know that I am asking if you would like to throw a *baseball* back and forth. "Have a catch" does not suggest other sports; football would be something like "Want to toss the football?" while soccer might be "Want to have a . . . kick?" No, when one references "catch," one is referencing baseball. "Play catch" works too.

The *action* of having a catch has also worked itself into our history as Americans. Over the past century (and beyond), parent-child relationships have been constructed through having a catch on the front lawn. MLB has begun to incorporate having a catch as a symbolic action in a game: these days; it is not uncommon to see professional players tossing the ball to a kid in the stands before the game starts. It's similar to throwing out the first pitch, in a sense. Yet in my opinion, nowhere is the emotional magnitude of having a catch better captured than in film.

The only movie out there that can make me cry on demand is *Field of Dreams* and simply because of its final scene. I tear up every time Kevin Costner's character, ridden with guilt at the way he treated his father before he died, gets one more chance to mend his tattered relationship when his dad returns to play on the field he built. And to what medium does Costner turn to do this?

"Hey . . . Dad?" he asks. "You wanna have a catch?" The tears in his eyes as he says this always mirror my own as I watch it.

I'm not suggesting that Andrew and Frazier were actually a father-son duo whose relationship had been frayed by years of differing ideals, but I *am* suggesting that the healing mechanism of having a catch was acting in the same manner. After only five or ten minutes, the two were laughing together again. The bird poop, the nuggets, the photography club jab—it was all water under the bridge. The only thing that mattered to each now was the ball, the glove, and the other person they were throwing to. From that red lawn chair, I caught glimpses of *Field of Dreams*.

"Is this heaven?" I surely asked myself, sheepishly referencing the movie.

No, it was Milwaukee. But as the *wsssssh-pop!* continued and the recently intense argument between my two friends healed, it was funny—I could have sworn it was heaven.

TOP OF THE THIRD
US Cellular Field

Ten Days?

8:45 p.m. | Tuesday, June 21

The rain pounded the concrete walkways. Small rivers formed, cascading their way down the steps toward the ball field like little waterfalls. The ferocious wind that had picked up was twisting the downpour sideways, showing no regard for our covered position in the concourse and drenching the four of us without mercy.

"It'll only last a few more minutes," an older man next to me said, spotting our shock at how quickly the system had moved in and delayed the game—which, only ten minutes before, had been proceeding nicely under open Chicago skies. "This happens all the time."

From our vantage point beneath the cement ceilings of the third-base concourse, US Cellular Field appeared dark. Yet this was not just due to the dingy weather; this place is normally dark. The home of the White Sox is made primarily of concrete, the majority of which has been painted black to match the team's main color. The railings are black, the scoreboards are black, the light fixtures are black—even every one of the more than forty thousand seats is painted black. Since we visited it, the stadium has had its name changed to Guaranteed Rate Field, a title that has combined with these dark confines to earn it the unfortunate nickname of "the Grate"—which actually might be a step up from its *former* nickname, "the Cell."

Opened in 1991, the twenty-eight-year-old ballpark still pays tribute to the White Sox's original home, Old Comiskey Park, which had stood directly across the street and housed the ball club for over eighty years. Pinwheels on the scoreboard spiral whenever a Sox player hits a home run, just as they did back at Old Comiskey. A showerhead in the center field walkway offers fans the ability to cool off during hot summer games, just as they were able to do at Old Comiskey. And before shifting titles to US Cellular Field in 2003, the stadium was called Comiskey Park, just as it had been at Old Comiskey (duh).

Even though we were uncomfortably crammed into that dark and wet walkway, we were entertained nonetheless because the atmosphere was wonderful. That evening's game, which was currently suspended between the fifth and sixth innings, was one of the annual meetings between the Chicago White Sox and their Northside rivals, the Cubs, in a series better known as the "Cross-Town Classic." It is one of only four series in baseball where teams from the same city meet up, joining the "Subway Series" (New York Yankees and Mets), the "Freeway Series" (Los Angeles Dodgers and Angels), and—if you count it—the "Bay Bridge Series" between the Oakland Athletics and the San Francisco Giants.

We were fortunate to also catch the Subway Series on this trip, but in all honesty, the Windy City's rivalry might top the Big Apple's. The L trains to get to the Cell had been abuzz with insults and the classic banter of hometown pride going up against hometown pride. The game itself had been a continuous chorus of chants, with "Let's go, Sox" and "Let's go, Cubs" echoing back-and-forth, making it difficult to discern which team truly had home field advantage. And the damp walkway in which we now stood was a sea of jerseys, as the black-and-white pinstripes of White Sox's apparel disagreed with the red and blue of Cubs' apparel. Some shirts stepped away from promot-

ing their teams and instead claimed pride to their neighbor-
hoods, broadcasting simple phrases like "Northside" or
"Southside." One woman standing near us wore a custom jersey
that was split down the middle, White Sox on the left and Cubs
on the right, representing her love for both teams. The name on
her back just said "Chicago."

Looking out at the tarped-up field through the steady stream
of water that dripped from the edges of the second terrace
above, my eyes fell on a scoreboard across the way. It was flashing notices for the White Sox's upcoming games, the next of
which was tomorrow's series finale against the Cubs. Reading
the date listed next to the start time, I immediately jumped.

"Oh god!" I said, scaring the woman in the two-toned jersey. "What date is it?"

"What?" Frazier asked lazily from my right.

"It's the twenty-first today?"

"Uh . . . yeah. Why?"

"I need to pay that speeding ticket!"

Andrew turned to look at me. "Speeding ticket?"

"Yeah, the one from the first drive."

"Oh no, I know it. But what on earth is making you think of
that right now?"

"I was looking at the scoreboard, and it says tomorrow's
game is June twenty-second, which means today is June twenty-
first."

"So?"

"So I was told to have that one hundred and seventy-five
dollars postmarked within ten days of receiving the ticket."

A pause followed this.

"You got that the day we left, right?" Michael asked.

"Yeah," I replied. "The eleventh."

"My god," he then said, his mouth falling open and his eyebrows rising uncontrollably. "We've only been on the road for ten days."

It was a statement of fact but also a statement of fear. At first, the thought of having been gone for only ten days just seemed crazy—time flies—but soon, the true weight of Michael's realization washed over each of us like the drenching rain we were staring at. A few more seconds of silence passed until Frazier spoke next.

"Jesus," he said, his voice now barely audible above the pounding of the rain and the whistling of the wind. "Ten days?"

"Yeah."

He let out a low whistle and then summarized what we each were now thinking.

"God, it feels like it's been so much longer."

Ten days? *Ten* days! That's all we had been traveling for? The feeling that hit me as I came to grips with this was not a happy feeling; it was one of anxiety, almost claustrophobia. Frazier was right: it indeed felt like we had been on the road for *much* longer than just ten days, and understandably so. We had already seen eight ballparks, received a speeding ticket, visited a mechanic, encountered a drug dealer, fought 108-degree heat a few times, and fought with each other a few times. That was all in ten days—and we had forty-three more left. The trip wasn't even a fifth of the way through.

"How many miles have we covered?" Andrew asked.

"Uh," Michael replied, scratching his head, "pretty sure we were a little over four thousand when I checked earlier today."

"God," I heard Andrew mumble. I didn't have to be told why. It wasn't just the things we had experienced over the first ten days that made the remainder of the trip seem so intimidating; it was also the things our *car* had seen that made the remainder of the trip so intimidating. In a little over a week of use, The Van had already shown many issues, from the omni-present brake lights back on that first drive, to the nearly con-stant clicking sound that had set in since, to the nonexistent air-conditioning and cruise control. Every mile we had rolled thus far had been filled with unease as to whether the next mile would even be a possibility.

"How many miles did we predict our route would require?" I asked to Michael, scared of the response.

"Over fourteen thousand."

"So we have at least ten thousand remaining."

"Yeah."

I looked back out onto the rain-soaked field, watching the puddles grow larger on the white tarp that was stretched out over the diamond. The storm was showing no sign of letting up, despite the local having told us that it would be over in a few minutes. Instead, the water continued to pound US Cellular Field, and the impromptu waterfalls kept rushing down the stepped, concrete walkways.

Somewhere in the parking lot, The Van sat drenched and aching.

MIDDLE OF THE THIRD
Busch Stadium

6:25 p.m. | Wednesday, June 22

"Meet me at Stan."

"Where?"

"*Stan.*"

It took us a good fifteen minutes to understand what the ticket scalper was talking about. Foreign to the city of Saint Louis—let alone its ballpark—we asked a few people what "Stan" meant as we walked around the grounds outside of Busch Stadium. We had struggled to find tickets to the game and had resorted to buying four from a bootleg seller on the street.

Like many sports, ticket scalping is totally normal in baseball. I often wonder whether I have purchased more tickets directly from the MLB box office, through an online sharing site such as StubHub or SeatGeek, or from street vendors (revendors?) who hold their product in the air and yell, "Who needs tickets?" It's always a crapshoot depending on the game, stadium, and your ability to bargain—but at times, scalping can be quite beneficial. If a game is sold out or you aren't trying to pay face value for entry, buying on the street is normally a decent option. In this particular instance, Busch Field was sold out for the Wednesday night Cardinals game against the Philadelphia Phillies. Michael had located a scalper, but the man claimed to have no more tickets left.

"But my buddy does," he said, whipping out a flip phone as if Michael had yelled *draw!* "Lemme call him and he'll tell you where to meet him."

Thus began our search for Stan. The first four or five people we asked claimed ignorance as well, but a man in a red Albert Pujols jersey soon perked his head up.

"Musial?" he said, taking care not to lose his spot in the entry line as he turned toward us.

"Maybe?" Michael replied.

"Yeah, I'll bet it's Musial." The man pointed farther down the road, toward the third-base side of the stadium. "That way, just outside the main entrance."

We followed his directions and sure enough soon came to a gigantic statue of Stan "the Man" Musial. There are twelve larger-than-life statues that honor Cardinal heroes circling Busch, but somehow Musial's monument has become the de facto rendezvous location for local fans, despite many of them not liking it at all. Regular game-goers, journalists, and even Musial himself have criticized the ten-foot bronze erection as being disproportionate and falsely representing the Saint Louis legend.[17] *Here stands baseball's perfect warrior,* the inscription reads, *here stands baseball's perfect knight.* Locals scoff at this statement, claiming it to be cheesy. I think it's pretty cool.

Our scalper was not there yet, but we waited patiently. It's part of the scalping procedure; honestly, buying scalped tickets is a lot like a drug deal. "He's never early, he's always late," Lou Reed once said. "First thing you learn is that you've always got to wait." True to his (and Reed's) word, our man showed up about ten minutes before first pitch with four tickets to the ballgame, each far less expensive than any of our previous offerings. We happily paid and made our way into Busch Stadium.

Red, red, red. Whereas the White Sox's field is almost entirely black, the Cardinals' is almost entirely red. The baseball players wear red, the fans wear red—even the stadium wears red. The brick walls that wrap the outside of the building are very much present within the gates as well, giving a rusted-rouge tint to the majority of walkways. The advertisements that look down onto the field have all incorporated red in one way or another, too, from the Big Mac sign that stood in center to the local real estate business billboard in left. And although Busch was proudly sold out on the night we visited, the stadium always *looks* full even when it is not, for the seats themselves are also painted red. From our scalped tickets in the upper deck we took in the red sea, as the Cardinals lost 4–0 to the (also red) Philadelphia Phillies.

Beyond the color, what I remember most about our visit to Busch Stadium was the man who sat next to Frazier. A fairly tall individual, he had to spread his legs open to fit them into the slim area between the seats. At one point, his left knee bumped the cupholder, knocking the cup within it and spilling beer over Frazier's shoes.

"Darn," the man said, "I'm sorry."

"No worries," Frazier said, waving off the accident and wiping his shoes. "I'm surprised my hair hasn't dipped into the beer of the guy behind me, to be honest."

This got a chuckle out of the tall man. "These things need to be bigger, don't they?"

"The beer or the seats?"

"Both," he replied with a smile. He introduced himself to Frazier as Max Entrien, and the two began to chat. Over the next couple of innings, Max learned our story, and in exchange we learned his. He had moved to Saint Louis only a few months ago, taking over a car dealership in the northern part of the city. The mention of cars sparked Michael's interest.

"You're a car guy, eh?" he asked, leaning over Frazier.

"You bet."

I watched Michael chew on his thoughts, debating whether he should pester this stranger about our vehicle's issues. He didn't chew long. "Any chance you might know what makes a car rattle?" he asked.

"Eh?"

"Rattling. Clicking. Our van . . . it's been clicking for about a week now. Like, a noise under the hood. We've been debating taking it to a mechanic, but nothing seems to be all that troublesome as of yet. Outside of the noise itself, that is."

"Clicking, you say?" Max seemed genuinely interested.

"Yeah."

"Does a change of speed vary it at all?"

"Actually, yeah. If we accelerate, it gets quicker and a bit louder. But we've been keeping it under sixty lately, and it seems to be fine, so we aren't thinking much of it."

Max took a sharp breath. "Ah, I wouldn't sit on that too long. Sounds like you guys might have an axle problem." The next thing we knew, he demanded that we bring The Van into his dealership tomorrow. I couldn't tell if this had been Michael's initial hope, but he reacted surprised and grateful—yet accepted the offer immediately.

"Glad we met you," he said, shaking Max's hand.

"Glad I spilled beer on your friend here," Max replied. He winked at Frazier and then said something about how he looked a bit like Wayne from *Wayne's World*. He wasn't that far off.

10:15 a.m. | The Following Morning

Max's shop was about ten minutes northwest on I-70, just outside of the Saint Louis city limits. It was surrounded by other car dealerships, each of which looked to be exactly the same, save for the brand of vehicle that they advertised. Max's was at

the far end, and it sold Land Rovers. We felt downright guilty
driving our shambolic camper through the parking lot that was
otherwise filled with nice, large, single-colored cars. At one
point, we even debated whether it would be too impolite to
reject Max's offer. Pulling up with The Van might be somewhat
embarrassing—not only for us but also for Max.

"Nah," Michael said, "he offered. Plus, we finally have
someone who can take a look at it." He paused. "You guys *want*
to fix this noise, right?"

"Yep."

"Yep."

"Yep."

We proceeded to the dealership.

"My word, look at that thing!" Max said as he came out and
caught his first glance of our car. He couldn't help but laugh as
his eyes wandered over the harlequin design. But fifteen
minutes later, The Van was up on the car lift, with two mechan-
ics inspecting its underbelly. Andrew and Frazier played catch in
the parking lot—it was now their thing to do to pass time—as
Michael and I sat on the curb and gazed into the distance. I regretted leaving the red lawn chair inside The Van as I sat and
looked at the Gateway Arch. It was barely visible above the
cloudy skyline, as a clump of Missouri haze was just beginning
to gather above Saint Louis. Two minutes passed in silence,
accompanied only by the now familiar rhythm of ball and glove.

"Think it's gonna make it?" I then asked.

"The Van?" Michael responded.

"Yeah."

"Yeah, man, I think so. Don't worry."

I paused another minute, watching as a few clients wandered
through the lot of the Chevy dealership across the way. "Think
we're gonna make it?"

"You sound like Andrew."

"I had a hunch you might've been awake during that conversation."

"Yeah, sorry."

"For the whole thing?"

"Yeah, sorry," he said again.

I took a breath. "I don't know, man. That thought's still in my head. I can't seem to get it out of there."

"What's worrying you? That we're not gonna be friends or something once this is all over?"

"Not that we're not gonna be *friends* but that we're not gonna be the same *type* of friends."

"What you mean?"

"I dunno, man. It's . . . I guess the thought of heading separate ways for something as big as college scares me. Maybe it's simply because I haven't done anything like it in the past—but I feel like stuff's gonna change."

"Stuff *is* gonna change," Michael replied sharply. "Stuff is already changing. But that doesn't mean we won't change with it." Blunt by nature, he then raised himself from the curb and clapped his hands together to free them of small bits of gravel. "Don't be a sap, dude. You think too much. We have other stuff to *actually* think about right now. C'mon, let's go check in on The Van."

We didn't make it very far, however, before The Van came to check in on us. Only a few seconds later, our car rounded the corner of the lot and bounded toward us, running through the rows of Land Rovers like a dog returning to its owners. It stopped about fifteen feet ahead of us, and we walked up quickly to pat it on its nose. But then a mechanic got out of the driver's side door, and Michael and I both took a step back. Other than the four of us, this guy was the first person who had driven The Van, and we felt weirdly threatened by him. It was as if he had touched something personal or had violated a sacred place.

"How'd it . . . go?" Michael asked, trying to mask his unease.

"We think we figured it out," the man said as he tossed Michael the keys. "One of yer tires was slightly off with the . . . with its alignment. So we replaced it."

A beat followed this before Michael spoke again.

"You replaced what?"

"The tire!" The guy was too enthusiastic about this for our liking.

"Which one?"

"Back right!"

At this, I could hear the breath release from Michael's mouth like a gasp of air being quickly let out of a balloon. Our clicking had definitely been coming from the front, not the back.

"Awesome," Michael said nevertheless. "Thanks, man—I really appreciate it. What do we owe you guys?"

"Nuthin."

"Nothing? Get out! You just replaced a ti—"

"Look," he said, cutting us off, "it was our pleasure to try 'n help. Max says you guys are good guys, and honestly if Max says it, it goes 'round here." He then grimaced. "But there *is* something I should warn you guys 'bout." With this, the mechanic gestured for us to follow him around to the right side of The Van, where he stopped and slid the door open, a gesture that once again felt weirdly violating.

"We aren't allowed to dispose of tires at this facility," he said, "so I had to leave the old'n with y'all. Sorry 'bout that . . . but hey, maybe it'll come in use as a spare if need be?"

Michael and I peered into The Van. There, plopped onto the back-bench seat, was a gigantic white plastic sack, holding the tire that had just been replaced. It stuck out over the edge of the seat about five or six inches and encroached significantly onto the other half of the bench.

"Ah," Michael said after a few seconds. "I see."

"Again, sorry 'bout that," the mechanic replied.

"No . . . worries . . ." He stared another few seconds before trying to pick up the tone of his voice a bit. "Well, thanks again, my man. Can we thank Max as well?"

"He had to take off, but I'll pass along the message."

"I appreciate it."

With that, the mechanic walked away, leaving Michael, The Van, and me standing in the lot of Land Rovers. I sat down on the floor of the vehicle, my feet resting on the pavement, and chuckled. I think The Van laughed as well. Andrew and Frazier, spotting the car's reemergence, soon wandered over too. We filled them in on all that the mechanic had told us.

"The *tire?*" Andrew asked, looking at the humongous sack on the bench seat. "C'mon, that definitely wasn't the problem."

"No, but it was kind of them to try," I replied.

"I'm not disagreeing with that. But now we're in charge of the stupid thing?"

"I mean, I guess so."

"Well, we should dispose of that immediately."

"Yeah, I think s—"

"Hold up," Michael interjected. "If they said that they couldn't get rid of the tire here, can we just dump it anywhere?"

"What do you mean?"

"If they can't dispose of it here, at an auto dealership, I feel like we can't simply throw it away as we please."

"Yeah," Frazier replied, "I actually think I read something about that once. Like, in the same way you can't just abandon a television in any old garbage can, you have to take it to a dump?"

"Or batteries," Michael said. "They need to be properly disposed of as well." And with that, the snowballing had begun.

"Yeah, batteries too," Frazier replied.

"I think car tires fall into the same category."

"Oh they definitely do."

"Right."

"I think it's a crime actually, right?"

"To dispose of them improperly?"

"Yeah."

"Yeah, I think you're right."

"You need to properly dispose of batteries?" I asked. "Huh, I've always just tossed them into the trash with everything else."

"Oh no," Frazier said. "No, you can't do that, man."

"You'd get in big trouble," Michael stated.

"*Big* trouble."

"Yeah, and the same goes for tires, I'm pretty darn sure. If the police find one on the side of the road, they can track it back to your car. And I don't wanna pay that fine."

"Me neither," Frazier agreed. The surefire rapidity of their discussion had convinced me too. The three of us turned toward Andrew, who stood propped against The Van. His mouth was hanging slightly open.

"You guys have to be kidding me," he said, an air of anger laced in his voice. "A *crime?* For a *tire?* Police tracking! Oh come on."

"Hey," Frazier said, putting his hands up in the air, "I'd rather be safe than sorry. We can't afford a police ticket right now, that's for sure." He nodded his head in my direction. "We've already had one too many."

With an ugly smirk, I flipped him off in response. Andrew shook his head again.

"You guys can't seriously think we're going to keep a *tire* with us in The Van, right?"

"What's wrong with doing that?"

"It's a *tire!* A massive, gigantic rubber tire! We're already cramped for space as it is!" He turned to Michael. "Look, just because you once corrected the teacher—"

"Oh shut up."

"—doesn't mean you know what's best for *everything.* I mean, come on, we've got four dudes in here, four big-ass backpacks, two sleeping bags, two blankets, a cooler, pots, pans, cutlery, and whatever other shit I've forgotten! Fitting a *tire* into this car as well is insane!" But Andrew's logic was outnumbered by our fear of the law and blind trust in Michael, and he soon had to concede.

The teenage mind is pretty darn gullible, isn't it? Look at how its perception of logic can spiral out of control, prompted only by an assumption and fueled by false support that simply *sounds* as if it could be correct. There is indeed a law somewhere that mentions something about improper disposal of tires—but it is not highly punishable, and we would likely have never felt its effects in the first place. But when you are young, you are so easily convinced of things that simply aren't true. All it takes is speculation, the classic phrase "I think I read it somewhere," and boom, the unraveling of sanity has begun. Out of nowhere, our fear of getting into trouble again had created a justification in our own heads, and we were now convinced that it was simply our duty to take the tire with us.

"Screw it," Andrew said, muttering as he slipped into the driver's seat of The Van and started the engine. "But I'm not sitting back there next to it."

He turned the key in the ignition and we took off, angrily bound for Kansas City. Twenty minutes later, the clicks returned, followed by a plethora of cursing.

"No wonder the work was free," Andrew grumbled. In the rearview mirror, he threw the discarded tire a mean look. Space was already at a premium in the tiny camper, and it was quickly beginning to feel like that gigantic thing and its plastic white sack took up more area than any of us did. We should have discarded the tire immediately. But we didn't. Instead, for some thickheaded reason, we held on to it for thirty more days.

BOTTOM OF THE THIRD
Kauffman Stadium

DEATH BY GPS

8:56 p.m. | Thursday, June 23

The large man next to me stood up and demanded I link arms with him. Utterly confused—but also completely intimidated by his humongous body mass—I obliged, angling my right arm into a triangle and hooking it around his left. The guy's biceps were the size of my neck, and hardly any of it was muscle.

"C'mon," he said in a gruff voice, "get yer friends to do it too!"

"What's going on?" I asked.

He looked perplexed, almost horrified at my ignorance. "It's the sixth!" he said. "It's Garth Brooks time!"

Garth Brooks time? As my eyes began to pan the rest of Kansas City's Kauffman Stadium, I noticed that many other fans were also standing up and linking arms with one another as a few familiar notes then blared through the speakers above my head. A few rows behind me, a woman grumbled.

"Why *this* song?" she lamented. "Why does it always have to be *this* song?"

Nobody else seemed to hear her, however, as the majority of the seventy-five hundred gathered in attendance for that night's Royals vs. Diamondbacks game belched out the first few lines of "Friends in Low Places," surprisingly on key. I had not yet been trained in country classics, so I merely observed the scene as my right arm slowly lost all feeling, suffocated into the armpit of the beer-guzzling giant who stood next to me.

Kauffman Stadium looks like a spaceship. Its pure white facade slowly ascends at an angle, beginning at the foul poles and reaching its peak behind home plate to make an arc that reminded me of the *Starship Enterprise*. Nearly every seat in the ballpark is held within this sleek curve, as outfield sections primarily house standing room areas and other attributes of the stadium, including the Royals Hall of Fame and a large fountain that erupts whenever a Kansas City player hits a home run.

By the time the Garth Brooks ballad was over (the participation in which far outnumbered "Take Me Out to the Ballgame" the inning after), the four of us were laughing. This was partially out of comedy, as the man to my right had proclaimed we were "true Kansas City locals now" and took a moment to "baptize" each of us using some of the beer in his cup as holy water. But the rest of our laughter was out of nerves; we were each ready to get this game over with. Nothing against Kauffman Stadium, but we had one hell of a drive facing us after it. Our nine ballparks in nine days section of the schedule demanded that we be in Detroit the following evening—and that was 763 miles away. However, whatever nerves we had about potentially not making it in time were soon replaced with nerves about potentially not making it at all.

1:41 a.m.

Death by GPS is a real thing, and we are here to raise awareness. I had heard this phrase once or twice before, primarily in articles about people doing wild things like getting lost in the desert or driving off a cliff simply because their GPS told them to do so, but had always assumed those stories to be some sort of cruel joke. Nope, it's real. We didn't *die* because of our GPS, but that evening in Missouri showed me that such a cause for fatality is indeed a possibility.

By now, we four teenagers had become completely devoted to our beloved Garmin, Tina. She was the only female presence in The Van and therefore held an unquestioned authority over us boys. Gone were the days of arguing with her; they had been replaced by such submissive phrases as "OK, Tina" or "Yes, dear" whenever she told us to do something like turn left or demanded that we make better life choices.

Michael had programmed "Detroit, Michigan" into Tina, and she had quickly calculated a fourteen-hour route that would lead us across Missouri and into Indiana before heading north toward Michigan. The first few hours of the drive were uneventful, as we merely made our way east from Kansas City on Interstate 70 through dark splotches of middle-America countryside. It was just after we passed Columbia that Tina's robotic, oddly sexy voice broke the silence and the excitement began.

"Rerouting."

This was never a fun word to hear from our dashboard girlfriend. Yes, it obviously meant she was attempting to avoid some sort of traffic ahead, but we had begun to interpret this word differently—personally. To us, *rerouting* now meant *reevaluating* in an almost existential sort of way, such as "I'm currently reevaluating your life decisions" if not "I see danger up ahead for you, dear, so I'm going to take over for a bit and reroute you toward a better future." And, of course, we had stopped arguing. Tina had never led us astray—yet.

"Take the next exit for Missouri State Route 54."

This was definitely a strange declaration, however. Outside of directing us to and from precise locations within cities, Tina had never yet led us off the interstates. Freeways are simply the quickest way to get from point A to point B in the gigantic country that is the United States of America, and Kansas City to Detroit was no different: I-70 continued on to Saint Louis and all the way to Indianapolis, where I-69 then headed north toward Detroit. This was what the GPS had originally declared to be the path. Surely that indeed was the fastest route?

But Tina wanted us to take the next exit, so we took the next exit. Assuming she had, in her clairvoyant beauty, predicted traffic ahead or calculated some sort of route shift that would allow us to shave a few minutes off our ETA, we succumbed to her tone like it was a Siren. The Van turned off I-70 and began heading northbound on Missouri State Route 54.

Fifteen minutes later, Andrew casually pointed out that we had not seen another vehicle since leaving the freeway. It was just the dark pavement, The Van, and The Van's still-frequent clicks. I stared out the rear window at the vast expanse of nothingness that our taillights dimly illuminated behind us. Something didn't feel right, but Tina told us that we were on the right course, so we questioned nothing. The time on the dashboard clock read 1:58 a.m.

ROAD CLOSED AHEAD
LOCAL TRAFFIC ONLY

The discouraging orange sign on the side of the road was gone too quickly for us to take it seriously. At one moment it had been visible, lit by The Van's headlights—and then it was gone, behind us, surely of no importance. Tina said to press on, so we pressed on.

"We're not too far from our next turnoff," Andrew said from the shotgun seat, nodding at the GPS. Silhouetted by the dull glow of her little screen, he had adopted the faint look of someone who had fallen into a hypnotic trance. Even his voice had changed slightly, as he now spoke with a monotonous drawl. "I'll bet we can pass as 'local traffic.'"

"Yes, we're local traffic," Michael said from beside me, his voice sounding eerily similar to Andrew's. What was this curse?

The Van proceeded obediently, acting as if it hadn't noticed anything strange either. A mile or two later, another orange sign appeared. This one, however, stood in the middle of the road and broadcasted a very simple, to-the-point message.

ROAD CLOSED

You would think that the sign's location and blunt communication would be enough to get our attention—but unfortunately, you would be wrong. We were in total submission to the tiny robot suction-cupped to the windshield, convinced it held a sliver of deity in its silky voice. Was there room for "local traffic" to continue past the sign? Of course there was room for local traffic to continue past the sign. Tina said to carry on, so we carried on.

BRIDGE OUT AHEAD
NO MORE THRU TRAFFIC

This one hung from a ratty rope draped across the two-lane highway. Proceeding further would have required us to consciously drive through the rope and tear down the sign—which, even in our entranced states, was going slightly too far for us. "Local traffic" was no longer a label of invincibility under which we could continue without fear; BRIDGE OUT AHEAD brought us down to earth pretty quickly. The Van came to a complete halt there in the middle of State Route 54, about six feet away from the sign hanging from the rope. We were close enough to see the frayed knots in the twine, which looked to have been weathered by a decent number of storms. And that's when the Twilight Zone hit.

The first thing that happened was that Tina shut off completely. We each had grown so accustomed to her presence in The Van that having it removed without notice left even the vehicle itself speechless.

"Wh . . . where'd she go?" Frazier asked. I could hear panic in his voice. I could feel panic in my own, as I replied from the back.

"Did one of you guys turn her off?"

"No . . ." Andrew replied, his voice still carrying that creepy monotone that I now realized I hated. It scared me. "No . . . she switched herself off." He tried rebooting her a couple of times and messed with her cords, but to no avail. "She's . . . gone . . ."

Danny's not here right now, Mrs. Torrance. I told my mind to shut up.

"All right," Michael said, "all right. Let's try to retrace our steps."

But as Frazier began to turn The Van began around in front of the rope, the true spookiness of our setting began to make its presence known. A couple of houses sat on either side of the road, their yards overflowing with weeds and their front porches scattered with dislodged planks. We had not noticed these houses initially. They were not part of a town at all but merely stood alone on this already isolated stretch of road. A crooked street sign next to one of them simply read HANNIBAL, with an arrow that must have once pointed in the direction we had been trying to go. But the sign was broken, and the arrow now hung limply from the signpost, pointing to one of the houses.

"Hannibal . . ." Andrew said from the shotgun seat.

"I think it's a town in the direction we were trying to go," Michael replied, much to my relief. But Andrew's mind was clearly where mine was now going as well.

"Yes . . . but isn't Hannibal also the name of—"

"Yes, Andrew. Stop that now."

The Van moved past the house and continued back down State Route 54, in the direction from which we had come. Headlights appeared suddenly in the distance. It was the first car we had seen since getting off the freeway—the freeway that we now so desperately wanted to return to. The car drove past us in the left lane and disappeared behind our taillights into the Missouri night. We never saw it again. It either ignored the BRIDGE OUT sign and tumbled to its death or it parked at Hannibal's house. I don't know which I would have preferred.

"Looks like we're running low on gas," Frazier mumbled from behind the wheel. This was a phrase that nobody in the car wanted to hear. Andrew turned his head slowly and craned his neck to look at the dashboard, his silence confirming Frazier's observations. I tucked my knees up to my chest on the folded-down back-bench and stared at the dark road ahead of us. Fireflies hit The Van's windshield and stuck there for a while, continuing to glow and adding a hazy, alien green light to what was otherwise dim headlamps and darkness.

MEXICO
NEXT RIGHT

What?

Like the first of the ROAD CLOSED signs, nobody acknowledged this obscure one as it passed us by on the side of the road. Apparently we had accidentally slipped through a portal of some sort and been transported much farther south than we were attempting to go. Future research taught me that Mexico is actually a tiny town in that part of the state—where the "Miss Missouri" pageant is held, of all things—but of course none of that was known at this moment. In our impressionable states, we were apparently on our way to the country of Mexico. Whatever. As long as there was a gas station nearby, we could have been heading anywhere. Tina remained dark on the dashboard, a casualty of midnight Missouri. Our headlights illuminated yet another sign a couple of minutes later.

BENTON CITY
Population: 126

The Van began to roll through what at first appeared to be a small town—but it soon became apparent that "town" (let alone "city") was a generous label. There was an old house on the left, an old house on the right, and then there was a graveyard. It stretched along the side of the road for a good three hundred yards and expanded back farther than our eyes could see or minds could imagine. For all we knew, that graveyard may have had no end. One house later, a sign told us that we were now leaving Benton City. Silently, we each wondered if the town's 126 people were living in the three houses or if the majority of them were six feet under. We didn't know, but we didn't care. What we *did* know was that we didn't drive through this place forty minutes ago.

Tension continued to rise in The Van as the road wound on for a few more miles. Suddenly a new light appeared—but it was not a friendly one, as the small *Empty* icon on the dashboard had now blinked on, its dim, depressing yellow shade joining the ghostly glow of the fireflies and headlamps. They all combined to illuminate a turn in front of us, the sharpness of which demanded The Van slow down to a creepy-crawling ten miles per hour. Frazier spun the wheel, and the headlights swept across the other side of the road, showing a grove of trees, a small gap, more trees—and then something that made The Van screech to a halt.

To the left, in the small gap between the trees, was nothing other than a second graveyard. This one was very small, with crumbling tombs and a rusty wrought-iron gate that seemed to stretch out toward the road like hands from the underworld. To the right, originally hidden by the sharp turn, was a rundown house, three stories high. Two smashed cars sat in the decaying front yard, and a single dull light shone from the very top room. And standing in the middle of the road, illuminated by The Van's dim headlights, was an enormous black dog. It looked to be pushing 140 pounds, it wore no collar, and its fur was matted and clumped, grizzled by what appeared to be years of roaming the Missouri countryside. The dog raised its ragged head slowly and looked at The Van, its eyes flickering yellow in the car's beams. It stared at us with a gaze that went straight through the windshield and entered our souls, exposing us completely. We were now entirely at its mercy. Ten seconds passed, elapsing in silence save for the surely audible thumps from our fast-beating hearts. Then the dog lowered its head and slowly skulked into the graveyard.

It was then that Andrew released a guttural scream that, to this day, is still the most raw and unrestrained noise I have ever heard emerge from a human being. Frazier hit the gas and The Van sped out of that nightmare, continuing down the road.

"Andrew?" Michael said, to no response.

I have never been so grateful to see the industrial lights of the freeway than when they appeared three minutes later. The moving headlamps of cars popped onto the horizon in a sudden manner, welcoming us back to the interstate's friendly, comfortable confines and lifting our spirits immediately. Almost on cue, Tina promptly sprang back to life from the windshield. As if nothing had happened, she immediately programmed a route that led us back to the freeway and then continued on to Indianapolis before turning left and heading north to Michigan—as had originally been the plan. A sign for gas appeared a minute later.

"Andrew . . .?"

TOP OF THE FOURTH

Comerica Park

MICHIGAN CENTRAL STATION

8:30 p.m. | Friday, June 24

Comerica Park is easily one of the nicest buildings in downtown Detroit. The exterior is a pleasant brick, lined with green gates and big glass windows that are filled with pictures of Tigers players, old and new. It sheds a feel of historic importance when you walk by the ballpark's grounds—a *you should be proud to be here* sentiment, regardless of whether you are actually going to the game.

Tigers are everywhere in Comerica. Yes, the park is obviously the host of the Tigers baseball team, but the mascot itself appears regularly in the stadium as well. Large stone tigers have been plopped sporadically within and without the ballpark, making sure no visitor mistakes where they are or what team plays here. The largest sits just outside of the main entrance, and my god it's huge. Caught in a pouncing position with paw extended, the beast guards Comerica and wards off fans of the visiting team. Andrew swung from one of its gigantic fangs before a guard told him to "get the hell down." Frazier laughed at him, they bickered, the world continued to turn.

Meanwhile, a large tiger-filled carousel can be found within the ballpark, in the left field concourse. It looks like something out of an amusement park or state fair, and I was slightly confused as to the purpose of this addition when I encountered it, seeing as the rest of the stadium felt somewhat modern. But even with the quirky merry-go-round, a ballgame at Comerica Park is a very enjoyable experience, for nearly every seat in the stadium has stellar views of the diamond and of the buildings of downtown Detroit that tower above it.

Andrew's terror from seeing the Benton City dog the night before was still with him as the game proceeded. "I don't mess with spirits, man," he said, taking a bite out of a sausage, "and I saw that thing. It saw me. It stared at me. It's an omen."

Frazier seized this moment to poke some fun at Andrew, who rarely showed signs of vulnerability. "Are you interpreting *Harry Potter* as real life right now?" he asked in an overly dramatic manner. "Just because a big black dog symbolizes death in the books doesn't mean that it's true in real life, you know."

"I know what I saw," Andrew replied. "That thing's gonna haunt me for the rest of my life."

"I'm gonna buy you a big black poodle."

"Stop it, Frazier."

By the time the next morning dawned, however, Andrew's proclaimed eternal fear had left him completely. In fact, I don't think he mentioned the dog again for the rest of the trip. Whatever "terror" it had instilled within him had been instead replaced by intrigue and fascination with the city in which he and I set out to explore later that night.

10:10 p.m.

I had been looking forward to visiting Detroit since the very conception of this trip. The draw I felt toward the Motor City was difficult to describe, as I was somewhere between excited and scared at seeing its modern ruins firsthand. It may sound like a cliché to many today—Detroit has recently been called "the world capital of staring at abandoned buildings"[18]—but to

an eighteen-year-old, it was as real as it gets. The juvenile attitude of "don't believe it until you see it for yourself" that coated
my logic at that age made me skeptical of the stories I had heard
about the city. Such descriptions as "bombed out" and "abandoned" simply seemed too foreign for me to grasp as a young
traveler. I had seen vacated buildings, yes, but could an entire
city really be that way? It seemed impossible. Somehow, through
both anticipation and fear, Detroit had continued to reel me in
like a fishing line as our trip proceeded.

After leaving Comerica, we drove around the city for roughly twenty minutes before winding up at West Riverfront Park
and declaring it our location to spend the night. Michael and
Frazier quickly stated their desire to go to sleep, but Andrew
objected.

"Come on," he said, "it's barely after ten o'clock! Don't you
guys want to see a bit of the city?"

"Not at all," Frazier replied.

"You sure, Frazh? This spot is filled with abandoned, ugly
things you can take pics of."

"Shut up."

Andrew turned to me. "How about you? You've been talking about visiting here since we began planning this whole
thing." He was right, but I was hesitant. As much as I wanted to
see Detroit, wandering the streets of the city at night understandably seemed precarious. But Andrew knew how to get to
me. "Come on," he continued, "it's something you'd regret if
you didn't. Don't pull a Pogues again." Triggered by anger at
my past self, I agreed to go with him.

"Watch out for scary dogs," Frazier said to Andrew.

"Fuck off," he crudely replied.

Andrew and I left The Van and began to wander north up
Trumbull Avenue, turning left after a few blocks onto Rosa

Parks Boulevard. Crowds of well-dressed people were wandering through the area, returning to cars parked on the street.

"Think a show just got out?" Andrew asked, as we passed a man in a three-piece suit and top hat.

"Must be," I responded. My eyes were fixed on the buildings that lined the boulevard on which we walked. Nearly all looked to be warehouses of sorts, and most looked entirely abandoned. A handful of them were encircled by chain-link fence, broadcasting their inactivity to passersby. A few even had entire chunks missing from their concrete or sheet metal walls. Their vacancy provided a strange contrast to the buzzing crowd.

Three blocks farther, the two of us spotted what appeared to be a nightclub on the corner. Its appearance suggested that it, too, was once a warehouse, but its vivid paint job and neon lights proved it was no longer devoid of life. A line of people about ten or so deep stretched from the building's entrance, which was marked with a purple-red door that matched the color of the velvet ropes that lazily dictated the line. Standing next to the door was the bouncer. He was a well-built man who wore a dark suit coat that covered a blindingly white dress shirt, the collar of which hung free, not bound by the restriction of a tie. Despite it being dark, his eyes were covered by black aviator sunglasses.

"Excuse me," Andrew said, approaching him. "Do you know of a place that sells food at this hour?"

The man turned and looked us up and down. At least, I assumed he did. I couldn't see his eyes through the tint of his sunglasses.

"Yeah," he answered after a few seconds, "matter 'o fact, there's a gas station right over there . . ." he gestured farther on down the road. "Yeah . . . matter 'o fact, keep going till you see the old Oyster House and turn left. It's close to the Station." He said it with a capitol *S*.

"OK," Andrew replied, "thanks."

But the man interjected before we could take off. "Matter 'o fact, there's a shortcut right through that road right there." He pointed to what looked more like an alley than a road. The dim light of the streetlamps did not make it look comforting at all.

"I think we're good," Andrew replied, trying again to depart politely. The bouncer had now turned his body completely toward us, and I watched as a few people in the front of the line snuck through the door and into the club. Seeming not to notice, he continued talking to us.

"Matter 'o fact, I can take you guys over there. I know the fastest route."

"I think you just told us," Andrew replied. "We'll take it ourselves. See ya—thanks again."

"Matter 'o fact, do you guys have any change to spare?" More people slipped into the club as the bouncer took a step toward us.

"Sorry, man, but I've got none on me. Maybe on our way back from the gas station."

"Ah, you don't?" Seeming totally confused at this statement, the man took a step back and turned his body, the movement of which blocked the club door slightly and forced those still in line to remain there. "Well, I should probably give *you* some then, shouldn't I?"

Now it was our turn to show confusion. "Huh?"

"I mean, matter 'o fact, how will you be able to buy food if you got no cash?" He then reached into the breast pocket of his suit coat and removed a money clip that, to our immense surprise, was packed thick with fifty-dollar bills. There was well over $500 in that thing; the small metal clip looked to be struggling to hold the wad of money. It eased only slightly as the man removed one of the fifties and tried to hand it to us.

"We're good—thanks, though. And thanks again for the directions." Andrew and I then promptly turned on our heels and continued to walk down the street. I glanced back over my shoulder after about fifty yards and saw that the man was once again checking IDs from the people in line for the club.

"Money is weird," Andrew said to me, as I turned my head back around to look forward once more. "Money is so, so weird."

I had no response for him; I could only nod my head in agreement to this statement. Money is indeed weird—but money is *extremely* weird in Detroit. It has a different feeling there than in other cities. It feels like it is needed everywhere, and it also feels like it should be kept away at all costs for fear of what it might do (again) to the city.

This strange aura of money and its polarizing necessity was nowhere more apparent, however, than in what Andrew and I stumbled on only a few minutes later. Heeding the bouncer's original directions to a gas station where we might find food, we headed up a few blocks, turned left onto Michigan Avenue, and began walking west. As the concentration of buildings started to thin, we debated turning around for fear of losing touch with the city. Yet as if hearing our whispered discussion, it was then that Michigan Central Station came into view.

Once the tallest train station in the world, this incredible structure had been abandoned for decades; having housed continuous railroad traffic from the 1910s until the late 1980s, it now housed only ghosts of years past.[iii] From our perspective at the tip of Roosevelt Park, the building shot up from the trees like an ominous, isolated mountain that watched over the dimly lit city from its dark, elevated perch. It felt like there was life in

---

[iii] Michigan Central Station has since been purchased by the Ford Company, which has vowed to attempt to restore it to some form of its prior glory.

there—and yet life like nothing we had ever encountered before.

"Let's go in," Andrew said.

I was reluctant for a second—but only for a second. This time, I didn't need anybody to remind me of the Pogues or of my plaguing tendency to dither when presented with an opportunity to live a little. Instead, I felt the umbilical cord that had connected me to that childhood hesitation sever. Snip, gone. This was what had been calling me to Detroit; this was the crux of the intrigue that I had been so confused by.

"Yes."

It took us about fifteen minutes to walk across the park to the base of the building. We kept an eye out for police cars that might be on the prowl in the area, extremely conscious of the sound of our feet crunching against the dead grass. But we saw nothing; police did not appear to patrol this space

"Why would they?" Andrew asked in a hushed whisper.

A chain-link fence surrounded the immediate building, but it looked to have been disregarded a decade ago. Holes the size of humans stood next to nearly every pole, and it was too easy for us to climb through.

Being on the other side of the fence was eerie. I felt as if I had walked into a new world, taking a step away from *hearing* about Detroit's reality and moving toward *seeing* it. I was no longer standing on the outside looking in—I was inside looking out.

We headed quickly for the building's main entrance, where a large arched doorway beckoned to us. Stepping in, I immediately felt my heart rise up through my chest. The rapid speed of its beat emulated the rhythm of the heavy locomotives that used to run through the building in which I now stood. I was feeling fear, yes, but I was feeling something else—I was also feeling thrill. I was feeling pleasure. We had emerged into what once was the main hall, a long, wide space lined with high-rising arches that naturally created domes in the ceiling. The way the faint light from the streetlamps beyond the building's property stretched into the space and dimly illuminated the interior area was enough to give me an idea of what was there as well as what *once* was there. Rubble littered the floor, and graffiti littered the walls. I couldn't make out any of the words that were sprayed onto the century-old concrete, but I didn't need to. The fact that such tags existed in the same place where bustling newspaper stands and automobile advertisements once stood was enough.

The glow from the streetlamps cast our shadows on the floor and pushed them forward, stretching them farther into the building until they blended with where the light ceased to shine. Andrew and I walked up to this point, hesitant to plunge into total darkness. We both took a second to simply stop and listen to the screaming silence of the building and its many, many memories. Then that feeling crept up again—that feeling of fear and pleasure mixed into one thrilling sensation.

"This is unlike anything I've ever experienced before," I whispered to Andrew. I didn't need to be able to see him to know that he nodded in agreement.

Schadenfreude: finding pleasure at somebody else's demise.

This is a hypothesis many academics hold when attempting to diagnose that sensation I was going through. When staring at ruins like those in Detroit, one often feels this intense conflict of emotions as a consequence of witnessing a space that has experienced a fall from grace. Also called *ruin porn,* this description carries with it a fairly negative connotation. As it should: many so-called urban explorers travel to such abandoned places purely seeking this thrilling feeling, thus exploiting the spaces for pleasure without regard for the reason as to why it fell into disrepair—just as Andrew and I were doing now. Even as I stared into the emptiness of Michigan Central Station, I couldn't help but feel guilty that I was getting a thrill out of wreckage. It was both horror and complete ecstasy—a simply addicting blend of hot and cold. Never again do I think I will experience something as pleasantly haunting as what I felt standing in that building, which was once booming in business and now creaks in emptiness.

MIDDLE OF THE FOURTH
PNC Park

THE MERCURIAL VAN

8:15 p.m. | Saturday, June 25

On days when the Pittsburgh Pirates play at home, the gorgeous Roberto Clemente Bridge is closed to cars, catering solely to pedestrians on their way to PNC Park. If you are lucky enough to cross it on a game day, take a minute to observe how the whole scene works together. The yellow hue of the bridge's ironwork matches the lining of the ballpark, which goes on to complement the stadium's primarily cream-brick facade. It all looks stunning when coated in a western Pennsylvania sunset.

The view from within the ballpark is even better than from the bridge. Any fan sitting in the upper level of the infield gazes out over the high right field fence, past the suspension cables of the bridge, and onto the skyscrapers of the Steel City that tower above the Allegheny River. It all glitters harmoniously when night descends and the lights come on.

It was in these seats that we sat, looking out onto Pittsburgh and enjoying every second of our PNC Park experience. A promised postgame fireworks show had combined with the Red Sox being in town to make for a lively atmosphere around the ballpark on that Saturday evening. The Boston fan base—which always travels well—went back-and-forth with the Pittsburgh locals, exchanging chants of "Let's go, Red Sox" and "Let's go, Pirates," with everyone enjoying a close game that eventually ended with the home team defeating the visitors, 6–4.

PNC was the final stop on our exhausting nine-in-nine stint of the trip. To celebrate, we drove The Van just beyond the city limits and promptly fell asleep at a roadside rest stop, just as we already had countless times on the journey thus far. The tire was my pillow, its white sack my pillowcase.

7:10 a.m. | The Following Morning

I woke up early the next morning to a cacophony of curse words erupting from Andrew in the front of The Van. We were already back on the road; heavy with exhaustion from the past nine days, I must have slept through the entire process of starting the car, leaving the rest stop, and returning to the freeway.

"What's wrong?" I asked, rubbing my eyes and lifting my head from the tire, which had left an indent in my cheekbone from the way I had slept on it.

"The Van's got a new problem," Andrew replied from behind the wheel. "This stupid thing is worthl—"

"Shut up, Andrew," Michael retaliated from next to him. He turned to look at me. "We just noticed that the clicks from The Van now come with a shaking sensation. Can you feel it?"

I paused and focused on the motion of the car. The clicking was certainly audible, but that was nothing new. That repetitive ticking noise had now become the metronome to our journey, keeping tempo with a stressful rhythm anytime we hit the road. Yet now it had indeed been joined by a new sensation, as the car shook ever so slightly, jolting rapidly from left to right. Like the clicks, the frequency of these shakes increased and decreased in concordance with the speed at which The Van traveled.

"Ugh . . ." Frazier groaned next to me.

Immediately, it was deemed that yet another mechanic visit was necessary. After making a few calls, Michael soon informed us that an auto shop on the southern outskirts of Toronto had offered to take a look. We drove straight there, The Van clicking and wobbling the entire way.

"This is going to be our third visit to the mechanic in fifteen days," Andrew stated, turning off the street and into the small concrete lot outside of the auto shop.

"Really?" Frazier asked.

"Yep. Los Angeles to fix the brake lights, Max's dealership to try to fix the clicking . . . and now."

"Wow. We're averaging a visit every five days."

"Good math."

"Shut up."

The Van pulled to a halt in front of the mechanic's shop, and Michael and I hopped out and entered the lobby. It was a small, impersonal place lit by overhead fluorescent bulbs, the buzz from which was the only noise other than the tones of a John Cougar Mellencamp song that came from somewhere in the back. Hearing us enter, a man stood up from behind the counter. He was roughly five eight and sported a gray shirt that hung loosely over his medium build. It was difficult to tell whether he was bald or had buzzed his hair that short.

"Walt," the man said, extending his hand to the two of us. "You guys the ones who called a few hours ago, eh?"

"We are," Michael replied. "Still a shot we can get in?"

"You bet. We're quiet today. What's the issue again?"

"It's this . . . well, it's a couple of things. Whenever we get above forty, the car starts clicking somewhere under the driver's seat and is soon followed by this wobbling, shaking sensation." I watched as Walt listened to him, using a pencil he had kept behind his ear to jot down a couple of notes on a small yellow notepad.

"Always been that way?" he asked.

"Uh . . . well, the clicks started about ten days ago. Maybe a bit more. It used to only happen when we would get above sixty, on the freeways and stuff, but we've noticed that it's definitely starting to happen more frequently now. And the shakes weren't a thing until earlier today."

"Was it clickin' and shakin' the way here?"

"Yeah, pretty much the whole way here from Pittsburgh."

Walt nodded his head enthusiastically. "Mind if I hop in 'n take it out with you guys?" he asked. "The best way for me to get a . . . uh, diagnosis for this thing is to hear it myself. And if she clicked and shook on the way here, sounds like I'll be able to."

"Yeah—absolutely."

Walt gave a thumbs-up and tucked the notepad into the front pocket of his greased-up mechanic shirt. After grabbing a pair of cheap sunglasses from a shelf beneath the counter, he yelled something about being out for a bit in the general direction of where "Jack and Diane" was still playing from and then gestured to Michael and I to show him to our car. We exited the lobby, and Walt stopped immediately upon seeing The Van.

"Lord!" he said with a laugh, which he followed with a light whistle. "Sorry—wowee. That thing is *loud.*"

It wasn't rare for The Van's disorderly design to spark this type of reaction from first-time viewers. I know I've mentioned it many times already, but the wrap job was just that absurd. Walt nearly had to shield his eyes as he quickly scanned all that was happening with the camper's exterior.

"OK," he said, "so you guys are trying to hit all the ballparks, eh?"

"We are," I replied, "if this thing can stay alive, that is." The Van shot me an angry glance.

"Gotcha," Walt replied. "In town for the Jays, I take it?"

"Yep."

"Love it." He then rolled up the left sleeve of his shirt, exposing a large Blue Jays tattoo on his forearm. "I'm one of their biggest fans."

"Nice," Andrew said, sticking his head out of the rolled-down passenger-side window and taking Walt by surprise.

"Whoa, how many ya got in there?" he asked.

"Four," I replied. I wanted to add "and a gigantic tire" but restrained myself; The Van was already looking angry enough.

"I see," he said before returning to the topic of the Blue Jays. "They suck right now, but I love 'em anyway."

"Hey, we're Mariner fans," I said. "We feel your pain."

"Yeah . . . that you do." Walt turned his head to look at Andrew. "Mind if I sit up there, buddy?"

"Sure thing."

Andrew slipped into the jump seat while Walt hopped up front and Michael walked around to the driver's side. I joined Frazier in the back, having to sit on the cooler since the tire was taking up the only remaining spot on the bench seat. After getting the OK from Walt, Michael twisted the key in the ignition and took us back onto the suburban Toronto boulevard. For the first time, we were each actually looking forward to hearing the clicks and feeling the shakes.

And damn it all, The Van drove perfectly.

Life has such a strange way of pulling little pranks like that on you. It turns your head one way, sets you up through repetition to expect a certain outcome, and then whips the carpet out from beneath you and laughs in your face. I need not describe the befuddlement and anger that quickly worked its way through the four of us when it became rapidly apparent that The Van was, for the first time in over a week, not going to show any problems at all. Michael tried everything, taking the old camper on the freeway, killing the engine a few times, and even going in reverse for a while in an abandoned parking lot. Nothing.

"Fuck you!" he screamed, banging the wheel in anger. "Why. *Why*—the *one* time we have someone in the car who actually *wants* to hear your stupid bullshit do you act normally?" It was the only instance that entire summer when I saw him lose it completely; cursing for Michael was such a rarity. "Sorry," he then said to Walt, catching his breath.

"No worries, man," Walt responded. "I'd probably react the same way." He then laughed aloud, but I couldn't tell whether it was in response to what he had just said or the ridiculousness of the situation. The Van had cried wolf with its clicks and shakes. In the rearview mirror, I saw the car wink at me. It was the most frustrating moment of the trip to date.

Still grumbling, Michael soon directed the camper back in the direction of the auto shop. Walt was extremely apologetic as he got out and informed us that there was unfortunately nothing he could do to fix a problem he couldn't identify.

"I can check yer wheels out, if you'd like?" he asked, holding the door open. "Maybe they're . . . misaligned?"

I heard Michael sigh, as Saint Louis surely flashed through his mind. "Nah," he replied, a grimace on his face. "I appreciate it greatly, man, but we already did that once. And honestly," he added, "it's us who should be sorry. We literally just took you on a joyride for nearly an hour."

Walt shrugged his shoulders. "Not at all. I told you, we were quiet today."

"Still though, I'm sorry. What do we owe you?"

The mechanic hesitated for a second.

"Nuthin," he then said with another shrug.

"No, no, no," Andrew replied from his spot on the jump seat. "We just wasted your time. We'd like to pay." I echoed his statement. We had already been given far-too-kind treatment at

Max's and didn't want to make a habit of receiving complimentary mechanical services. It didn't feel right. But Walt insisted.

"I already told ya, I wasn't doin' anything! Plus, I love what you guys are up to with the ball fields." He nodded at the side of The Van.

"We'd like to pay, man."

Walt crinkled his nose and squinted his eyes a bit as he pondered how best to answer our desire to provide reimbursement for his time. "Tell you what," he said after a few seconds, "I'm not gonna accept money from y'all. But," he added with a smile, "you can take me to the Jays game tonight, eh?"

"Done," Michael said. He turned to us. "Sound good?"

"Yep."

"Yep."

"Yep."

BOTTOM OF THE FOURTH
Rogers Centre

THE FIRST TIME I EVER SAW NEW YORK CITY

8:25 p.m. | Tuesday, June 27

Two obscure pieces of art stand outside of Toronto's Rogers Centre, offering a unique welcome for those walking into the stadium. Created by artist Michael Snow, the works are a collection of identical busts that depict the many moods of fans attending a game; some are cheering, some are laughing, and some are blatantly taunting the visiting squad, giving Bronx cheers and wagging their fingers in front of their noses. Appropriately titled *The Audience*, they are one of a kind.

It takes inside access to the Rogers Centre to appreciate the gigantic size of the home of the Blue Jays. The stadium checks in as the second largest in all of MLB, with a capacity of over fifty-three thousand (trailing only Dodger Stadium, which can seat roughly fifty-six thousand).[19] This high capacity allows the Blue Jays to draw impressive crowds when the team is good. And in the early 1990s (when the team was *very* good), the Jays achieved an astounding record, as they became the first and thus far only sports team to draw over four million people in three consecutive years.[iv]

This is incredible because four million in *one* year—let alone three in a row—is astonishing. However, it's something that can

---

[iv] This measurement looks at basketball, soccer (including international), baseball, football, and hockey.

happen only in baseball. Although football stadiums regularly attract single-game crowds that are far larger than baseball ones, these places get to host only eight regular season games a year. This means that it is difficult for an NFL team to draw more than *one* million fans in a season, let alone four.

Perspective: The Dallas Cowboys have the largest stadium in the NFL, with a capacity of over ninety-two thousand (thirty-six thousand larger than Dodger Stadium). Yet the Cowboys' attendance total last season came in at just over 1.3 million fans.[20] Meanwhile, in the *other* football, England's Manchester United plays at Old Trafford—the largest stadium in the Premier League—and drew a little over 1.4 million in the same year.[21]

With eighty-one games a season played at each team's ballpark, MLB stadiums can rack up some impressive numbers—and when you have a good team and a big stadium, large sellouts become common. It's therefore not abnormal for ball clubs to crack the three-million mark in seasonal attendance. String together a few *really* good years at a *really* big stadium, and you are the Toronto Blue Jays. The seasons of 1991, 1992, and 1993 each drew over four million fans, as Toronto was one of the best teams in baseball and the Rogers Centre was packed with well over fifty thousand fans a game.

Yet even with its attendance capability and oddball statues, Rogers Centre's most recognizable attribute has nothing to do with baseball. Above the batter's eye in center field sits the Marriott City Centre, a hotel that is built into the stadium. Here fans are welcome to sit down and have a few drinks while taking in batting practice or a few innings of the game. You do not need to have a ticket to the game itself to be here—the hotel is its own property—however, the food and drinks often cost far more than an entry fee. Meanwhile, many of the Marriott's rooms look down onto the field, and it is not unusual to see people propping up desk chairs at the foot of their beds to watch a bit of baseball while they are in town on business.

"It's really weird when the patrons forget they're in front of a whole crowd," Walt said to my left, gesturing at the hotel. "Sometimes you see . . . well, a bit more than yer ticket price suggests."

Walt turned out to be one of the more fascinating people we met on the trip. A mechanic by day, he morphed into an impromptu pit boss at night, organizing underground poker games for big-time Toronto business workers who wanted a bit of action. He was also incredibly genuine; after learning more about the nomadic nature of our journey and the many on-the-spot decisions we made regarding where we would sleep nearly every night, he offered his driveway as a location for that evening.

"Y'all can take showers in the morning."

Say no more, Walt. The last time I'd showered was at a dirty truck stop between Chicago and Saint Louis.

From there, the night seemed to extend indefinitely, as we learned poker tricks, listened to old Bruce Springsteen records, and drank beer with Walt and his wife, Julia. Despite our frustration with The Van, none of us wanted to leave Toronto the morning after, but Walt had to return to work that afternoon and we had to return to our schedule: our next game was the following evening in New York City.

2:00 p.m. | The Following Day

Click . . . click . . . click . . .

The cursing that then erupted in The Van would have made George Carlin proud. We were only twenty minutes outside of Toronto, and the all-too-familiar noises had returned—along with the shakes. The camper had dropped its pants and mooned us completely, officially offending the four of us. Our anger at it persisted for the duration of our time in Canada and continued for a good thirty minutes after reentering the United States. It only increased as we entered a bumper-to-bumper traffic jam on I-90, just east of Buffalo. From our vantage point at the top of a small hill, we could see a few miles ahead—and we could see that nobody was moving.

"What's going on?" Andrew said beside me, throwing his hands at the windshield, through which only red taillights were visible. "We're gonna lose a ton of time here."

The four of us had originally hoped to be in New York City late that evening, but as the hours slipped by and the traffic remained stagnant, the likelihood of that happening quickly disappeared. We moved three miles in three hours. Night began to descend, and with it came a fog the thickness of which I had never seen before.

"God," I said, squinting my eyes from behind the wheel. "I can barely see ten cars in front of us."

"This is weird," Andrew remarked. "Throw the brights on."

"We don't have brights."

"I hate this car."

The Van creaked as if offering a word of caution, but I tuned it out angrily and focused on the dense fog. It lowered itself lightly on the unmoving cars like a detached spiderweb drifting along with the wind, floating down and wrapping around us. Through the windshield, I could see the wisps of condensation as they drifted slowly past, cueing visions of Stephen King movies in my head.

"I'm actually kind of glad that we're still in this jam now," I said to nobody in particular. "I'm not sure I'd be able to drive safely through this thing." The traffic moved forward a couple hundred feet, only to come to a stop yet again. "See? Now I can only see one, maybe two cars in front of us."

"Maybe the fog is the cause of the stoppage," Frazier hypothesized.

"Nope," Andrew replied tartly. "We've been stopped longer than the fog's been here. But it's definitely not helping." Looking ahead, I saw a blue sign on the side of the road that advertised the upcoming exit. Logos beneath it suggested that food and gas could be purchased there. I tilted my head to look at the fuel gauge.

"We may need to pull off for gas soon," I said.

"I wouldn't mind that at all," Andrew answered. "Would give us a break from this traffic, if nothing else."

We reached the off-ramp for the exit about thirty minutes later, and I pulled The Van off to the right. For the first time in hours, the car began rolling at a speed higher than five miles per hour—but with it, of course, came the clicks.

"Yikes," Michael said, referencing the noise. "We aren't even going twenty right now. It's getting even more frequent." My knuckles tightened on the wheel as my anger with The Van increased. It creaked again.

I squinted to try to see ahead, hugging the lane indicators on the right side of the road for guidance while relying on the brake lights of vehicles ahead to indicate their presence. Andrew leaned over the dashboard, hunching his shoulders and lowering his head as he attempted to locate the promised gas station. It appeared a few hundred yards later on the left. I threw on the blinker and turned into the lot—

BAM!

The front left wheel of the Van hit the curb hard, causing the hood to scrape against the cement as the rest of the car jumped awkwardly up onto the pavement. Whining in pain, the camper then rolled through a small portion of grass before eventually crawling into the gas station's parking lot and coming to a full stop at the nearest pump. I killed the engine and swore under my breath. What had I done? Had *I* done this? Or had it been the fog, or—

The sound of Andrew's door slamming jolted me back to earth. I quickly got out as well, leaping down from my seat to assess the damage. Horror images flashed rapidly through my head as I began to fear what this latest incident might have done to the poor, noble camper. Ah, how quickly emotions can change.

"You OK, baby?" was a phrase that actually came out of my mouth as I patted The Van's hood. It looked back at me, but it was a look I could not read.

We spent a good twenty minutes examining The Van, but strangely, no damage was noticeable. A walk around the car showed nothing but a small chunk of grass wedged into the front bumper. Andrew even slid his entire body below to check for any damage that might have occurred to The Van's under-belly—nothing.

"Huh," I said, more to myself than to anyone else. Had we dodged a bullet? I turned around and began filling the car up with gas while Andrew, Michael, and Frazier entered the convenience store to grab some coffee for the upcoming late-night shifts. As the fuel began to flow through the pump, I walked around again to the front of The Van.

"I . . . I don't know what you're up to," I said, "but I don't know how I feel about it." It looked back at me with the same indecipherable look.

"What?" Frazier's voice made me jump as he appeared behind me.

"Nothing."

"Were you talking to The Van?"

"No."

He gave me a confused look. "Here, I got you a sandwich." He handed me a moist-looking sub wrapped in cellophane. "Want to take the graveyard shift with me?"

"Thanks. And yeah, I'd like that."

"Awesome. Let's let Michael and Andrew cover the next few hours then, and we can hop up after that." He slid open the door and folded the bench seat down into its makeshift bed position, taking care to move the tire all the way to the back before doing so.

The pump clicked off and Andrew and Michael returned a minute later. Cracking open a lime green energy drink, Andrew hopped into the driver's seat as Frazier and I climbed into the back, Frazier lying down on the bed and me positioning my back against the tire so that I could see out. The fog had begun to lift and The Van began moving again, cautiously, bracing itself for more traffic, clicking and shaking.

But no cars were to be seen. We had been at that station for only thirty, maybe forty minutes, and somehow in that time frame, the incredible congestion that had halted our progress for hours had disappeared. Poof, gone. I blinked my eyes a few times from the back, making sure I wasn't hallucinating.

"There *had* been cars there before, right?" I asked.

"Yeah . . ." Michael said from the passenger's seat. "At least, I think so . . ."

"Whoa. Ghosts, man."

Ten minutes later, the fog cleared completely. Still no traffic was to be seen—but even more amazingly, no clicks were to be heard and no shakes were to be felt from The Van. None of us mentioned this for fear of jinxing the apparent good luck we had stumbled on; only a half hour ago we had feared that the bump at the gas station would certainly have compounded our problems, but oddly, it was looking to be the opposite. Forty-five minutes soon passed, and The Van continued to drive as if it had just been purchased. I shifted nervously in the back, still picturing the uneasy way the car had looked at me.

"Remember old tube TVs?" Andrew then asked from behind the wheel.

"Yeah," Michael replied. "Why on earth would you ask about that right now?"

"Well . . . remember how sometimes they got really bad signals, and to make the image clearer, you just banged the monitor as hard as you could?"

"Yeah," Michael said again, opening his mouth to speak before thinking of what had just happened with our old camper and the cause of its apparent fix. "Ah . . ."

We didn't actually believe The Van had been miraculously fixed—but we wanted to believe The Van had been miraculously fixed, so we chose to believe The Van had been miraculously fixed.

4:45 a.m.

I will never forget the first time I saw New York City. As had been the plan, Frazier and I manned the graveyard shift as The Van, still eerily silent after its scare with the gas station curb, made its way east. It was close to 5:00 a.m. and we were god knows where—"Upstate New York" is as specific as I can get. I was behind the wheel and Frazier sat next to me with his feet kicked up onto the dashboard and his hands pinned behind his head, propping his slouching body up in the shotgun seat. Together we watched the cars on the other side of the freeway median fly by us, illuminated for only a split second by our headlights before they were gone.

"Do you ever wonder at how many people there are in the world?" Frazier asked as a silver sedan whirred by on the left.

He turned his head, following the red glow of the car's taillights until they disappeared.

"How many people there are?" I replied, trying to keep my voice to a whisper to allow Michael and Andrew to continue sleeping in the back. My eyes glanced up to the internal mirror. Andrew lay stretched out with his head all the way in the back while Michael slept propped against the tire.

"Yeah," Frazier said, "there's just . . . I dunno. There are just *so* many people out there." He sat up straight in the seat. "I mean, look at us right now. Here we are, driving at some absurd hour on a Tuesday night—"

"I think it's Wednesday morning now."

"Is it? I wouldn't even know. But that's my point. We're driving in the middle of the night—or morning, whatever—and we're driving in the middle of nowhere. Nobody else should be out at this hour in a place like this. And yet, here they are . . ." His voice drifted off as another car drove past us.

"Go on," I replied.

"I dunno," he said again. I could hear the gears turning in his head. Frazier loved to ponder life's big questions and often loved to do so out loud. "Since we've started spending so much time on the road at ungodly hours of the day, I've become amazed that *other* people are *also* driving at times like this. And I can't help but thinking that it's just because there's so many people in the world. If you were to speak to someone and ask if they'd ever be in . . . wherever we are . . . on a Tuesday night or Wednesday morning, they'd say, 'Good god, no. Why would I be?' And yet since there's *so many people* in the world, somebody is bound to say yes!"

"I'm not sure I'm following you in the slightest."

"Like, what's *their* story?" he asked as a black SUV passed The Van. "What are the people in that car up to? Are they coming home from work? Are they also on a big trip of some sorts? Are they just out for a drive . . .?"

"OK, now I might be following you. A bit."

"Ah, I might be just spitting nonsense. Night drives always cue up strange thoughts, but it's something I've begun to think about more and more." Twenty seconds of silence followed this before he spoke again. "Ever think you've seen the same person twice?"

"Like, of the people who are passing us?"

"Yeah. Ever think you might have passed the same car before—but have had no idea that you did? Like, the one that just passed us right there, that big black one . . . maybe the person driving it just also *randomly* happens to have been someone who we stood next to in line at the game in Phoenix, or sat next to us in Minnesota, or . . . I dunno. But we'd never know, would we? Nope. They all blend together."

I chuckled at the way his mind worked. Frazier always had some sort of novel observation, something new that made him question something else. I realized that the two of us had not been isolated all that often on the trip thus far; on drives like this, I normally found myself accompanied by Andrew or Michael. This realization nudged its way into my subconscious and back to the question that had pestered me ever since that midnight drive in Arizona when we passed Joseph City.

"Think we'll stay in touch after we all get back?"

"You sound like Andrew."

"You were awake for that conversation as well?"

"Yeah."

I smiled faintly. Nothing was ever private in The Van. "Well?" I continued. "What's your take? Think we'll all be the same after we head off to college here in a couple of months?"

Frazier did not reply right away. I sensed an air of hesitancy and nervousness engulf him as he shifted again in the seat, slouching back down a little bit and crossing his left leg over his right leg. He turned his head to look out of the right window of the car, away from the road.

"I'm not going to college," he then said.

"What?"

"I'm not going to college."

"What do you mean?" My voice was now louder than a whisper.

"I'm not. I'm sorry, man. I . . . I didn't know how to tell you guys."

"Wait, I . . . what are you doing instead?"

"I'm drifting down to Peru for a while."

"Drifting to P—what the hell? What are you going to do in Peru?"

Frazier continued to look out the window to the right of the road, where no passing cars were to be seen. I wondered what he saw in the blackness.

"I'm not sure yet, but I'll figure it out," he answered. I could hear more nerves in his voice. "I met a guy last year who runs a hotel somewhere near Machu Picchu, so I thought maybe I'd try to work there for a while. Practice my Spanish, get a better feel for the world."

Five seconds passed. "Wow," I said, returning my voice to a low level. "How long have you known you were going to do this for?"

"About a month or so. Maybe a bit longer."

"So since before we left."

He didn't respond to this at first but instead took another breath before turning his head to look forward once again. "I guess I just wasn't ready for college, you know? Well, maybe you don't. But I started panicking at the end of high school and wondering where all my time was going. And why I haven't seen the world yet."

"What are you doing right now? What are *we* doing right now?" I felt myself getting angry with him. "Are we not seeing the world right now?"

"I know, I know—I just had an itch. An itch to see *more* of the world, not just what's here in the States. Plus, like you asked earlier, I feel that once you head off for school and stuff, things change and are never the same. People normally wind up falling into a job and then into a relationship and then into a family, right? Andy said the same thing when you were chatting with him that night in Arizona." I opened my mouth to say something, but Frazier continued. "And I know it's getting to you, so that's kind of why I didn't want to bring this up, but . . ." His voice trailed off. Light music played in the background.

"Do you know how long you'll stay down there?" I asked.

"I don't know. A year?"

"And you think you'll go to college after that?"

"I think so."

"So I'm moving to Wisconsin, Andrew to Oregon, Michael is going to California, and now you're off to Peru." I let out a low whistle. When this ended, I wasn't just going to see my three best friends heading off to live in different states from me, I was now going to see one head off to live in a different *country*. I drummed the steering wheel lightly, watching the approaching headlights of another car in the distance. I wondered if I had ever seen that car before or ever would again. Even if I did, would I ever know?

It was then that I saw New York City for the first time in my life. As the headlights of the car rushed by The Van as quickly as all the others had, a new light appeared way, way off in the distance. It started out very dull, a reflection against the otherwise dark sky, muted and drab in the blackness like the power light of a device that is nearly drained of battery. But then the light began to grow.

Neither Frazier nor I spoke as we watched the dark 5:00 a.m. sky slowly give way to New York. Within thirty minutes, all of which passed in swallowing silence, the tall buildings began to pop individually into view, shimmering with lights that had not been turned off for decades. The city was backlit by the approaching dawn, which went unnoticed at first but soon began to make itself known through the faint shades of purple and pink that started to stretch above the horizon. We remained silent as The Van moved east. Almost thirty minutes passed before I felt myself subconsciously pressing the pedal down more, making the car go faster, faster.

Then, as if knowing what we were waiting for, the sun rose behind the city. It looked molten at first, glowing at the base of one of the nameless skyscrapers and reflecting harshly against its glass windows and metallic frame. But as it slowly rose, the sun's rays began to stretch through the thin cracks between the buildings, popping out wherever they could find a gap. They looked like they were reaching to us.

I will never forget the first time I saw New York City. An image as magical as that is impossible to erase from anyone's memory—but that magical image also brings me back to Frazier and the spacious geography that was quickly getting in between where my best friends and I would be in just two months. To this day, New York City brings back feelings of excitement and nervousness: excitement for the amazingness of the now and nervousness for the uncertainty of the future.

TOP OF THE FIFTH
Yankee Stadium and Citizens Bank Park

THE YEAR OF JACKIE

7:10 p.m. | Wednesday, June 29

Yankee Stadium is the courthouse of America's pastime. Every decision on how a baseball team's season is going to unfold comes from the Bronx; the Yankees dictate the law of the league just as the judge dictates the law of the land. If a team is going to make it, they will have to go through New York at one point or another. It seems to have always been this way: since becoming a team in 1903, the Bronx Bombers have established themselves as the best franchise in baseball history, solidified as the eternal gavel-striking rulers of MLB. One of their best players is even named Judge.

But the ballpark *physically* feels like a courthouse as well. Maybe it's the gigantic columned marble archway that proudly greets visitors to the home plate entrance. Or maybe it's the formal white fencing that arches itself around the upper edges of the outfield sections. Whatever it is, when you step into Yankee Stadium, you immediately know that you are stepping into a place of importance—a place filled with history, money, and pride. It's fitting: the Yankees have won the World Series twenty-seven times, easily doubling the total of the Saint Louis Cardinals, who are runners-up with eleven titles. A man sitting next to us in the upper deck sported a T-shirt that read *Got Rings?*

But the power this ballpark holds goes beyond its team and even its physical appearance, trickling all the way down to its name. Being called "Yankee Stadium" means that the building is completely and totally devoted to the team that plays there, and nothing else is in the way. There are no sponsors meddling with the stadium's title, as is the case for the majority of other parks (think Coors Field, PNC Park, or Rogers Centre). Yankee Stadium is Yankee Stadium, and that's that. Some even call it just "the Stadium," perhaps the highest superlative a sports venue can achieve.

Everything is personal to Yankees fans. Anybody walking into the Stadium sporting the gear of the visiting team is going to be heckled instantly, with insults tossed their way that can toe the line of flat-out harassment. When the boys in pinstripes take the field for the first inning, the bleacher bums out in right begin collectively calling the first name of each starting player as they take warm-ups at their respective positions. The chant for each repeats and grows in volume until that player acknowledges the section by tipping their hat or waving their glove. The game then continues in a similar atmosphere of player-fan interactions: when a Yankee makes a great defensive play or hits a home run, the chants of adoration return—and if a Yankee screws up, the chants shift to those of extreme displeasure. It's an intense atmosphere. It's fun. Surrounded by the big lights of the Big Apple, taking in a game here is something that every baseball fan should experience at least once.

6:30 a.m. | The Following Morning

We slept three nights in New York City, camped in a parking lot in the Upper East Side of Manhattan. The overnight parking rates had been decent, and we convinced ourselves that it was the best place for us to crash those three nights, each of which we were hoping to spend in New York. The only time we left the city was the following morning, Thursday the thirtieth, when we quickly popped down to Philadelphia to catch that day's matinee game between the Phillies and the Red Sox. We departed early in the morning, expecting traffic—yet found nothing but open lanes, a bit of rain, and another argument between Andrew and Frazier.

"I'm just saying," Andrew stated from behind the wheel, "he loses a ton of momentum when he pauses during his windup. He could easily gain an extra three or four miles per hour on his fastball if he just continued it in one fluid motion."

"He's a major leaguer for crying out loud," Frazier responded next to him, fumbling with his camera. "I think he knows what he's doing." The two of them had been discussing one of the pitchers who had appeared in the Yankees game the night before—or maybe it had been the Blue Jays game two days ago. I didn't know; they were all beginning to blur together. Whatever it was in reference to, the conversation had started in fairly docile tones but quickly escalated from there.

"I'm not saying he doesn't know what he's doing," Andrew retaliated. "I'm just telling him that he could throw faster by simply not stopping."

"But he probably doesn't *want* to throw faster, seeing as he throws mainly curveballs and changeups." Frazier then nodded to the dashboard. "Oh and by the way, you're way over the speed limit."

"As if you can tell me what speed to drive—you're the one who is always pushing it on the roads," Andrew said, scoffing. "Plus, it's OK right now. I can go about ten over the limit on an arterial in New Jersey."

"One, you're a dick. Two—how the hell do you know that? Either way, take it easy. It's raining outside and I don't want The Van to start clicking again."

"I don't think it will. It was an issue with the axle beneath the driver's side wheel, and hitting that curb probably jolted it back into the right place."

"Again, how the *hell* do you know that? And why are you so adamant?"

"I only argue things when I know I'm right."

Frazier threw his hands into the air, and the strap of the Nikon nearly whipped Andrew in the face. "So all of a sudden you're a pitching coach, a driver's-ed instructor, and a mechanic?"

"I just know I'm right." A few seconds went by as The Van moved past a rusted sign on the side of the highway, advertising the various food options that could be found at the upcoming exit. "Ooh look," Andrew said, a heavy tone of mockery lacing his voice. "We're passing an exit—an *exit,* Frazier! Quick, take a photo—"

"Enough, man."

"—maybe they'll take it in the next club you apply to—"

"Shut up, you two," I said from the back. The conversation was teetering on the edge of eruption, and Michael and I could feel ourselves becoming angry as well, although neither of us could discern exactly why. We didn't want to be mad—we didn't have any *reason* to be mad—but we were getting mad regardless. It was a very strange sensation to feel your emotions slowly slipping out of your control while consciously recognizing that they were doing so. I felt powerless, like there was nothing I could do to fight it.

Recognizing the need for a respite, we took the exit and The Van soon came to a halt in the parking lot of a McDonald's somewhere near Applegarth, New Jersey. It was our ninth visit to the fast-food chain already on the trip, which meant we were on pace to visit a McDonald's about every two days. But you know what? We were fine with it. McDonald's was one of the few statics we could rely on during the trip. Whereas scenery always changed, moods always changed, and prices always changed, everything under the golden arches was always the same. A McFlurry was the same in Charlotte as it was in Chicago; the dollar menu was the dollar menu whether we were in New Mexico or New England. It sounds lame—it *definitely* sounds unhealthy—but McDonald's was comforting to us in a strange, strange way.

Eager for some separation, Michael and Andrew stayed behind to "clean up The Van" while Frazier and I went into the restaurant to place a group order. We ran across the parking lot in an attempt to avoid getting drenched by the persistent rain, and we both slipped on the slick tile upon entering the building. Every eye in the place turned to look at us as we approached the counter and ordered.

"Pardon me," a voice behind me soon said, "but are you guys the ones driving that bright-colored thing I saw out there in the parking lot?"

I turned around and came face-to-face with an old man in an even older Yankees hat. He looked to be about eighty or so, with eyebrows that raged in unkempt brilliance and a classic smile that was highlighted by deep dimples. Beside him was a second man who looked to be just about the same age. He wore a ratty pinstriped Thurman Munson jersey that draped down to cover the tops of his jeans, which looked as if they had seen decades of wear.

"The bright-colored thing?" Frazier asked innocently.

"He means The Van," I replied.

"Oh! Yes, we are."

"My," the man in the jersey said, a cackle of laughter slipping from his mouth, "I didn't know if I was lookin' at a car or takin' a color-blind test!"

Something about the comic harmlessness and total under-standability of this comment immediately lifted Frazier and me out of our dark moods. The Van was just that chaotic in its de-sign: many people we encountered had attempted to describe its absurd wrap job to us. "Color-blind test" was right up there with "psychedelic camouflage" and "a Twister board on wheels" for the best of them.

"So y'all are going through with that, eh?" the man in the hat inquired, nodding his head enthusiastically. "The ballparks?"

"We're trying!" I replied, trying to keep an upbeat tone. The-se were always slightly awkward conversations, as I could rarely discern between those who appreciated what we were doing and those who were annoyed, thinking we were completely nuts and perhaps somewhat ignorant. However, I soon recognized these two to be members of the first category.

"Just came from New York, I assume?" the man asked.

"That's right—wonderful time."

He tugged the bill of his hat. "What'd ya think of our Yan-kee Stadium?"

"Oh, we loved it—" I began to say, but at that exact mo-ment, the cashier called our order number and our bag of food appeared on the counter. "That all for *you* guys?" the man in the jersey asked, his eyes widening at the size of the bag.

"No," Frazier replied, laughing, "there are two more of us out there." He nodded toward the window, in the general direc-tion of the color-blind test.

"Ah, I see," the first man said. "Well, have fun! Was a pleas-ure to chat with you, albeit too briefly. Good luck wherever you're off to!"

We thanked the two men, grabbed the bag, and made our way for the door. But then both of us stopped without saying anything. A brief moment passed during which Frazier and I subconsciously asked ourselves the same questions: What was the point of leaving so soon? Hadn't we come on this journey to see places *and* to meet people? It was only 8:00 a.m.—yes, we were already ordering burgers—but we had experienced no traffic; what was the rush to get to Philadelphia?

"Actually," Frazier said, spinning around, "do you guys want to eat with us?"

The two men turned, as if confused. "What about your friends?" one of them asked.

"They can wait."

"Oh . . . well yeah, then, if you're serious—we'd love that."

And so it came to be that two eighteen-year-olds and two eighty-year-olds stuffed themselves into a corner booth at a McDonald's just off Interstate 55 somewhere near a place called Applegarth. At first, the elderly gentlemen wanted to hear about our trip—and we told them—but in truth, we wanted to hear more about *them*. How had they come to be at this same McDonald's, and what was their connection to baseball?

"Well," said George, the man in the hat, "we both grew up in the same small town just about a half hour away from here, just down the road."

"Farmingdale," the other interjected. "That was the name of the town."

"That *is* the name of the town, Lester."

"Oh yeah," Lester replied. "Yeah, I guess we still live there, eh?" They both chuckled. Their laughs were wonderful.

"Neither of us left," George continued. "Something about the place was sticky, and we couldn't get out . . . but then again, I'm not sure we ever really wanted to."

"I went to college at Fordham—"

"And I went to Saint John's."

"—but that was really the only time we left the town and the only time we ever really were separated in life."

"We sound like an old married couple, Les."

"We practically are." Frazier and I laughed along with them this time, as Lester took a bite out of his burger before continuing. "We both had wives, yeah, but we were always married to the Yanks."

"Yep, yep," George replied, his eyes staring off into the distance as a smile crept across his face. "I grew up just down the street from Les and can remember getting together almost every day durin' the summer to watch the games."

"They didn't get lights till the mid-40s, so a lot of games were played during the afternoon."

"When we had school, we would play hooky sometimes and go down to the restaurant to watch." George smiled again, his eyes twinkling a little. "There was this old diner . . . it's not there anymore."

"Life felt so small in Farmingdale," Lester said, a similar look passing over his face. "And we liked it that way, don't get me wrong—but the Yankees provided us with an escape to the bigger world. When the team traveled to play the Cubs, I felt like I saw Chicago; when they would go out to the West Coast, I felt like I was there as well, seeing Hollywood and the Golden Gate Bridge."

"Some people watch travel shows, we watched baseball."

As the conversation continued, a communal pool of french fries from our orders began to accumulate in the middle of the table. "Were you just up in New York for the past Series?" I asked.

Lester shook his head. "Other way around—we're on our way there right now. Yep, we go every year to see the Subway Series. Unfortunately it's at Citi this year, but we'll get to see it at our spot next year."

"What'd you guys think of the Stadium?" George asked. He said it with a capital *S,* as many Yankee fans do.

"Loved it," Frazier and I replied, almost simultaneously.

"And Citi?" he asked.

"Haven't seen it yet," I said. George did not seem satisfied with this response.

"Can't be as good as the Stadium, though," Frazier added, using the local lingo much to the appreciation of the older men. They both smiled again at each other, as if proud that their ballpark would surely exceed that of their cross-town rival.

"Man," Lester stated, "I'd love to see 'em all. Must be like roundin' the bases of the States, eh?" He then cupped his hands together and mimicked the voice of a baseball broadcaster: "Touch 'em all, young man . . . touch 'em all."

"We haven't exactly seen *none*," George responded, nudging Lester in the shoulder. "C'mon, we've been to our fair share of parks!"

"Yeah, but they keep buildin' new ones! I'm too old to keep up with the league and their new stadiums, it appears. Lights at Wrigley, stadiums in Tampa Bay . . ." The two chuckled again. Frazier and I smiled. Why had we been arguing all morning?

"Yes, seeing 'em all would be wonderful," George said, taking a handful from the pool of fries, "but first, I'd rather see another Yankees title."

"Hey now," Lester added, laughing sheepishly. "These guys are Mariners fans—they haven't won a title in . . . wait, they've never won."

"I was born in 1929. I'll rub anything I want in."

"You were born in '30, old man."

"I was indeed born in 1930," George replied with a laugh. "Whoops. Let's see, Philadelphia won that year. We won in '32—I was a toddler, that's when I became hooked on the Yanks—and then I got treated *real* nice when we won four in a row in '36, '37 . . ."

"We remember the years based on who won the World Series," Lester said, as George continued counting ("'38, '39 . . .").

"It's incredible to think that you can mark your days based on what happened in a sport, eh? Let's see, '40 was Cincinnati, '41 was us . . ."

"'42 was Saint Louis *over* us . . ."

"But then '43 was us over *Saint Louis.*"

"You're right. The Cardinals took it again the year after that, then the Tigers over the Cubs . . . Cards again in '46 . . . then we won in '47 of course."

"Ah yes—of course." They both smiled.

"What?" Frazier asked.

"Well, that was the year of Jackie."

"What was that like?" I asked immediately, speaking up for the first time in a while. George and Lester paused for a second before answering.

"What do you mean?" Lester asked.

"Jackie Robinson, the color barrier . . . What was it like living during that?"

Lester took a breath before opening his mouth. "It was one of the few moments in life when I recognized that history was happening," he stated, nodding his head along with his words, which he spoke slowly, with meaning. "I've lived through wars—many wars—but none of that is my passion. Of course not. For many people my age it is . . . but me, no sir. I'm not a man for overseas. What I care about's right here, in America, and especially in America's pastime. And when you get the chance to see history unfold right before your eyes . . . well, there's nothing like it."

"It showed the differences of America quite . . . well, quite bluntly," George said. "They played us in the World Series that year. The Dodgers, that is. Jackie's Dodgers. And let's just say not everyone in this country was rooting for Brooklyn that year. I can't say we were, but that's because we wear pinstripes, not because the other team had a black man playing for them. No, in fact, I actually think that was the first and only time where I wouldn't have minded if the Yanks had actually lost the Series."

The conversation then came to a natural break, as each of us reflected on the timeline of baseball. The sport's longevity has allowed it to string together different phases of the United States, leading the country from one era into the next. No matter what America went through, its pastime was always there to maintain some sort of normality. It saw World War I escalate into World War II and from there slip into the Cold War, Korea, Vietnam, and every other international conflict that has emerged since the beginning of the twentieth century. When atrocity occurred overseas, baseball always stood as an unmoving force back home—a reliable constant amid a changing world.

But most powerfully of all, baseball found a way to turn a country's head away from its international involvement and demand it look inward. For me, the signing of Jackie Robinson by the Brooklyn Dodgers in 1947 is *the* moment in this wonderful sport. It is when America's pastime forced people to examine America's present time, as the dividing and strangling issue that is the color line was finally placed on the field, no longer held in a separate space. It's simply erroneous to say that baseball has succeeded in curing bigotry and profiling, as racism unfortunately does not appear to be disappearing. But I would like to think that baseball has helped, if maybe just a little.

As I recognized the bonds that linked the four of us at that McDonald's booth near Applegarth, New Jersey, I couldn't help but smile. Here sat two completely different generations: one that grew up with images of soldiers playing pickup baseball when Victory in Europe was announced and one that grew up with images of their local team huddled together in center field surrounding an American flag in the immediate wake of September 11. One generation happily amazed that Jackie Robinson broke the color barrier, the other struggling to imagine a world in which the sport *had* a color barrier. And uniting it all was the great constant of baseball.

9:41 a.m.

The Van pulled into the lot of Citizens Bank Park a little after 9:30 a.m., still with three hours to go before the game started. We each tried to take naps to catch up on sleep, but this only resulted in Andrew and Frazier arguing about who had to sleep with their head propped up against the bulky tire. Any sleep we did manage to steal that morning was quickly erased in quality by the drenching pools of sweat that rapidly accumulated below our bodies anyway; the temperature was already pushing one hundred degrees. Soggily stumbling out of The Van, we found ourselves blinded by midday sunlight and submerged in a crowd of fans in their early twenties. Nearly every one of them was carrying bottles of booze, playing drinking games, and shouting anti–Red Sox chants. In our dreary, stuffy states, it was a horrible juxtaposition.

Citizens Bank Park sits on the edge of South Philadelphia, about three blocks from the banks of the Delaware River and the New Jersey border. This area of the city is completely devoted to sporting complexes: adjacent to the ballpark sits Lincoln Financial Field (home of the Eagles football team) and Wells Fargo Center (where both the Flyers hockey team and the 76ers basketball team play). Although there is not much appeal to the surrounding area (the stadiums are right next door to the CSX Rail Yard), the actual aesthetics of Citizens Bank Park are quite inviting. The outer facade is primarily composed of warm brick and large glass windows, which blend together to form a design like that of Saint Louis's Busch Stadium. The interior of the ballpark, meanwhile, feels open and spread out. While some stadiums, restricted by area, are built *up,* Citizens Bank took advantage of its fairly suburban location and built *out.* Standing from the concourse above home plate, the yard spreads itself before you, with the bleachers ascending slowly to three decks on either side. A low, flat walkway connects the left field foul pole and center field batter's eye, topped by a restaurant, a large scoreboard complex, and a neon Liberty Bell that sits atop a scaffolding-like structure. In the far distance, the skyline of Philadelphia can just be seen peeping its head above the ballpark's outer walls.

The tire-induced bickering session between Frazier and Andrew did not cease when we woke up, nor when we left The Van, nor when we entered the ballpark and wandered through the crowd looking for our seats. At this point, it seemed like one argument between the two of them simply led into the next. The heat did not help, nor did when we soon remembered that we didn't actually have *seats* to the ballgame. The sold-out crowd for the matinee against the interleague powerhouse Boston Red Sox had forced us to purchase standing room only tickets, and we therefore perched ourselves at a railing for the majority of the game. Frazier, tired and disgusted by the company he was being forced to stand with, declared that he was going to wander off in search of a bit of isolation.

"Isolation?" Andrew replied in mockery. "It's a sold-out game, man. You won't find isolation anywhere in this place."

"Isolation from you is all I need right now," Frazier answered in a biting tone. He left without saying anything more.

With what Frazier had revealed to me about his Peru plans still in my head, I could not help but think that I might now be watching my childhood friendships unravel before my eyes. And you know what? I wasn't doing anything to help keep them sewn together. To be honest, I was starting to find that I didn't give a damn. It was hot, I hadn't had a comfortable night's sleep in weeks, and I was yearning for isolation as well. I didn't blame Frazier as he walked away into the sea of fans. I was jealous of him.

MIDDLE OF THE FIFTH
Citi Field

THE DEFEAT CIGAR

6:30 p.m. | Friday, July 1

If you live in New York City, you probably don't own a car. Owning a car there is essentially pointless; traffic is a 24-7 thing in the Big Apple, and parking is wicked expensive, even if you manage to get to where you want to go on time *and* somehow find an open spot. No, if you live in New York, you take the subway. With no traffic, no search for parking, and no parking cost, it's simply the best way to get around. Yeah, it's dirty and can be unreliable at times, but this is New York we're talking about. Everybody uses the subway, which means the mood on the trains varies by time of day: it's filled with suits at rush hour, drunks after bar close, and bickering sports fans before games.

"Jeter," a large man dressed in pinstripes said next to me.

"Reyes," replied his counterpart, who was donned in blue and orange. I couldn't tell if the two men actually knew each other, but their banter about which New York shortstop was having the better season was quickly heating up. Both players were good, and both fans were biased.

"Jeter."

"Reyes."

"How can't ya say Jeter? He's the classic, man."

"Sure, but Reyes is better this year. Hittin' .330."

"I'm takin' Jeter any day."

"'Course y'are, you're wearin' his jersey, aren't ya?"

The debate continued in this manner for the duration of the ride out to Citi Field, with the two men's conversation eventually escalating into a bet on which team would win that evening's game. Others in the subway car asked if they could get in on the action as well, but the men resisted, insisting that this was "between the two of them." A few minutes later, we arrived at the penultimate stop of the Flushing-bound #7 line—a stop that's simply called "Mets."

Opened in 2009, Citi Field is essentially a modern reconstruction of the Mets' old home, Shea Stadium. Nearly every part of the new ballpark is an ode to the old one: it still boasts orange foul poles (the only ones in the majors; all others are yellow), it has a pedestrian bridge that's bluntly named "Shea Bridge," and it still incorporates the darn home run apple. This thing is probably the most recognizable element of the ballpark: when a Met goes yard, a large red sphere that apparently looks like an apple rises out of a circular platform in center field. It doesn't twist or light up or do anything spectacular—it just sits there, weighs forty-eight hundred pounds, and then gets lowered back down.[22] Whatever—fans love it. Go Mets.

Speaking of fans: the crowd that packed Citi Field on that Friday evening was the largest in the young ballpark's history to date, as the Mets hosted the Yankees in the annual Subway Series. The only people I could see who weren't wearing some form of New York apparel were Michael, Andrew, and myself. Frazier was out there somewhere, but not with us. Like in Philadelphia, he had decided to sit alone during the game.

10:45 p.m.

Have you heard of cabin fever? I'm sure you have. But in case you need a reminder, *cabin fever* is a term that denotes the feeling of claustrophobia one encounters when isolated in a small space for an extended period of time. Think of finding yourself in a tiny, simple cabin in the middle of nowhere and being snowed in for a while. If alone, cabin fever normally brings about boredom, as you grow incredibly restless, faced with the prospect of nothing but yourself and a tight, enclosed space for an indefinite duration. But if experienced in company, cabin fever normally triggers extreme irritation toward the others stuck in that space with you. With nowhere to go and nobody new to talk to, you grow to hate those with whom you share the little cabin. The smallest things tick you off and your anger erupts out of nowhere. Arguments are a product of forced proximity instead of actual opposing viewpoints. It is one of the most frustrating, helpless feelings out there.

Allow me to introduce you to *van fever*. It's the same as cabin fever, but you're stuck in a camper van—which is even *smaller* than a cabin. And there were four of us in there.

But at least the scenery changes in a van, right? Isn't that better than being stuck in a static location, like you would be in a cabin? Yes—and no. It would be appropriate to assume that the views that changed every second were a freeing distraction for us, but in all honestly, they proved to be more like a tease: while the outside of The Van shifted every minute, our claustrophobic confines remained the same. We would look out at wide-open plains and look up at large skyscrapers, but that only reminded us that we were in a sweaty camper with three other testosterone-filled eighteen-year-olds. It was always hot; I never knew if it was my sweat I felt on my body or somebody else's.

In New York City, van fever claimed victory over each of us. It had been chipping away for weeks now, sparking disputes ever since we departed. Yes, Andrew and Frazier had been hit the hardest by it—the tire fight in Philadelphia was just an extension of the pitching spat in New Jersey, which stemmed from the bird poop incident in Milwaukee, which was really just the whole trip—but van fever had officially worked its way into the subconscious of Michael and me as well. What I had been feeling at the game in Philadelphia had now become constant; by this point in the trip, there came a point at least once a day when I simply hated the guys I was traveling with. Anything that they would say, even if I agreed with it, caused a red dot of fury to erupt somewhere deep within me. I couldn't explain what was wrong, so instead I just got mad. And I know the others felt the exact same way. The layers upon layers of passive comments and buried frustration had continued to stack precariously on top of each other, and our visit to the Big Apple was when this unstable tower of pent-up anger came crumbling down.

After the Yankees defeated the Mets 5–1, we met back up with Frazier and wandered through the crowds to board the subway back to Manhattan. Hardly a word was exchanged between the four of us as the #7 train approached Times Square.

"Wanna get out and take a look around?" I suggested, sensing that a bit of fresh air might do us some good. Silently, the others nodded in agreement, and we rose out of the subway station and into one of the busiest intersections in the world. "Fresh air" was a pipe dream here. Even at night, I could see the East Coast summer haze illuminated by the blinding neon billboards that changed colors every other second.

"Man, it's an amazing sight, isn't it?" Andrew asked. He was the only one of us who had visited New York City before, and he had been looking forward to returning since we had left Seattle.

"I hate it," Frazier replied. Michael and I immediately exchanged glances filled with nerves. But then we replaced them with shrugs filled with indifference.

"Why do you hate it?" Andrew retaliated, his voice verging on a quiver. It was difficult to tell whether he was trying to defend Times Square or was simply spoiling for a fight. Looking up at the sensory overload that encircled him, Frazier took a deep breath before responding. He knew that anything, *anything* he would say would cause Andrew to erupt, so he took his moment to cue up perhaps the most pretentious phrase he could muster.

"It's a . . . it's a concrete jungle that's been overrun by commercial weeds."

That was all the fuel Andrew needed. "Oh my *god,* Frazier," he screamed. "You're such a fuck, you know that? You think you're hot and all with the way you can word things and with the supposed *insights* you've got about the world and about the people who fucking *fill* the world—but you're really just making fun of yourself." Michael and I should have stepped in right there, but we didn't care enough. Andrew had more to say, and he clearly had wanted to say it for a while now. "You like to take that camera of yours and wander off and take artsy pics of stuff like graffiti and rundown buildings—but you know what? No wonder none of them were ever accepted by your stupid photo club. 'Cause you're just taking pictures of garbage. Of shit. Shitty pictures of shit. I'm tired of it."

What happened next was a flurry of flailing limbs and jabbing insults, the intensity of which was enough to muscle Michael and me out of our indifference and force us to intervene. I held Andrew back. He was much smaller than me, but all of a sudden he seemed stronger too. The passion he had for the anger he felt was clear, and he soon broke away from my restraining grip and rushed at Frazier. I can still hear the sound of the punch he landed, the clack that echoed around noisy Times Square as his fist hit Frazier's jaw.

Silence ensued. It was a moment of extreme contrast: the four of us were motionless while the loud advertisements and electrified billboards continued to rotate in their ceaseless energy. A few tourists standing near us turned to watch, having seen the punch and becoming intrigued by what might happen next. The flash of someone's camera illuminated Frazier's jaw, where a cut the size of Andrew's finger now glared red in blood. It wasn't bad, but it was enough.

"God," Andrew said, breathing heavily as he reached out and patted his friend. "God, I . . . I'm so sorry, Frazh. I . . . I don't know why I did that." Michael and I looked at each other again, still unsure of what to do. This was new territory for any of us: we had fought *verbally* many times, but it had never turned physical. Andrew's punch was the first of its kind in the history of our friendships. "Here, man," he said, reaching toward Frazier. "Here . . . let me help you up."

But Frazier put his hand up. "Stop" was all he said. The calm tone with which he spoke was frightening.

Clearly at a loss for words, it took Andrew a good thirty seconds before thinking of what to say next. "Here," he eventually said again, "let's . . . let's go back to The Van. We can figure stuff out from there. Let's grab the mitts and have a catch! I think that the lot we're sleeping in has pretty good lighting. We can throw for a while . . . that's worked for us befo—"

"Stop, Andrew." The monotony of Frazier's answer told me that this incident was not something he was willing to wash over with the classic ball-and-glove remedy. He rarely called Andrew by his full name; I think that was the first time I had heard him say something other than *Andy* for years.

"You OK, man?" Michael asked sincerely. Frazier nodded and removed his hand from his face. A small splotch of red was visible on his fingers. "Ah, good," Michael continued. "There isn't that much blood!"

Frazier smiled, but it wasn't a happy smile. He then stood, placed his bloody hand onto the Broadway concrete, and picked himself up. A grimace now spread over his face.

"Yeah . . ." he said, not making eye contact with any of us. "Yeah, I'm taking off."

"Back to The Van?" I asked.

"I don't know." And with that, he turned and walked away, slipping through the small crowd of people who were still watching. I turned to Michael and Andrew.

"Should we follow him?"

"No," Michael replied, his eyes following Frazier's head until it disappeared into the throng. "No, let's give him space."

"I don't know what got into me," Andrew said quietly. "I can't believe I did that."

"It's OK, man. We've all been stressed lately. Something's been eating at us."

"I can't believe I punched him."

"It's OK, man."

"We've been friends forever," Andrew stated, now slouching down to sit on the curb next to where Frazier's drops of blood still reflected the bright lights. "If you had ever told me that I would punch him one day, I would have punched *you* in the face. Oh god," he continued, now placing his head in his hands. "Oh *god,* what the hell is going on?"

"I don't know," Michael said, patting Andrew's back. "I . . . I don't know."

11:50 p.m.

About an hour later, the three of us made our way back to the Upper East Side parking lot and approached The Van. We each hoped to see a light on in our car and Frazier sitting there, having taken some necessary space and now ready to move past the Times Square incident. But The Van shook its head slowly at us, as if it knew. Michael unlocked the door, slid it open, and looked inside.

"His bag is gone."

The only noise I heard for the minute that followed this statement was a slight groan from Andrew, which slowly worked itself into an under-the-breath "No." The fluorescent glow of the overhead streetlamps seemed very impersonal as the three of us stood there in that dirty parking lot, unsure of where our fourth was—or indeed where he was going. A few calls to his cell phone rang through, and the voice mails that were left were ones of apology and desperation. But as the hours ticked by and no reply came, we were forced to spend that night in The Van without knowing where Frazier was. Andrew went alone to the top area, but I don't think he ever actually slept.

It was not until we woke up the following morning that a text message from Frazier popped up on our phones:

> hopped a train at Penn Station. i just need to get away from you guys for a while.

A separate message from him then said:

> i'll probably see you in Boston.

That day was the longest of the trip. The up speed of New York City clashed harshly with the down mood Michael, Andrew, and I felt as we roamed the streets of Manhattan, hoping that sightseeing would distract us from our current situation and sentiment. It couldn't. The hours dragged by, and nobody in that city seemed to notice us. The worst thing about it was that even with the eruption that had occurred the night before, the three of us still felt tinges of animosity toward one another. There was simply nothing we could do: van fever had won, even after already eliminating one member of our company.

"Dare I even ask about things staying the same after we leave for college?" I voiced with a light chuckle, trying to ease the mood while also addressing what I felt to be the elephant in the room. We were standing on the Brooklyn Bridge, staring at the "love locks" that adorned the railings, poking fun at the cheesy superstition to make us feel better. The New York sky-line stared back at us, condemning our criticism.

"I don't think anything will ever be the same now," Michael said bluntly. I could tell he was annoyed with me. I could tell Andrew was annoyed with me too—just as I could tell that he was annoyed with Michael as well. And they could both tell that I was annoyed with the two of them. It simply never stopped. It was exhausting.

"Let's go find some food," Andrew eventually said. "All in favor?"

"Yep."

"Yep."

We each paused, waiting for the customary third "yep." But of course it didn't come.

A walk back across the Brooklyn Bridge plopped us by City Hall, at which point we turned right and aimlessly wandered a few blocks into Chinatown before grabbing sandwiches and eating them on the curb in front of a closed seafood market. A man selling hand-rolled cigars then walked by and offered us one. We bought it, thinking that it might raise our spirits a bit. It didn't. None of us smoked.

Yet we passed around that stick of tobacco nonetheless, af-ter struggling to light it with the matches. As the fumes wafted over us, we each reflected on the past forty-eight hours in silence, our thoughts floating lazily up with the cigar smoke and disappearing into the already-hazy New York night. Hardly any of the street signs around us were written in English. Cars honked but we barely heard them, each of us totally consumed by our current states of depression. This moment not only felt like the end of the trip but also the end of our friendships.

People often celebrate big accomplishments with "victory cigars," making a point to light up an expensive Cuban to honor a triumph of some sort. Well, there on that corner in China-town, we smoked a "defeat cigar." Victims of van fever, we were totally at a loss for what was going to come next.

"You want anymore?" I asked, offering the half-smoked stick to Andrew and Michael. They both shook their heads curt-ly, suggesting they felt the exact same way I did. Standing up to leave, I snuffed out the cigar on the curb and threw it into the sewer.

BOTTOM OF THE FIFTH

Fenway Park

MID-DRIVE DRIVER CHANGE

2:35 p.m. | Sunday, July 3

The monsoon of a storm that drenched the East Coast on the morning of July 3 was the only thing that welcomed Andrew, Michael, and me to Massachusetts as we crossed the state line from Connecticut. No welcome sign was visible on the side of the freeway. It was there, but we couldn't see it through the dense sheets of water that crashed onto the pavement of northbound I-84. The only thing we could make out were the temporary rivers that gushed down the side of the road, and even those were barely visible through the rain that streaked rapidly down The Van's windshield. The wipers waved furiously, but those old, thin pieces of plastic were hardly effective.

Not a word was exchanged in The Van as we continued driving north; anger and indifference still coated our moods completely. From behind the wheel, my mind inevitably flashed back to that prevailing conversation of where our friendships were going and the statement Michael had made the day before.

"Damn," I muttered aloud. It was the first word spoken in The Van in over an hour.

"What?" Andrew asked from the passenger seat.

"Nothing."

The rain continued to fall. The Van felt more like a boat than a car as we drove slowly in the right lane of the freeway, hydroplaning at times over puddles that could easily have been mistaken for ponds if placed elsewhere. My knuckles were turning slightly white as I gripped the steering wheel tightly and leaned forward, squinting to try to see farther. The intense conditions required us to roll at a sluggish thirty miles per hour, with the slow pace of the car mirroring the slow pace of the trip.

Soon enough, the sea of water I was looking at and the copious amount of coffee I had consumed that morning mixed together, and I really had to pee. I informed the rest of the group of this and began looking for an exit to pull off at. The Van grumbled slightly, protesting stopping in the torrential downpour.

"Really?" Michael said from the back, echoing the camper. "It's disgusting outside, man, and we just stopped an hour ago."

"I know," I replied guiltily.

"And we still have nearly a full tank of gas."

"Again, I know."

"Can't you go in the hand urinal?" Andrew asked from the passenger seat.

"How would I do that? I'm driving."

A few seconds of silence followed my statement, during which I could hear the gears turning in Andrew's head beside me. I feared what he was thinking, and sure enough he then voiced it.

"Why don't we just . . . change drivers right now?"

I gulped. "Get out. How would we do that?"

Andrew pursed his lips as he looked at the driver's seat, the naiveté of his eighteen-year-old mind taking over from his perception of safety. "Well," he said, "if you scoot up in the seat, I could position myself right above you. If you then let 'er coast for a second, you can slip to the right and into the passenger seat—while holding the wheel—while I slide down and take over completely."

"That's insane, man." I looked at the mirror to Michael for support—but, as a surprise to me, found him only nodding in agreement with Andrew.

"Yeah, man," he said, somewhat bluntly. "I really just don't want to stop again right now." The rain continued to pummel the windshield.

Raising my eyebrows at both of them, I soon gave in. The stress that was swallowing the rest of the trip made this small driving maneuver seem totally insignificant. In light of our journey potentially unraveling at the feet of our own dissolving relationships, what was a mid-drive driver change going to do?

"Fine."

Within ten seconds, Andrew had climbed onto the armrests of the driver's seat as I moved my body to the front of the chair. My eyes fixed on the road ahead, I gunned the gas to give The Van an extra boost before coasting, gripped the wheel with my left hand, and then slid to the right and into the passenger seat. Simultaneously, Andrew plopped down into the position I had just vacated and took over the pedals while I handed off control of the wheel. Incredibly, the maneuver went as smoothly as our stupid minds assumed it would.

After then exchanging places with Michael so that I could pee in a (slightly) more private manner, I held the little plastic bottle up to my waist and looked out the window. I could still barely discern the trees that lined this section of the highway for the thickness of the raindrops in between. Then The Van skipped over another puddle, its wheels losing touch with the pavement for a brief second. Simultaneously, a gust of wind slapped the side of the car, jolting it to the side and forcing Andrew to jerk the wheel to bring us back into the lane. During those two seconds, the bottle shifted from my grip, and I pissed all over The Van and myself. Michael and Andrew pretended not to notice. Or maybe they just didn't care that there was now exposed pee in the same place that we slept. It was that bad.

As I stood there, covered in urine, I hit rock bottom. Something about the smell of my own piss and the recognition of how terribly the mid-drive driver change could have gone if the same jolt of wind had happened in the middle of it mixed together, and I suddenly realized that I needed out of the trip. I didn't need out for good, but I needed out for a bit. I made up my mind right then and there that I would return to Seattle during the upcoming All-Star break. When we reached Boston a few hours later, I booked a flight as quickly as I could and was soon scheduled to leave Thursday morning from Washington, DC.

1:05 p.m. | Saturday, July 4

Fenway Park is perhaps the most recognizable stadium in all of Major League Baseball. The ballpark's uniqueness begins with its age: built in 1914, it is the oldest in baseball. And—although it has indeed been modernized in certain parts to keep game watching a predominantly twenty-first-century experience—like Wrigley Field, the majority of Fenway still pays tribute to its ancient origins, making fans feel as if they are enjoying a Red Sox game amid echoes of the early 1900s. A hand-operated scoreboard in left is still the primary means through which to track the game while poles supporting the upper concourses stand freely in nearly every infield section, completely obstructing the views of a few unfortunate seats behind them. And yet although these archaic elements contribute well to the standout nature of Fenway, the park's true character shines through in its dimensions.

Down the right field line, the wall slowly curves into foul territory as opposed to turning at a sharp corner (which is the case in every other stadium). This curve starts in fair territory at 380 feet from home plate and eases into the foul line at 302 feet, where the foul pole stands. What's funky is that this lack of a true corner creates some strange circumstances with game-play; here it's not uncommon for a batted ball to end up in foul territory yet still actually be considered a home run, as it wrapped around the shallow foul pole. This distinctive marker has been dubbed "Pesky's Pole," a nod to longtime Red Sox infielder Johnny Pesky, who used to cater his swing specifically to hit the ball to right field in hopes of using the pole's shallow (and slightly controversial) positioning to his benefit. He was quoted as saying that the pole feels far more like 295 feet away from home plate than 302.

But the oddity of Fenway's dimensions does not stop there—in fact, Pesky's Pole is only a warm-up. The 302 feet to right field checks in as the shortest outfield distance in all of baseball, but Fenway's other measurements continue this trend as well. It is 380 feet to straightaway center and 310 to left—both of which are *also* measured to be the shallowest distances to their respective fields in all MLB stadiums.

And then there's Fenway's wall.

In right, the wall stands a meager three feet high as it curves out from Pesky's Pole. Three feet! That's the size of most bats used by Major League hitters. This short height has tabletopped many outfielders as they crash into the fence trying to catch a fly ball, flipping them into the bullpen that lies beyond as the small wall chops their legs out from beneath them. (Google "Jay Buhner Fenway Catch" for a better idea.)

From there, the wall begins to ascend in height, reaching seventeen feet in center field before losing all sense of baseball reality in left. Famously dubbed "the Green Monster," this portion of the (green) wall soars up to thirty-seven feet high and stretches 231 feet wide, 228 of which are in fair territory. Right-handed hitters love to target the Monster, knowing that its shallow dimensions and absurd height will often allow them to get a hit by slapping fly balls and line drives against the wall, which would otherwise be caught by the left fielder in every other MLB park.

. . .

We reunited with Frazier at the game, but it was completely underwhelming. Our number had returned to four, but our insouciance remained the same. We handed out brochures for the Martinez Foundation outside Fenway after the final out was recorded, doing so in an absentminded daze and completely forgetting that it was the Fourth of July and we were in the revolutionary city of Boston. I was probably the happiest of the four of us, propelled by the knowledge that I was going to leave in a few days. I couldn't wait.

TOP OF THE SIXTH
Nationals Park

The Fan Happiness Scale

10:10 p.m. | Wednesday, July 6

This chapter takes a brief step away from the carousel of depressing narrative that the past few have been littered with—however, it also comes with a warning. In a book that uses baseball as its spine, it feels almost compulsory to include a section that takes a deep dive into statistics, for baseball is indeed a statistician's dream. With so many minute numbers that have been meticulously recorded for well over a century, America's pastime lends itself to the passionate and the analytical alike. Sometimes arguments based on these statistical deep dives seem fairly pointless, if not obscure or completely irrelevant to the actual game; I once saw a measurement on runners who stole after the pitcher threw over to first base.[23] Does anybody—fan, manager, or general manager—really need to know that? Maybe, maybe not. But the numbers are there, and my initial argument remains: you can't talk baseball without at some point unraveling into a statistics-heavy tirade.

Warning: in this book, this chapter is that tirade.

. . .

With the exception of the Washington Monument, no building in DC is allowed to exceed the height of the United States Capitol Building. This means that the majority of the city's structures are a similar height, floating regularly between six and ten stories tall. Nationals Park is no exception. With its highest point being 130 feet tall, the stadium has got to be one of the shortest in the majors. But because every other building in Washington is relatively the same height, the views from the ballpark's concourses are stellar. From right field, you look out to Virginia; from left, to Maryland; and from the upper-deck sections of the infield, you are treated to a sweeping view of DC.

The Nationals were relocated from Montreal (where they were the Expos) in 2005, with immediate construction of a new field being one of the mandates in the agreement. The existing ballpark, RFK Stadium, hosted the team temporarily, but it was by no means fit to house an MLB squad long term, with exposed wires hanging down from the concourses and a PA system that sounded like it was broadcasting from underwater. At first, the city of Washington considered building its new stadium on the outskirts of town next to RFK but soon decided it wanted a more urban ballpark. So it opted to place Nationals Park in the Navy Yard area, just south of the Capitol.

This decision was a curious one at first, for in 2005, the Navy Yard was certainly considered a rough neighborhood. Crime had been prominent in this part of Washington for decades, and the choice to flood it with tens of thousands of spectators eighty-one times a year initially drew skepticism. But as soon as the location for Nationals Park was announced and construction broke ground, innovative developments began to pop up in the down-and-out Navy Yard. What was once a vacant lot was now a valuable piece of land, and brand-new apartment units, commercial complexes, and office buildings began to spring up. The price of construction was cheap, and the addition of a new baseball stadium suddenly made the area attractive, as the foot traffic to baseball games would surely mean future business. Now, just a decade later, the Navy Yard is one of the more hopping places in the city.

Nats Park is not the only example of a ballpark influencing a neighborhood. In fact, plenty of cities have strategically decided where to build a new baseball field in hopes of revamping a struggling part of town. San Diego's Gaslamp Quarter was revived when the city opted to build Petco Park just below it, and Seattle's SoDo district was resurrected through Safeco Field. It just proves one more element of magic that baseball can have— not only on its fans but also on its city. *If you build it, he will come.* In this case, "he" is more like "they/business," but you get the point. Good job, Washington.

We saw the Nationals win that night, beating the Chicago Cubs in a tight 3–2 pitchers' duel. Yet it was not enough to appease the man sitting to my right, who grumbled even as closer Drew Storen recorded the final out and secured the home team's victory.

"Doesn't matter," he said, muttering into what was left of his beer. "The win only brings us up to .500. We're still ten games out, or something like that."

I asked him how long he had been a Nationals fan. "Since '05," he said, before downing the rest of his beverage. "I grew up in Baltimore and followed the O's even when I moved down here in '98, but once the city announced that we were getting our own team again, I switched immediately." A look of sadness then came across his face. "But I fear I might've made the wrong choice. This city's cursed . . . our sports teams never win it all.[v] I'm sure Nats fans will become some of the most miserable in the Bigs, even as the franchise develops."

Maybe it was the lowly moods I had been experiencing lately, but my mind hung on the word *miserable* during my walk back to The Van. In 2011, DC fans had seen only seven years of Nationals baseball—how could this guy already be condemn-

---

[v] This occurred before the Capitals won the Stanley Cup in 2018.

ing himself to a lifetime of sadness? I felt that, being a Mariners supporter, I knew something about misery. As mentioned in the introduction to this book, I—and my friends—had slowly grown immune to the regular failure of the hometown M's. Every year, we latched onto the many iterations of "this season might be the one" fed to us by *Seattle Times* writers in March, tried to find solace in sub-.500 records in July, and always became excited for the September roster expansions, convincing ourselves of promising young talent and repeatedly adopting the phrase: "Just you wait: in two years, we'll be great." But two years came, and two years went—and this happened again and again . . . and again. It's still happening. The M's have never won the World Series and are one of only two current teams to have never even *played* in one—with the other, ironically, being the Washington Nationals.

But there are plenty of other fan bases out there who have experienced a similar historic woe. The Pittsburgh Pirates, for example, only recently ended an abysmal stretch of eighteen consecutive losing seasons—the longest such streak in the history of baseball. The San Diego Padres, meanwhile, have never won a World Series and have made the playoffs in only five of their fifty seasons as a ball club. The Tampa Bay Rays have also historically been just really, really bad.

To be honest, quality arguments could be made for a good seven to ten MLB teams as to why they are the "most desperate" for a World Series ring, if not just an appearance in October. So as I walked, I tossed around the question: Which baseball fan base is the least happy? And which is the happiest?

Let's find out.

Now *happiness* is a phenomenon that is simply impossible to gauge. In sports alone, the happiness a fan feels hinges on everything from watching victories, to experiencing big wins over rivals, to how their squad's season measured up to what their initial expectations were—with many ups and downs in between. ESPN recently released an index that attempted to incorporate similar factors while calculating the top twenty-five most miserable fan bases in American sports[24]—yet although I felt a lot of their measurements were spot-on, I also felt that they fell short in the baseball category, primarily because they did not take advantage of the historical statistics that are available to make such arguments, in particular the simple category of wins versus losses. As this chapter's introduction mentioned, America's pastime is a statistician's dream. These numbers go back well over a century and are here for making arguments as pointless and disputable as measuring fan base happiness. Here's mine.

The closest I have come to any sort of potentially accurate measurement of happiness is a calculation I developed in 2016 called the MLB Fan Happiness Scale, or FHS for short. It's an index that, through statistical observations of the history of all thirty Major League ball clubs, attempts to gauge the current level of contentment (and woe) of each fan base in baseball by ranking them in comparison to the other twenty-nine.

The entire system of value is based on your team's success. It's no secret that a lot of your happiness as a sports fan comes from watching your team succeed: when your squad does something well, you have a reason to cheer. In baseball, success is most plainly measured simply by winning baseball games (more than losing them). The next step of success comes in a team's ability to wrangle up enough wins to make it to the playoffs—followed by pennants and then titles. In concordance with these observations, the FHS measures fan happiness based on how often they get to watch their teams do all these things: how often fans get to watch their teams win a game, how often fans get to watch their teams make it to the playoffs, how often fans get to watch their teams win their respective leagues, and then how often fans get to watch their teams celebrate a World Championship.

Pause.

Before proceeding further, it must first be understood that *fan bases* are not to be confused with *franchises*. It's understandable to assume that the relative success of every franchise would automatically relate to the relative happiness of its fan base—but in reality, these two things are quite different. The term *franchise* encompasses every year in existence since the specific organization was created. This obviously includes current location, yes, but a franchise also might have played ball in a completely different city before relocating to where they are right now. And when this happens, supporters from the franchise's old location for the most part dissolve. (A Seattle franchise example: I used to root for the Supersonics; I now despise the Oklahoma City Thunder.)

A *fan base*, on the other hand, refers to the supporters of the team since its most recent relocation—that is, the fans who have cheered on their home teams since they began playing in their hometown. Name changes are one thing—the Boston Americans are the same team as the Boston Red Sox, just as the Devil Rays are still the Rays—but total relocation creates a different fan base altogether. The Nationals fan mentioned earlier became a supporter of the team when they moved to DC, not when they were playing up in Montreal. Therefore, when assessing happiness, the Expos' abysmal statistics would not transfer over to that man's ultimate happiness, as he is a *Washington* fan, not a *Montreal-Washington* fan. Meanwhile, the Milwaukee Brewers' statistics do not include the success of Hank Aaron and the Milwaukee Braves—a franchise now in Atlanta. The numbers for the Dodgers began when they moved from Brooklyn to Los Angeles—but the Brooklyn numbers do not correlate to the Mets' history—you get the point.

Resume.

Because baseball is old (really old) and some teams are older (far older) than others, some teams therefore have had more of an opportunity to succeed (or fail) than others. Example: The Cleveland Indians and the San Francisco Giants have each won six pennants in their team histories—but does that mean that they are equal in this measurement? No, because the Giants have existed for 61 years while the Indians have been around for 118—nearly twice as long. Therefore, San Francisco has been more successful in winning pennants than Cleveland because SF achieved the same total in almost half the time it took the Tribe.[vi]

Because of instances like this (of which there are many), analysis based purely on totals cannot be conducted for this measurement, as it is unfair to the fan bases who have existed for a shorter (or longer) time than others. Therefore, the Fan Happiness Scale levels the playing field by weighing historic *averages* as opposed to historic *totals*. These averages come in a team's overall winning percentage as a ball club during the regular season, their playoff appearance rate, pennant rate, and title rate. Once each average has been calculated, the FHS then ranks each team based on where they stand against the other twenty-nine Major League ball clubs. If team X has the worst

---

[vi] A few explanations. First, the FHS calculations go as far back as the 1901 expansion, which many consider to be when the "modern era" of baseball started. Second, all statistics here were taken from Baseball Reference. Third, you'll notice that some teams that have been around for the same number of years have played different amounts of games. The reason for this is this calculation does not factor in ties (which—although rare—did occur sporadically in the early part of the twentieth century) and because occasionally teams will have a game or two postponed and then wind up *not* making it up at the end of the year, as scheduling the makeup game was initially difficult and in the end resulted in having no playoff implications anyway.

rate in the MLB, they are given a ranking of 1—and if they have the best rate, they get a 30. Finally, the FHS adds up all the rankings: the higher the number, the higher the team's success rate—and therefore, the happier the fans.

Let's start with the basics. The following table takes into account every regular season baseball game each current team has ever played, and shows their historic winning percentages.

FHS 1: Winning Percentage

Fan Base (Created)	Years	Games	Wins	Losses	Win %	FHS
NY Yankees (1903)	116	18,056	10,275	7,781	0.569	30
LA Dodgers (1958)	61	9,726	5,244	4,482	0.5391	29
St. Louis (1901)	118	18,360	9,582	8,778	0.519	28
Boston (1901)	118	18,348	9,518	8,830	0.5187	27
Oakland (1968)	51	8,131	4,216	3,915	0.5185	26
San Francisco (1958)	61	9,725	5,021	4,704	0.5163	25
Atlanta (1966)	53	8,442	4,336	4,106	0.5136	24
Cleveland (1901)	118	18,352	9,384	8,968	0.5113	23
Baltimore (1954)	65	10,318	5,252	5,066	0.509	22
Pittsburgh (1901)	118	18,355	9,330	9,025	0.5083	21
Detroit (1901)	118	18,376	9,299	9,077	0.506	20
Chicago Cubs (1901)	118	18,370	9,278	9,092	0.5051	19
Chicago WS (1901)	118	18,337	9,211	9,126	0.5023	18
LA Angels (1961)	58	9,266	4,637	4,629	0.5004	17
Cincinnati (1901)	118	18,375	9,181	9,194	0.4996	16
Washington (2005)	14	2,266	1,129	1,137	0.4982	15
Toronto (1977)	42	6,679	3,316	3,363	0.4965	14
Minnesota (1961)	58	9,257	4,579	4,678	0.4947	13
Houston (1962)	57	9,105	4,494	4,611	0.4936	12
Arizona (1998)	21	3,402	1,678	1,724	0.4932	11
Texas (1972)	47	7,478	3,682	3,796	0.4924	10
Kansas City (1969)	50	7,961	3,842	4,119	0.4826	9
Milwaukee (1970)	49	7,806	3,760	4,046	0.4817	8
NY Mets (1962)	57	9,094	4,362	4,732	0.4797	7
Colorado (1993)	26	4,151	1,962	2,189	0.4727	6
Seattle (1977)	42	6,679	3,151	3,528	0.4718	5
Tampa Bay (1998)	21	3,400	1,590	1,810	0.4676	4
Miami (1993)	26	4,142	1,933	2,209	0.4667	3
Philadelphia (1901)	118	18,339	8,536	9,803	0.4655	2
San Diego (1969)	50	7,974	3,677	4,297	0.4611	1

My first reaction is that, apart from perhaps Philadelphia—
which, for a team that's been around for 118 years, has a simply
awful record—the bookends of this chart make sense: the Yankees, Dodgers, and Cardinals belong at the top while the Padres, Marlins, and Rays belong at the bottom. But my peak intrigue lies in the middle of the table, particularly with the two
teams that have the FHS rankings of 18 and 19, respectively.
Look at the Chicago teams: both brought in the modern era,
both have played over 18,000 games (eighteen *thousand* baseball
games!), and yet over 118 years, the Cubs have established a
winning percentage that is only .0028 higher than the White
Sox.

What's important for this analysis, however, is that you keep
an eye on the handful of teams at the bottom of the table. Philadelphia's historic win percentage is bad, yes, but they have
found ways to make up for it. The Padres—along with a few
others—have not.

Up next comes a glimpse at how often each team reaches
beyond its historic winning percentage and accumulates enough
victories in a season to earn them a berth in the playoffs. This
measurement is the Playoff Appearance Rate (PAR), which is
calculated by Years Active/Playoffs Made to show the average
number of years that each fan base waits between watching
their teams in the postseason.

FHS 2: Playoff Appearance Rate

Fan Base (Created)	Years	Playoffs Made	PAR	FHS
NY Yankees (1903)	116	54	2.15	30
Atlanta (1966)	53	20	2.65	29
LA Dodgers (1958)	61	23	2.65	29
Oakland (1968)	51	19	2.68	27
Arizona (1998)	21	6	3.5	26
Washington (2005)	14	4	3.5	25
St. Louis (1901)	118	28	4.21	24
Houston (1962)	57	12	4.75	23
Minnesota (1961)	58	12	4.83	22
Boston (1901)	118	24	4.92	21

Fan Base (Created)	Years	Playoffs Made	PAR	FHS
Baltimore (1954)	65	13	5	20
San Francisco (1958)	61	12	5.08	19
Colorado (1993)	26	5	5.2	18
Tampa Bay (1998)	21	4	5.25	17
Kansas City (1969)	50	9	5.56	16
LA Angels (1961)	58	10	5.8	15
Texas (1972)	47	8	5.88	14
Chicago Cubs (1901)	118	20	5.9	13
Toronto (1977)	42	7	6	12
NY Mets (1962)	57	9	6.33	11
Pittsburgh (1901)	118	17	6.94	10
Detroit (1901)	118	16	7.38	9
Cincinnati (1901)	118	15	7.87	8
Cleveland (1901)	118	14	8.43	7
Philadelphia (1901)	118	14	8.43	7
Milwaukee (1970)	49	5	9.8	5
San Diego (1969)	50	5	10	4
Seattle (1977)	42	4	10.5	3
Miami (1993)	26	2	13	2
Chicago WS (1901)	118	9	13.11	1

My *god*, White Sox fans. Wow, I'm sorry. As supporters of a 118-year-old ball club that has made the playoffs only nine times, you wait an average of 13.11 years between getting to experience October baseball in South Chicago. I used to turn north in the Windy City to shed sympathy, but perhaps I was slightly blinded and should pay a bit more attention to Southside. Yikes.

So the White Sox get the 1 in this FHS category, but as was the case for Philadelphia in the last table, it's all up from here. As was *also* the case in the last table, take a look again at the handful of teams circling the drain right above Chicago. Recognize a few?

Once teams make it to the playoffs, do they flop immediately—like that Nationals fan was talking about—or do they go on to be crowned champions of their leagues and get to play in the World Series? The next FHS category takes this all into account,

analyzing the Pennant Success Rate of each team, which is calculated by Playoffs Made/Pennants Won.

FHS 3: Pennant Rate

Fan Base (Created)	Playoffs Made	Pennants Won	Pennant Rate	FHS
Miami (1993)	2	2	1.00	30
NY Yankees (1903)	54	40	0.74	29
Detroit (1901)	16	11	0.69	28
St. Louis (1901)	28	19	0.68	27
Chicago WS (1901)	9	6	0.67	26
Cincinnati (1901)	15	9	0.6	25
Boston (1901)	24	14	0.59	24
NY Mets (1962)	9	5	0.56	23
Chicago Cubs (1901)	20	11	0.55	22
Pittsburgh (1901)	17	9	0.53	21
Philadelphia (1901)	14	7	0.5	20
San Francisco (1958)	12	6	0.5	20
LA Dodgers (1958)	23	11	0.48	18
Baltimore (1954)	13	6	0.46	17
Kansas City (1969)	9	4	0.44	16
Cleveland (1901)	14	6	0.43	15
San Diego (1969)	5	2	0.4	14
Oakland (1968)	19	6	0.32	13
Toronto (1977)	7	2	0.29	12
Atlanta (1966)	20	5	0.25	11
Minnesota (1961)	12	3	0.25	11
Tampa Bay (1998)	4	1	0.25	11
Texas (1972)	8	2	0.25	11
Colorado (1993)	5	1	0.2	7
Milwaukee (1970)	5	1	0.2	7
Arizona (1998)	6	1	0.17	5
Houston (1962)	12	2	0.17	5
LA Angels (1961)	10	1	0.1	3
Seattle (1977)	4	0	0	2
Washington (2005)	4	0	0	2

Reaction one: My eyes are immediately drawn to the zeroes at
the bottom. What this means is that these two teams—the
Washington Nationals and our dear Seattle Mariners—have
never clinched a pennant in their histories, meaning that their
fans are still waiting for their first World Series *appearance*, let
alone title. Yeah, Nats fans are still relatively young (and have
been fairly successful since the franchise's move from Montre-

al), but for the purpose of this study, both the Nats and the Ners get 2s in this FHS category. (They would get 1s, but technically they're both tied for second-to-last place, and the extra FHS point is mere consolation at this stage.)

Reaction two: the Yankees' record of 74 percent pennant rate is incredible, especially once you wrap your mind around the fact that they have made the playoffs *fifty* times and have thus missed out on the World Series on only fourteen of those occasions.

Reaction three: Check out the solid 100 percent that the Marlins hold. OK, yeah, they have made the playoffs only twice (their PAR is terrible), but they have won the National League both of those times—and it didn't stop there.

FHS 4: Title Rate

Fan Base (Created)	Pennants Won	Titles Won	Title Rate	FHS
Miami (1993)	2	2	1	30
Toronto (1977)	2	2	1	30
Arizona (1998)	1	1	1	30
LA Angels (1961)	1	1	1	30
NY Yankees (1903)	40	27	0.68	26
Minnesota (1961)	3	2	0.67	25
Oakland (1968)	6	4	0.67	25
Boston (1901)	14	9	0.64	23
St. Louis (1901)	19	11	0.58	22
LA Dodgers (1958)	11	5	0.56	21
Pittsburgh (1901)	9	5	0.56	21
Baltimore (1954)	6	3	0.5	19
Chicago WS (1901)	6	3	0.5	19
Cincinnati (1901)	10	5	0.5	19
Houston (1962)	2	1	0.5	19
Kansas City (1969)	4	2	0.5	19
San Francisco (1958)	6	3	0.5	19
NY Mets (1962)	5	2	0.4	13
Detroit (1901)	11	4	0.36	12
Cleveland (1901)	6	2	0.33	11
Philadelphia (1901)	7	2	0.29	10
Chicago Cubs (1901)	11	3	0.27	9
Atlanta (1966)	5	1	0.2	8
Colorado (1993)	1	0	0	7
Milwaukee (1970)	1	0	0	7

Fan Base (Created)	Pennants Won	Titles Won	Title Rate	FHS
San Diego (1969)	2	0	0	7
Tampa Bay (1998)	1	0	0	7
Texas (1972)	2	0	0	7
Seattle (1977)	0	N/A	N/A	2
Washington (2005)	0	N/A	N/A	2

Not only do the Marlins *make* the World Series every time they (infrequently) make the playoffs but also they *win* the World Series every time they make the playoffs! In their young history, the Fish have played in October twice and both times have come home with the Commissioner's Trophy. The awful PAR of 13 suggests that they won't make the postseason again until 2032, but don't worry Marlins fans: you'll be champs then!

The N/As for Washington and Seattle are obvious elephants in the room as well. But the explanation is quite simple: it's impossible to calculate a title rate for either, as you can't divide by zero (Title Rate = Titles Won/Pennants Won). When you have never even played in a World Series, how could you win one? The zeroes above them, meanwhile, represent the remaining MLB fan bases that have never celebrated their teams winning it all.

So how does each team and fan base stack up? The final chart provides the overall happiness rating for each, adding up the teams' rankings from the four measurements, giving the cumulative FHS in historic winning percentage (Win %), Playoff Appearance Rate (PAR), Pennant Rate (PR), and Title Rate (TR). With four categories that each have 30 possible FHS, the highest possible total would be a 120 (4 x 30), and the lowest a 4 (4 x 1).

Fan Happiness Scale

Fan Base (Created)	W% FHS	PAR FHS	PR FHS	TR FHS	Total
NY Yankees (1903)	30	30	29	26	115
St. Louis (1901)	28	24	27	22	101
LA Dodgers (1958)	29	29	18	21	97
Boston (1901)	27	21	24	23	95

Fan Base (Created)	W% FHS	PAR FHS	PR FHS	TR FHS	Total
Oakland (1968)	26	27	13	25	91
San Francisco (1958)	25	19	20	19	83
Baltimore (1954)	22	20	17	19	78
Pittsburgh (1901)	21	10	21	21	73
Arizona (1998)	11	26	5	30	72
Atlanta (1966)	24	29	11	8	72
Minnesota (1961)	13	22	11	25	71
Detroit (1901)	20	9	28	12	69
Cincinnati (1901)	16	8	25	19	68
Toronto (1977)	14	12	12	30	68
LA Angels (1961)	17	15	3	30	65
Miami (1993)	3	2	30	30	65
Chicago WS (1901)	18	1	26	19	64
Chicago Cubs (1901)	19	13	22	9	63
Kansas City (1969)	9	16	16	19	60
Houston (1962)	12	23	5	19	59
Cleveland (1901)	23	7	15	11	56
NY Mets (1962)	7	11	23	13	54
Washington (2005)	15	25	2	2	44
Texas (1972)	10	14	11	7	42
Philadelphia (1901)	2	7	20	10	39
Tampa Bay (1998)	4	17	11	7	39
Colorado (1993)	6	18	7	7	38
Milwaukee (1970)	8	5	7	7	27
San Diego (1969)	1	4	14	7	26
Seattle (1977)	5	3	2	2	12

First: Oh how nice it would be to be a Yankees fan. Yeah, we know that and all—but wow! On average, Yankees fans see more wins than any other fan base, they see their team in the playoffs every 2.15 years—and from there there's a 74 percent chance the Yanks take home the AL pennant and then a 68 percent chance they win the World Series. Twenty-seven titles and forty pennants. With a 115 on the FHS, fans of the Bronx Bombers are at 95.8% possible happiness (115/120). Numbers don't lie.

Second: ah, the Mariners.

MIDDLE OF THE SIXTH
Progressive Field

BRANDON

8:10 a.m. | Thursday, July 7

I parted ways with Michael, Andrew, and Frazier early the next morning, hopping a train at Union Station to Baltimore-Washington International Airport. My departure was bland because it was expected; unlike Frazier's dramatic separation, I had planned mine (slightly) ahead of time. I don't know if that made it any better, though—in fact, it might have made it worse. For me to schedule a hiatus and actually stick with it as opposed to acting on a spur-of-the-moment decision was a testament to my own sentiment toward the trip.

Maybe it was homesickness. Yeah, that was certainly a part of it. To be eighteen and facing the imminent departure for college is a unique stage in one's life; for most who encounter it, it brings the first true leap out the door of your childhood home and into the "real world"—an exciting but also a scary prospect. And suddenly I had realized that my final summer at home before this leap was not being spent at home at all. By climbing into The Van back on June 11 and departing Seattle, I had already made my leap out the proverbial door, but it had snuck up on me; I hadn't realized it. It wasn't until a few days ago, while standing in The Van with my own urine running down my leg and the swells of depression surrounding me, that I realized what had happened. And to be honest, I panicked. I got scared, I got nostalgic, and I needed a break to simply go home for a bit.

But the part beyond homesickness was sheer fatigue at the demanding nature of what we were doing. I was tired of traveling like we had been, and I was also tired of being angry. After the defeat cigar, urine incident, and many recent fights I had watched and participated in with my best friends, my dream summer wasn't feeling much like a dream anymore. The lows of the drug of travel had overwhelmed me completely. So I boarded my flight and headed to Seattle, where I passed the All-Star break and rebooted for almost a week.

Looking back today, I wish I hadn't left. My absence meant that I missed our visit to Cleveland, which meant that *my* part of the trip was never truly completed. My childhood dream, built out of a baseball fantasy chalked up with my best friends, remained unfinished because of my inability to gut it out and withstand the stresses of traveling and simply growing. I didn't see all the ballparks at once, and to this day the journey still feels incomplete. I still haven't made it to Progressive Field.

But at the same time, I also now recognize that to truly enjoy something, you must sometimes take the time to find room to breathe. And although I'm not proud that it had to be this way, I also honestly know that if I hadn't elected to take that hiatus and go home, I wouldn't have enjoyed the remainder of the trip after I returned. What's more is that I was not the only one of our group who felt this way. After I announced my departure from Washington, Michael soon followed suit and decided that it was also in his best interests to skip Cleveland and use the All-Star break as his own break from the trip. Following the game in DC, he took the Metro to Union Station and boarded a late-night bus to New York City to go do I still don't know what. Breathe, too, I guess. Recollect some sanity as well. Traveling is hard; watching your best friendships unravel as a consequence of it is harder.

This left Frazier and Andrew alone to head to Cleveland. At first I had assumed that they both would also opt to forgo Progressive Field and take some solo time, but they seemed intent on going. Maybe they both wanted to outlast the other, thinking their counterpart would cancel first, but in the end, the two of them proved to be too dedicated to the cause. I still commend them for this. Andrew and Frazier were the real champs of the trip. Yet seeing as they were also the duo who easily fought the most, Michael and I were understandably nervous about leaving them to gnaw at each other's necks without either of us there to run interference. To be honest, we would not have been surprised if only one person had come back in The Van after the All-Star break.

We were thus extremely surprised when three people did.

3:55 p.m.

I'm still not entirely sure what happened in Cleveland. I could never get the full story out of Andrew and Frazier; it seemed some sort of personal secret between the two of them, and maybe appropriately so. To me, however, it remains an unsolved gap in the trip. I stopped asking questions years ago.

As was perhaps expected, Andrew and Frazier didn't speak to each other for the first part of their drive to Ohio that afternoon, their lingering animosity toward one another prevailing. But as the hours passed and maintaining passive-aggressive silence became boring and pointless, conversation began to bud yet again. Slowly, the tear in their relationship that had been left by the punch in Times Square was temporarily stitched back together once more. By the time four o'clock rolled around, they had made it to Cleveland, and Andrew texted me that he and Frazier were "boys" again, chatting about baseball and love and the world and the future and all those kinds of things, as if no bad blood had ever existed between them. I smiled, unsure if I fully believed it. But the positive mood only continued to grow as they parked The Van somewhere in downtown Cleveland and wandered to Progressive Field. They scalped the two extra tickets that were originally for Michael and me to a vendor on their way to the ballpark and entered the gates.

Progressive Field is supposed to be beautiful, sitting just a few blocks in from the banks of Lake Eerie on one of the many bends of the Cuyahoga River. A towering grandstand in right field and a gigantic scoreboard in left make the ballpark feel big to those sitting within it, but in reality, Progressive is fairly small. Its seating capacity of just over thirty-seven thousand makes it one of the smallest parks in baseball—but for big games, the stadium can expand to roughly forty-five thousand through selling standing room only tickets and housing thousands of more fans at its many pavilions and bars.

The Friday night crowd was large, and the only empty seats in Andrew and Frazier's section were the two next to them, vacated by the scalped tickets. When the third inning rolled around, a young man wandered down the aisle. He was tall, roughly six two, with dark skin and hair that was picked into a small Afro. In his hand he held a ticket stub, and he paused at Andrew and Frazier's row.

"Twelve or thirteen?" Frazier asked.

"Sorry?" he replied.

"Do you have seat twelve or thirteen."

"Yeah . . . seat twelve, row G?" He indicated to the seat next to Frazier. "How'd you know?"

"You scalp 'em?" Frazier asked.

"Yeah?"

"We sold 'em."

"Ah," the guy looked taken aback. "Well, in that case . . . thanks, man. Big crowd tonight for some reason, and I couldn't find any cheap seats."

Frazier flipped down the seat next to him, motioning for the young man to sit. "Just you?" he asked.

"Yeah, just me."

"You been to Progressive before?"

"Many times. I live just outside the city. Go Tribe."

"Mind telling us a bit about the ballpark?"

"'Course, what you wanna know?"

"Everything."

"Everything?"

"Everything." He reached his hand out for a shake. "I'm Frazier, by the way."

"Brandon. Alright, well let's start with the size. Progressive's actually pretty small, you see . . ."

It was as simple as that. The game soon turned into background noise, as the three entered into conversation. Brandon had ventured into Cleveland by himself earlier that day, biding time before he returned to college in Atlanta for his sophomore year.

"I finished up with my summer job 'bout a week ago," he continued, "and am now just waitin' to head back down. Figure'd I'd come in for the game 'cause I hadn't been to one yet this year. I take it y'all have never been here before?"

This naturally prompted Andrew and Frazier to speak about their own reason for being there. Brandon's eyes lit up as he learned about our trip, his enthusiasm for what we were trying to accomplish becoming apparent immediately. He soon began asking questions about the parks we had seen, The Van, and all that had happened since setting out from Seattle almost a month prior. When he learned of the unfortunate reality of the past week and me and Michael's temporary departures, he expressed sympathy.

"So now it's just you two?"

"For the time being, yeah," Andrew replied. "Until after the All Star break."

What Brandon said next was both unexpected and perfect.

"Need a third?"

At first, Andrew and Frazier didn't take him seriously. There was no way they were about to let a complete stranger join the trip, were they? Surely not. They laughed off the offer and soon re-entered into a light chat with Brandon, this time about *other* ballparks he had been to. Yet as the conversation continued to grow, Andrew and Frazier both silently began to consider. Would it be all that bad to have another face join the trip? It might actually be quite nice—a little shake up of the tense reality we had grown to know and grown to hate.

"Man I already told you, I'm just killin' time right now," Brandon said. "I'd have to head home and pack up some of my things before takin' off with y'all, but I could do that in a day or two. You said you don't need to be back on the road 'til after the break, right?"

"Right. Our next game is in Baltimore on the fourteenth."

"I mean what's today, the seventh? So that's not for another week." Brandon shrugged. "It's up to you guys, of course, and I don't wanna pressure nothing. But all I gotta do is be in Atlanta by the end of August. How I get there . . . or *when* I get there . . . that's all up in the air." By the time the game ended, Andrew and Frazier had invited him to join the trip.

. . .

As the nervous one of the group, I was initially skeptical about this addition when it was mentioned to me. A stranger? On our trip? *Our* trip? It felt wrong and intrusive. I had always envisioned this baseball odyssey to be about us, about my friends—a celebration of our childhood friendships through accomplishing our dream.

But dreams often look different in the rearview mirror. Brandon joining the trip brought me to my biggest realization of that entire summer: contrary to my initial thoughts, this trip wasn't about who we *were*. It wasn't about celebrating our childhoods, the time we had spent together, or what our friendships had evolved into—hell, it wasn't even about seeing ballparks.

No, this trip was about discovering who we were *becoming*. All the fights, all the disagreements, and all the stresses of travel were merely a product of coming to realize that, despite my fears, things were *never* going to be the same. Our lives were about to shift drastically; our friendships were already changing, and we were caught right in the middle of it. This trip wasn't a fantasy of high schoolers taking one last blast into the great wide open—it was an introduction to real life. And real life is better than any sort of fantasy.

I'll say it: Brandon Burke was the best thing that happened to our trip. When I returned six days later, I recognized this immediately. Not only was his company flat-out enjoyable but also Brandon provided a fresh enthusiasm that was similar to what the four of us had felt during our first couple of weeks on the road. He was not yet spoiled by the stresses of travel, and his optimism spread to the rest of us almost immediately. Suddenly, after weeks of incessant arguing, Andrew, Frazier, Michael, and I seemed to be completely immune to any animosity we had clearly felt toward each other just one week before. And for the duration of Brandon's stay, it remained that way.

BOTTOM OF THE SIXTH
Camden Yards

THE BALLPARK THAT FOREVER
CHANGED BASEBALL

7:30 p.m. | Thursday, July 14

There are thirty ballparks in baseball. You know this. Many of these fields, a good chunk of which I have already described, are wonderful places to enjoy a game. Designed specifically to host baseball, they have welcomed the lack of dimension restrictions with open arms and incorporated creative, unique features to their venues that set them apart from all others. Simply put, such places feel like *baseball* fields.

This was not always the case. A century ago, parks like Wrigley or Fenway were created in this "baseball-only" mindset, but fifty years later, such places were anomalies in MLB. By the mid-to late 1900s, the idea of designing urbanized, specialized ballparks had been turned down by owner groups who instead favored rural, multipurpose stadiums. Out were the days of the distinct; in were the days of the disgusting.

Remember the King Dome, Seattle? Remember Veterans Stadium in Philadelphia or County Stadium in Milwaukee? These all are examples of what was then considered to be *the* venue for baseball teams—because they were *the* venues for sports teams in general. Football, baseball, soccer . . . monster truck rallies, ice skating competitions, equestrian shows . . . everything could take place here. The buildings were heartless and lacked creativity of any kind, instead standing as truly modernist approaches to athletic complexes, the epitome of form follows function. Former MLB commissioner Bud Selig claimed such buildings had "no character"; journalist Reid Forgrave was slightly more to the point, calling them "drab concrete dough-nuts."[25]

And you think the list of those stadiums ends with the three I just mentioned?

San Diego: Jack Murphy Stadium. Pittsburgh: Three Rivers Stadium. Minnesota: the Metrodome. Houston: the Astrodome. Washington: RFK. Cleveland: Municipal Stadium. I could continue.

Google any of these things and try to tell me that they don't each look exactly the same. They were not *baseball* stadiums, they were *big* stadiums. They were places where baseball was merely played, not places built *for* America's pastime. There's a big difference. The names of all these venues each ended with "dome" or "stadium," inherently straying from being a ballpark specifically and instead making them a multipurpose sports complex. And if you are still struggling to remember what one of those places felt like, there are still a few surviving today: visit Tampa's Tropicana Field, Oakland's Alameda Coliseum, or Toronto's Rogers Centre, and you'll better grasp the picture. It goes without saying that the ballparks we have now are so, so, *so* much better.

San Diego: Petco Park. Pittsburgh: PNC Park. Minnesota: Target Field. Houston: Minute Maid Park. Washington: Nationals Park. Cleveland: Progressive Field. Milwaukee: Miller Park. Philadelphia: Citizens Bank Park. Seattle: Safeco Field. I could continue.

See any "stadiums" or "domes" in that list? These days, venues for baseball are venues for *baseball.* The labels "field" and "park" have returned, clearly indicating once again that such a place is meant as a home for America's pastime. There are, of course, a few exceptions to the suffix, as the word *stadi-*

um no longer solely denotes big, gross, and multipurpose. It's merely a convenient title here and there; I would argue that Yankee Stadium, Busch Stadium, and Kauffman Stadium are still *baseball* stadiums and match up right alongside today's ballparks, which are far more interesting and fan friendly than the drab concrete doughnuts of yesteryear. And they all have one ballpark to thank.

In the late 1980s, the city of Baltimore needed a new place to play baseball. Memorial Stadium, the old multipurpose venue that stood just north of Charles Village, was not cutting it anymore as a host for the Orioles—or even as a place for sports fans of any kind to visit. Its nicknames reveal this negative sentiment: it was called "the old gray lady of 33rd street" for its bland aesthetics and "the world's largest outdoor insane asylum" for its horrible atmosphere (mixed, probably, with how bad the Baltimore Colts football team was in those days).[26]

With the Orioles clamoring for a new home, the city made a bold move and opted *not* to reinvest in Memorial Stadium. Instead, they decided to construct a *baseball* field. The architects, HOK Sports, turned away from the multipurpose plague and instead looked back to the country's oldest ballparks for inspiration: Wrigley and Fenway. They did not want to impose a stadium onto the city; they wanted to fit one *into* the city. They desired to blend memory with practicality and create something that fans would fall in love with instead of have to deal with. And, man, did they succeed.

Camden Yards—officially Oriole Park at Camden Yards—is the ballpark that forever changed baseball. It is fit snugly into Baltimore, located just three blocks off the Inner Harbor on Eutaw Street. The place emerges from the city just like any other building; walking down Eutaw, you suddenly stumble on a baseball field. Meanwhile, the old B&O Railroad Warehouse is as much a part of the stadium as the diamond or the seats themselves. Iconic in its red-brick glow, the warehouse is representative of everything that Camden stands for: incorporating Baltimore into its creation. Ballpark shops and restaurants line the concourse level of the old building while office flats above remain populated with nine-to-five workers. In front of the warehouse is a large standing room only patio, where fans can gather and look out over the field from up high while enjoying a beer.

We have now grown used to ballparks incorporating city buildings or placing beer landings into concourses—but just three decades ago, such things were unheard of. Nearly every single ballpark that has been built since Camden Yards opened in 1992 has used it as inspiration in one way or another. San Diego's Petco Park has a warehouse of its own in left while Seattle's Safeco Field has a standing room only beer patio in center. They, along with the likes of PNC Park, AT&T Park, Nationals Park, Coors Field, and many more, have been constructed not for sports in general but for *baseball* in particular—all thanks to the model set forth by Camden.

Sprinkled around the Yards are a few attributes that commemorate special events that have occurred here. Every single seat in the stadium is dark green in color, save two beyond the outfield wall, which are bright orange. One marks the spot where Eddy Murray hit his landmark five-hundredth career home run, the other where Cal Ripken's 278th dinger landed, which at the time was the most of any shortstop in MLB history.

But speaking of honoring home runs.

One year after it opened, Oriole Park at Camden Yards hosted the 1993 MLB All-Star Game—which of course was accompanied by the trivial-but-fun Home Run Derby. On July 12, fans packed the stadium for the Derby, eager to see that year's biggest sluggers literally take their shot at the Orioles' new home. And while Texas's Juan Gonzalez would go on to win the competition, the most memorable moment of the event belonged to Seattle's very own Ken Griffey Jr.

Somewhere in the middle of his round, Griffey launched a ball to right that, for a split second, entered orbit. By the time it came down, it had landed way beyond the heightened beer patio above the tall right field wall—and suddenly, fans gathered on the patio went ballistic, waving their arms like maniacs. Now this is by no means a foreign gesture at the Home Run Derby, where mad scrambles for baseballs often result in what looks to be a concert mash pit erupting somewhere in the stands until a lucky fan raises their hand, clutching the souvenir in victory. But something about the reactions to Griffey's home run were different.

"That might have hit the warehouse . . ." the broadcaster said hesitantly. He sounded uncertain at first, but soon the camera zoomed in and confirmed his suspicion, as fans were pointing at the base of the old B&O building. Griffey's ball had hit about six feet up, on a stone pillar that supports the brick warehouse above. It was the first and to this day remains the *only* home run to hit the icon of the iconic ballpark.[27] I smiled as I wandered up and looked at the plaque that marks the spot where the ball landed. It's a little bit of Mariner influence stamped onto the ballpark that influenced all other fields that came after it.

TOP OF THE SEVENTH
Great American Ballpark

CHOOSE OPTIMISM

10:30 p.m. | Friday, July 15

Mark Twain would have loved Cincinnati's Great American Ballpark. Not only does its name bluntly honor the country the author loved to feature in his work but also the building itself would have appealed to him. The Reds' stadium feels like a turn-of-the-century steamboat that is making its way up the Ohio River through Twain's America, passing roaring factories before moving on in blissful transit to pastoral countryside. This feel primarily comes from the center field complex, where an actual nineteenth-century riverboat has been placed just above the batter's eye. It has now been converted into a party deck reserved for events and is flanked by two large steamboat smokestacks that light up and spout flames when a Red hits a home run or the team claims victory. Meanwhile, the majority of the park's concourses feature stellar panoramas of Cincinnati and the surrounding bits of Ohio and Kentucky—Great America spreading out from Great American, if you will.

If the Mark Twain visions are difficult for you to imagine, this ballpark seems to have been built for another figure as well: Pete Rose. Yes, Rose has an embattled history with that whole betting thing, but one cannot take away from the phenomenal baseball player he was during his twenty-four years in the sport, nineteen of which he spent in Cincinnati. A sixteen-time All Star who hit a lifetime .303 and racked up 4,256 hits is a simply incredible career—and Great American makes sure everyone recognizes this. Those smokestacks I just mentioned are both flanked by seven sculpted baseballs, fourteen in total, which represent the #14 that Rose wore on his jersey. But that's just the beginning.

In 2003, a gigantic three-piece mural was unveiled on the back of the left field scoreboard, depicting the bat Rose used and the ball he hit when he broke Ty Cobb's all-time hits record in 1985. (The mural, along with Rose's reputation, faded away slowly as the years passed. It was replaced before Cincinnati hosted the All-Star Game in 2015.) Meanwhile, just next to the stadium stands the elaborate and pun-loving "Rose Garden," located in what would have been the infield of old Riverfront Stadium, where the Reds played until Great American opened in 2002. Along with functioning as the team's Hall of Fame, the garden houses one single white rose in the middle of its plethora of red ones. This marks the exact spot where Rose's aforementioned record-breaking hit landed, standing in what would have been the shallow outfield of the ballpark in which he played so many games. And just when you thought there was no more that could be done to broadcast Rose's legacy, inside the building adjacent to the garden stands a massive glass case displaying 4,256 mounted baseballs—one for each hit Pete Rose ever recorded. It is a record that still stands today, and Great American is here to make sure that you never forget it.

The game we saw that evening was one of the best of the entire trip. A Brandon Phillips walk-off home run electrified the Friday night crowd, us included. Yet somehow, even with all the cheering and game-ending fireworks, it also sparked another bit of bickering between—who else—Frazier and Andrew.

"Best game of the trip," Frazier stated.

"Nah, the Dodger game was better."

"What? No way—tonight's was a walk-off!"

"Better atmosphere at Dodger Stadium."

"There was hardly anybody there!"

"Yeah, and the people were more electric, which speaks volumes."

"You just liked it 'cause it was our first stadium."

"Are you stupid? It was our second!"

"Man, stop," Brandon said calmly, as the five of us exited the gates of Great American. I turned to glance at him, but he wasn't looking at either Frazier or Andrew, despite addressing them. He just kept speaking. "Remember what that woman said."

1:15 p.m. | Earlier That Day

I'll get to what Brandon meant in a second—but first, a traveler's note: two-lane roads are far better than freeways. In retrospect, the four of us each wish we had opted to abide by this mentality more than we did that summer, but time restraints often required us to take interstates. Yet even when we *had* time on our hands, we often fell victim to habit and normally calculated the fastest route to our destination, taking freeways in order to save some time.

But there is a difference between saving time and spending it. Some of the best moments in life on the road come *on* the road, when you have thrown the importance of your ETA away and allowed for whatever obstacles that might arise to do so, tackling them with an adventuresome spirit. Such obstacles can end up being more like doorways, offering new experiences and unpredictable encounters. You never know where your next amazing moment might come from.

Cue: two-lane roads. They allow you to see real America, the guts of the country that you inherently desire to see as a US road tripper. Freeways are like bypasses, showing you nothing but the same bland vistas and rest stops complete with Burger Kings and Subways; a Pennsylvania freeway can look a lot like an Oregon one. Two-lane roads are different because they're local and personal. They wander you through wacky towns, drag you by national parks, and drop you off at food joints that show the true flavor of the area you're in.

There was no direct freeway to take from Baltimore to Cincinnati, so after stints on I-68 and I-79 led us through a good chunk of Maryland and West Virginia, Tina dumped us onto State Route 50 to Parkersburg, where we crossed into Ohio and changed onto State Route 124. We passed through small towns bordering the Ohio River before moving farther into the state, eventually ending up in a place called Rutland. It had one main street, on which there was a post office and a gas station—that was pretty much it. As The Van idled in the right lane of the road, Andrew spotted a local walking our way and stuck his head out of the driver's side window.

"Excuse me," he said. "There a café of any sort around here?"

The man paused on the sidewalk. Roughly sixty years old, he wore weathered overalls covering a light-red T-shirt that was splotched with what appeared to be bleach stains. A tattered Reds cap was jammed onto his head, hiding the little hair he had remaining. The man's hands were filled with calluses that looked to be the product of decades of hard work with a heavy tool. I watched as his eyes slowly shifted from staring at Andrew to staring at The Van and its lawless design. He squinted as he took in the car's tie-dye color job, reading our brief description on the side of the vehicle.

"Wow," he said, finally speaking. His voice was a slow drawl that suited his physique. "So you young men . . . are . . . are doing all this?"

"Yes, sir!" Andrew replied enthusiastically.

"My . . . baseball games, eh?"

"Yes, that's right. Been a dream of ours."

"Y'on yer way to Cincy, I assume?"

"That's right."

"Can I ask you a question?"

"Of course!"

"What the fuck are you doing here in Rutland."

It wasn't a question at all. The man uttered the sentence with a tone that was more an insult than it was an inquiry, and it took each of us by surprise. He moved on immediately, and out of the back window of The Van, I watched as he shot one last glance at our car before continuing down the sidewalk, proceeding at the same slow pace he had been moving at before hearing Andrew's question.

For about fifteen seconds, nobody spoke as The Van idled on the street. The village seemed not to move either—I don't know the last time it did. We each followed the old man with our eyes as he turned the corner at the end of the block and disappeared off the main street, heading somewhere remote in the already remote town of Rutland. Andrew soon spoke again.

"Wow, what an asshole."

In the immediate aftermath of the overall-wearing local cursing us out, this at first seemed a fair statement. But then Brandon opened his mouth.

"Yeah, that was weird for sure," he said, "but you gotta imagine all that went through his mind right there."

"What do you mean?" Andrew replied. "I just asked him if there was a café around."

"I ain't suggesting you did anything wrong. But c'mon, that guy looks as if he hasn't left this place in decades, man. For him to see a bunch of teens roll through his tiny town in a wildly colored camper van on a trip like this . . . that's gotta be a bit off-putting, don't ya think?"

"Not really," Andrew replied, unwilling to cave. The Van continued panting in the right lane of the street as a car passed.

"Well," Brandon continued, "here you are. Here *we* are. Five teenagers on the trip of a lifetime! It's somethin' you've clearly dreamed of and somethin' you've certainly worked hard for, no doubt—but also somethin' that you're each very fortunate to be able to dream of *and* work hard for. Those who come from other backgrounds, or who live in a town like this—like Rutland— they probably don't got the same means as y'all. I mean, that guy right there might've never even dreamed that he would be able to get out 'n see the country. His life looks to have been completely contained here in ol' Rutland, Ohio, and he probably just assumed that other things—like cross-country road trips—are reserved for big cities and stuff he's never seen. So when he sees a car like this pull through, he probably catches a glimpse, ya know? A glimpse of a life that was never made available to him. And he gets a bit angry. Not at you, but at the *situation*. But he can't curse at the situation, so he curses at you."

At no moment on that trip did a bit of education hit me harder than it did right there. In my eighteen-year-old state, I was at a loss for speech as I chewed over Brandon's words, each of which rang true. Since departing from Seattle, we had often been victims of one-track minds, experiencing the effect the places we visited had on *us* but failing to consider the effect *we* might have on those places. Big cities were normally indifferent, having seen the likes of us plenty of times before. Ballparks would occasionally turn their heads, intrigued by the nature of our trip and comparisons between the thirty temples of baseball around North America. But small towns were different. Small towns took notice when things like us passed through—because it was uncommon. Frankly, our story didn't sit well with some.

"I guess, maybe," Andrew said after thirty seconds of silence, but I could tell that was just his combative self prevailing. Deep down, he wholeheartedly agreed with what Brandon had said—as we all did. We were indeed fortunate to be able to do what we were doing. Yes, we had dreamed up this trip by ourselves, had labored to raise the money necessary to execute it, and had put all our effort in trying to benefit the Martinez Foundation along the way—but that does not detract from the pure fact that we were fortunate to simply have the *opportunity* to do all this in the first place. I scowl at my past self for not realizing it earlier. Perhaps it goes without saying, but sometimes teenagers like we were need a bit of perspective to slap them in the face and force them to realize how lucky they are. As Brandon stated, the four of us worked hard to make the trip happen, sure, but we were lucky to be able to work hard. We were lucky to come from the backgrounds we did, lucky to have this chunk of time between high school and college—and, my god, we were lucky to have *gone* to high school and to be *going* to college. That moment there in Rutland taught us to never forget our position and to never be distracted from how we might appear to others. Rutland taught us to observe.

But Rutland also taught us that optimism and inspiration can peek out from any pocket of this country. After recovering from the man in the overalls and his blunt declaration of our out-of-place status, Andrew put The Van back into drive and we continued rolling down the main street. Only a hundred yards farther down the road, we spotted the word PIZZA on a wooden sign sticking out from a red-brick building. It beckoned to us. We parked The Van in the one parking spot out front and walked in.

Nobody else was in the pizzeria. There were five tables inside, each square, each the same size, and each made out of the same white plastic. Sitting on the tables were red rubber placemats and plastic cups that look like they had come from a high school cafeteria. The walls were covered with sky-blue wallpaper and multicolored balloons that floated lightly in suspended happiness. A ceiling fan spun lazily from above, providing the only sound in the small restaurant other than the muffled ding that rang when we walked in.

The door to the back opened and a woman appeared. She was shorter than each of us and slightly plump, with curly brown hair that looked to be in danger of turning white at any moment. Behind her walked a young girl. She was about ten years old, with long hair pulled into a ponytail that bobbed against the small of her back when she moved. The girl wore tortoiseshell glasses that were slightly too big for her face, forcing her to push them back up the bridge of her nose every few minutes. Both she and the woman, whom we assumed was her mother, had stunning green eyes and smiles that were contagious on first encounter.

"Can we help you?" the woman asked.

"We'd like to . . ." Michael started, before confirming: "Do you . . . do you do pizza?"

"Of course," she replied with a smile.

"Oh, great! Um . . . well, we'd like to order some pizza," he muttered, "if that's OK." I could tell he was rattled by the incident with the local on the street and the ensuing comments from Brandon. It was one of the few times I saw him stumble over his words that summer.

The woman chuckled. "Yes, of course it is." She whispered something to the young girl, who ran back through the door and disappeared quickly into the rear part of the restaurant before returning with a few menus. Each was an 8.5x11-inch piece of paper with five selections of pizzas printed on them. We ordered three.

"Is that your guys' car out front?" the woman asked after directing us to a table. She then picked up the menus and handed them back to the young girl, who once again retreated through the rear door.

"It is," Andrew replied. Like Michael, there was hesitancy in his response as well.

"Wow. Very cool. So where are you guys from?"

"Uh, Seattle."

"Seattle! *Really?*"

"Yes."

The woman then turned her head to the back door and yelled, "Hey, Charlotte! Come back in here!" The young girl walked back into the main area a few seconds later.

"Yeah, Mom?"

"These boys are from Seattle. What state is that in?"

"Washington."

"Good—and what's the capital of Washington?"

"Olympia?"

"Very good!" She then turned back to our table and flashed us a sheepish smile. "We're working on states and capitals at school right now."

"Are you now?" Brandon replied. He scooted his chair closer to Charlotte and spoke to her. "What grade you in?"

"Going into third," Charlotte responded, taking a step toward her mother and hiding herself a bit behind her leg.

"Nice. Where's your school?"

"Just that way." Charlotte pointed out the pizzeria and down the street.

"What's the capital of California?"

"Sacramento."

"Arizona?"

"Phoenix."

"Let's see—Kentucky?"

"Frankfort."

"Is it?" Brandon replied, now looking at Michael. "I thought it was Columbia."

"That's Missouri."

"Oh."

Charlotte giggled, amused that she knew more about state capitals than someone nearly twice her age. I looked at Brandon. From his sly smile, I couldn't tell if he had meant to screw up the capitol of Kentucky on purpose or if his mistake was genuine.

"Your teacher's doin' a good job," he then said with a nod.

"Thanks," Charlotte replied, looking up at her mother. "It's my mom."

"Your mom's your teacher?"

"Yeah, she teaches the first, second, third, fourth, *and* fifth grades here in the town."

"Oh . . . wow." Brandon now turned his head toward the woman. "And you work this pizzeria?"

"Yep," she said with a smile. Her green eyes flashed their beautiful gaze again. "Mainly during the summer, though."

"Y'all close up once school begins?"

The mother nodded. "Pretty much. Dan's out of the picture, so it's just Charlotte and me now—which means there aren't exactly many hands to work the shop *and* the school at the same time. Especially since we're both *in* school at the same time!"

Brandon smiled, apparently unfazed by the woman's outward sharing of her current situation. Instead, he expressed appreciation for her resilience.

"Thank you for your service."

"Bah!" she replied. "*Service?* Oh stop—that's what we say to our heroes overseas."

"It's what we should also say to people like you."

The woman did a small double take at these words, perhaps taken aback by the assertiveness of a total stranger who was at least twenty years her junior. I could see the gears in her head turn as she registered what Brandon's statement had meant and evaluate whether it actually applied to her or not. Yet regardless if she decided yes or no, she quickly returned to her prior statement of dismissal.

"No, no, no, I'm not to be compared to such people." She added another smile. "Plus, it's easy once you wrap your mind around it!"

"How's that?" Brandon asked. "I'd love to learn."

The mother turned her head down toward her daughter. I think I saw her wink. "What's the key, Charlotte?"

"Huh?" Charlotte responded.

"What do we teach in school?"

"Uh . . . states?"

"No, dear. What's the motto?"

"Oh!" Charlotte blushed slightly. "Optimism." She pronounced every syllable diligently.

"Optimism?" I asked. Charlotte nodded.

"Yeah. *Choose optimism.*"

"*Choose optimism,*" I repeated, swishing the words around in my mouth. "I like that."

"Choose optimism," the mother said, freeing herself from Charlotte and heading to the back of the restaurant to begin making the pizzas. "Because no matter where you are or what you're facing—optimism is an option. It's always an option."

SEVENTH INNING STRETCH
Turner Field

BREAKDOWN

5:50 p.m. | Saturday, July 16

When we entered "Turner Field" into Tina, the brief description that popped up on the Garmin labeled it as a "nostalgia-filled modern baseball stadium." Yet when we *visited* Turner Field, we quickly discovered that nearly every bit of this so-called nostalgia was directed solely at Mr. Ted Turner, the TV billionaire who funded the stadium's creation. Originally, the ballpark was supposed to be christened "Hank Aaron Stadium" after the longtime Braves legend, but somehow money got in the way and the name shifted to follow the finances. In an attempt at consolation, the Turner Corporation renamed the avenue outside the ballpark "Hank Aaron Drive" and was able to finagle the stadium's address to be number 755, a nod to Aaron's outstanding home run total—which, until Barry Bonds and his asterisk rolled around, was the record for most all-time dingers in a career.

Turner Field is an absolutely massive place. Although its capacity pushes fifty thousand, the stadium's expansive layout makes it feel even bigger—and makes it feel quite dark at times as well. When the Braves drew small crowds, the ballpark would actually turn off lights in distant sections to try and shepherd fans closer to the field. I speak in past tense because the Atlanta Braves do not play at Turner anymore, having closed out their last game there on October 2, 2016. They now play at SunTrust Park, a slightly smaller stadium with more of a modern, *brighter* appeal—and one that is *not* owned by the Turner Corporation. Yet Turner Field itself isn't all that old (it was constructed in 1997), and usage rights for "the Ted" have now been passed along to the Georgia State football team, which is currently converting it into their new stadium.

As I hope you have been able to grasp from this book, different ballparks host different atmospheres within their confines. I have already described the call-and-response pregame festivities that take place at Yankee Stadium, the beer-inspired in-game promotions at Miller Park, and the late-arriving and early-departing crowd at Dodger Stadium. Yet many ballparks have different atmospheres *outside* their confines as well. Yankee Stadium: vendors mob you as soon as you get off the subway, trying to sell their latest collection of anti–Red Sox T-shirts. Miller Park: tailgaters mob you as soon as you park your car, essentially forcing beers and brats into your hands and demanding you come and have a good time with them. Dodger Stadium: nobody mobs you in the parking lot, as scalping and vending is illegal there and hardly anybody has made it for first pitch anyway.

In Atlanta, we experienced perhaps the most eclectic atmosphere outside of any park we visited. After taking a woman up on her offer for five-dollar game-day parking that was advertised on a cardboard sign, we were directed to park The Van in a grassy area that we soon discovered to be her front yard. It was roughly a half mile away from the entrance to Turner Field, the walk to which was amazing. Some guys sitting on coolers sold normal drinks, such as bottled water, sodas, and beer—but one guy sitting on a cooler sold unmarked bottles filled with an electric-green liquid. His sign simply read JERRY'S JUICE: $3/BOTTLE. Some guys sitting on lawn chairs sold normal ballgame paraphernalia, such as knockoff Braves hats, key chains, and cheap T-shirts—but one man sitting on a lawn chair sold Braves hubcaps. His sign simply read HUBS: $20/EACH. $70/4.

Yet nobody outdid the man sitting on a stool at the end of the block. Straying from normality of any kind, this vendor (if that's what we can call him) had a small white tub in front of him out of which he sold turtles. Live, swimming turtles. The handwritten sign next to him read:

TURTLES: $10

CAN TAKE INTO STADIUM.

Can take into stadium? Normally one would see this phrase scrawled next to an advertisement for kettle corn or sunflower seeds, assuring fans that they would be able to enjoy their purchase while watching the game. (Drinks normally cannot be brought into ballparks, but some snacks can.)

Turtles? I mean, I guess so. In Seattle, we have "Bark in the Park" night, where fans are encouraged to bring their dogs to the game; the Frisco RoughRiders, a minor league team, have a promotion called "Take Meow to the Ballgame," where attendees can buy a ticket for their cats; looks like "Turner Turtle Night" was just around the corner in 2011. Shoot, if only the ballpark had remained the home of the Braves.

"Ten bucks for one," Frazier said, eyeing the sign as we walked past. "That's a good deal, guys."

Andrew literally stopped in his tracks.

"Frazier . . . what?" He held his hands out as if hopelessly begging for an explanation. Even Brandon laughed as Andrew continued. "You say this as if you've purchased turtles before. And not only that you've *purchased* turtles before but that you've purchased *enough* turtles before to know when to spot a good deal!"

Frazier shrugged. "I'm just saying—ten dollars? C'mon, that's cheap."

"They're turtles, bro."

"So?"

"So?" Andrew laughed as he started walking again, slowly. "*So?* So what the hell are we gonna do with a turtle?"

"I dunno. Use it as a pet in The Van? A symbol of the trip?"

"We already have five people and a gigantic tire." At this, he turned to Michael and me. "Which is *still. In. The. Van!*" His point was a good one: Even with the addition of Brandon, we still hadn't disposed of the tire. Seeing as three people now had to somehow fit onto the main level foldout mattress to sleep, we had just been placing the tire outside The Van at night. I think we were each hoping somebody would just steal the stupid thing already, but our hopes were yet to be fulfilled. Andrew continued: "We have no space for an extra cup of coffee, let alone a live animal that needs a tub of water to survive. We can't keep track of our own wallets in that vehicle; we would surely lose a turtle and find it weeks later, curled up and dead in a sleeping bag or something."

"Oh god," I said, shuddering in reaction to this prediction.

Frazier, apparently unfazed by Andrew's reasoning, merely shrugged his shoulders again.

"I dunno, man, I think it'd be funny."

The Atlanta Turtle Debate, although short lived, was yet another reminder of the many nonsensical thoughts that crossed through our minds as eighteen-year-olds trekking across the country without a real sense of what was right and what was stupid. I'll be honest: for a split second, I was totally behind Frazier's declaration that purchasing a turtle outside of a ballpark would be a wonderful story to pair with the many others we were quickly accruing on this summer trip. Imagine if I was now telling you about what life in The Van was like when we decided to add a Testudine to our company for the final four weeks of the journey. But the vision of the poor thing suffering at the hands of our ignorance and the eternal chaos of our car changed my mind immediately. I'm still humored that such a purchase was even a possibility, though.

10:55 p.m.

We had to say goodbye to Brandon that evening after the game, as Atlanta was his predetermined final destination. This was, needless to say, extremely difficult for each of us. Despite not being a part of the original plan, Brandon's company and the perspective he brought with him was one that we grew to hope would stay with us for the duration of the trip—even if meant continuing to sleep five in The Van. But, even though his schooling was not set to recommence for another month, the man stayed true to his word, grabbing his duffel bag and hopping a bus into Atlanta, leaving our company as quickly as he had entered it. We gave him a Mariners hat to remember us by. I haven't heard from Brandon for about four years—but I'll bet he still has that hat, and I hope he roots for the M's.

Hardly any words were exchanged as The Van departed Atlanta. We had initially hoped to make a dent in our drive to Tampa that night, but the group mood had now returned to low and we barely made it an hour before pulling off into another nameless freeway rest stop and spending the night.

11:54 a.m. | The Following Morning

We got a late start the following morning, as none of us could find ways to wake up because we couldn't find ways to cheer up. This unhappiness continued as the day proceeded and The Van continued to move south. By the time we entered Florida, the positive energy of the past week had disappeared completely, and the anger of the weeks before was back.

"You purchased a haircut?" Andrew screamed from behind the wheel. He shot his eyes into the dashboard mirror, trying to make eye contact with Frazier. Michael's most recent examination of our expenses showed that a twenty-five-dollar haircut had been purchased with the debit card that accessed our collective bank account, the funds of which were supposed to be used only for gas, food, and tickets. The rest we were saving to donate to the Martinez Foundation.

"I said my bad," Frazier replied, avoiding Andrew's piercing gaze. "I didn't remember the PIN to my own card, and I had to pay the barber somehow."

"Who the *hell* doesn't know the PIN to their debit card?"

"I've remembered it since then," Frazier claimed. "I just couldn't in the moment."

The Van said something in warning, but nobody seemed to hear.

"What do you need a haircut for, anyway?" Andrew said, his momentum building. "You haven't cut your hair since 1999!"

"I needed to trim a few strands."

"I mean I could've done that. For free. Hell, I'd have *paid* you to let me chop some of that mess off."

"As if I'd have let you near me with scissors."

"You're such a piece of shit sometimes, man."

"Shut up. I said I was sorry, OK? It won't happen again. Plus, it was only a small stupid little sum. I'll repay the money once we get to a bank."

Again, The Van spoke. Again, we ignored it.

The back-and-forth continued for a few more minutes, escalating into a heated evaluation of the two's ethical approach to the trip and the Martinez Foundation. Michael and I were soon drawn in as well, fighting for Andrew to understand Frazier's innocent ignorance while at the same time fighting for Frazier to recognize his own stupidity. The volume of the argument increased like an operatic crescendo—until The Van decided it had had enough.

BANG!

"Jesus! What was that?"

The noise had sounded like a gunshot; the bump had felt like we hit a land mine. Immediately, The Van began slowing down, whimpering in a tone that none of us had heard before. It sounded like a dog in pain. Andrew pumped his legs furiously from behind the wheel, looking down to the pedals in confusion and fear.

"I . . . I can't do anything," he said, panic rising in his voice. "We have no breaks—no gas!"

Somehow calm as ever, Michael twisted around from the jump seat and stuck his head up front. "Throw your hazards on and pull onto the shoulder," he said. "This is a long stretch of road and there's hardly anybody behind us—we'll be fine." Andrew followed his directions, and after about a minute of coasting, The Van rolled over the cautionary rumble strips and came to a halt on the side of the freeway, its right wheels on a patch of grass and its left wheels still on the pavement. "Now pull up the emergency brake," Michael continued, "and let's figure out what the hell just happened."

We failed at this, however, as our examinations of the car were in vain and our attempts to restart it yielded nothing but silence. I soon wandered around to the front and asked The Van what was wrong—but it spoke not a word.

"It hadn't even been clicking," Frazier said. "Had it?"

"I don't think so," Andrew replied. All the animosity he had been holding only minutes before appeared to have vanished. "Maybe it had and we didn't hear it?"

"Maybe."

"Maybe it was like the calm before the storm?"

"Maybe."

One thing was for sure: The Van was dead. The four of us were now stuck on the shoulder of southbound I-75, somewhere in Florida north of Gainesville. A sign in the distance showed an exit for O'Leno State Park.

It took a good ten minutes for each of us to comprehend the magnitude of the situation. The Van was obviously our method of transport, our communal home, and—whether or not we wanted it to be—had become the overarching symbol of the trip. To have it die was to have the trip die. Gone was our ability to move; gone was our ability to continue. As Andrew, Frazier, and I sat in the grass staring at the incapacitated vehicle with dazed looks on our faces, Michael phoned AAA and requested a tow truck. The company said a driver would be deployed, yes, but given our remote location, it could take at least three hours for someone to arrive.

"Man," Frazier muttered, clicking his camera to snap a picture of the rusty freeway barrier. "That's gonna feel like forever in this heat."

I hadn't realized the truth of this statement until he said it. The thermometer on the dashboard had read ninety-eight degrees just before we broke down—but what it did not read was the humidity. I felt like I was breathing corn syrup as I laid my head down on the grass and looked up at the sky, fearful of our ability to continue. I could hear the sound of cars drive by, as the afternoon Florida traffic passed us in an indifferent nature. Beads of sweat began to appear on my brow instantly. And then, as quickly as the sweat had come, the bugs arrived. Mosquitos the size of quarters flocked to the scene, forcing us to jump up from our positions on the grass and flail our arms like pinwheels to try to swat them away. It must have been quite the sight for the cars that whirred by: four teenagers standing next to a broken-down, colorful camper van, waving their hands like interpretive dancers. Unable to fend off the bugs for very long, we were forced to retreat back into The Van and wait for the tow truck to arrive.

So there we were, squished into a stagnant automobile that slowly roasted like a pressure cooker in the exposed Florida sunlight and heavy humidity. The bugs only increased in number, thus eliminating any possibility of leaving The Van; the only shade offered in the moment came from the mosquitos stuck to the windows, which now looked like the coat of a Dalmatian. We were totally at the mercy of a tow truck driver whom we had been told was coming to get us—but when, we did not know. And even if the man did come, we knew nothing about what would happen after that: whether The Van could be fixed and whether our trip could continue at all. All we knew was that it was hot, and we had to wait. The only method of entertainment we had was playing Hearts with a soggy deck of cards.

7:44 p.m.

Three hours came, and three hours went. As the sun descended and the clock approached 8:00 p.m., each of us began to exchange nervous glances, implicitly fearing the same thing. Was anybody actually coming to get us? If they were, would they be able to find us? Michael had not been able to give a location other than "somewhere on southbound I-75 near the turnoff for O'Leno." Perhaps the driver had been deployed but could not locate The Van. At what point did we call again?

"Your trick," Frazier said, breaking this concerned string of thoughts. Confused, I looked his way. "You take the hand," he explained to me. "It's your turn."

"I don't feel like playing anymore," I replied. Truer words had never been spoken.

"Why not?"

"I feel like I'm swimming, man. I feel like the air I'm breathing is thicker than the sweat that's dripping effortlessly from my hair. I feel like this seat I'm sitting on is a waterbed without the bed part. I feel—"

"All right. All right. I get it."

My god, how slowly the minutes ticked by. I watched from the driver's seat as the sun began to set behind what seemed to be endless fields of grass, morphing the color of the blades from dark green to golden brown. The bugs persisted, sucking themselves to the windshield's moist surface and further obstructing my view of the surrounding scene. As the four of us continued to roast within the vehicle, the inside pane of the windows began to bead up with liquid as well. It was difficult to tell the difference between our own sweat and the condensation.

Knock, knock. The sudden sound of a tapping on the side door startled each of us, causing Frazier to drop his cards in surprise.

"Tow truck's here," Michael said. "Gotta be." Distracted by the literal heat of the moment, we must have somehow failed to notice the tow truck's approach. I turned to see Michael reach for the door, slide it open, and come face-to-face with the person outside.

At first, I thought that the man was removed from the film *Deliverance*. Standing beyond the open door of The Van was an individual who sported nothing but overalls, steel-toed boots, and a tattered blue ball cap that was tilted off to the side. His chest hair flowed freely from beneath the denim straps of his outfit while coarse bristles of his unkempt beard curled around his crooked mouth. He was missing two teeth.

"Trip' A?" he said, with a wonky smile.

"Yes," Michael replied, having to take a second to decipher the man's question.

"Alri.' Let's see wha' we got 'ere." He used very few consonants when he spoke.

We each filed out of The Van and watched as the driver stuck his head under the rear of the vehicle before popping up quickly. "Whoops," he said, "thought this wa' the front." We each laughed the moment off, desperately hoping that the man was joking. After locating the correct end of the car, he then returned to the tow truck and pulled it around to the other side. Within two minutes, the nose of The Van was hoisted up onto the truck's bed, with its rear wheels freely rolling behind it.

"Alri'," the driver said again, stepping out of the cabin. "Gay'rville, right?"

This one none of us could comprehend. "What?" Michael replied.

"I'm a' take you to Gay'rville, right?"

"Gatorville?"

"Yeah."

"Oh—*Gainsville!*"

"Ri'—but it's Gay'rville to tha locals!" the man said with a guffaw, before proceeding to clap his hands in a large vertical motion.

"Ah, right," Michael replied, watching him continue to clap. "Right, because of the Florida Gators . . . I see." He then grew a little nervous. "No, not Gains—er, *Gator*ville—we were told that we would be taken to Tampa?"

"Tampa!" The driver stopped clapping and threw his hands up in the air as if we had just offended him. "Tampa! D'y'know how far Tampa is?" Not waiting for an answer, he turned around and returned to the truck's cabin, rummaging through some papers behind the driver's seat. He removed a map and began scanning it, muttering beneath his breath the entire time: "Tampa . . . Tampa . . . frickin' *Tampa*." Five seconds later, however, his head popped upright from the map, and his attitude changed completely. "Yep!" he said, his voice now a light and fluffy tone. "Yep, I can definitely do that. But wer' gonna have ta stop for gas, 'kay?"

Taken aback, Michael replied a few seconds later. "Er . . . yeah, man, that's totally fine."

"An' it'll cost ya an extra fifty—cash."

"Huh?"

"I'm bein' paid to drive ye to Gay'rville, not Tampa. Pay me un'r the table in cash, 'n wer good."

A confused minute passed as we each continued looking at our de facto decision maker. "Whatever," Michael eventually said. "Fine. But you'll take us to Tampa?"

"Pay me, 'n I'll take ye to Tampa."

We were each obviously bewildered by the ragged-looking man's sudden mood swing and demands for backdoor cash, but what choice did we have? Darkness now blanketed the scene, The Van was already hooked up to the tow truck, and we had nowhere else to turn. Collecting some money from our wallets, the four of us handed him the sum and then crammed into the tow truck's cabin. "One of ya can sit up wi' me," the man said, stuffing the cash into the cupholder in the central console. "Bu' the other three'll have to squeeze into the back seat. Sorry." Michael hopped up to shotgun while Frazier, Andrew, and I stuffed ourselves into the small area behind him, which felt as if it used to be the holding section of a police car. Our legs stuck to the plastic covering of the crusty bench seat while our knees overlapped with one another's. Off we went.

Nobody spoke during the next forty minutes, as our obscure companion drove farther south down I-75. Among our tangled web of limbs, I could feel Andrew's hand beneath my forearm. His fingers were clenched tightly into a fist. The driver's mannerisms and the fact that we had just handed him cash didn't sit right with him. It didn't sit right with any of us. Not long after, the driver began to pull the tow truck off the freeway and onto an exit that led to a two-lane road. Throwing on his blinker, he turned right and continued driving. No lights shone from ahead.

"Where the hell are we going?" I heard Andrew mutter from next to me. I shifted my head a bit and shrugged my shoulders. I was confused too: the man had said that he would need to stop for fuel, but we had already passed numerous exits that advertised gas stations. Now we were completely off the freeway and appeared to be driving into the countryside. Into god knows what. A forest soon engulfed the road, and it was only then that the driver began to slow down. I watched as he scanned the trees. It seemed that he was looking for something—but following his eyes, I could see only darkness.

"Here we are," the man then said, breaking the tense silence. Still, I saw nothing. Even as the truck began to pull off the vacant arterial, I could not make out the small road we were turning onto. Apart from the car's headlights, it was totally dark.

It was only then that I truly came to my senses and absolute fear set in. Nobody was anywhere near us, nobody knew that we were here. It was just the four of us teenagers and this strange, depraved-looking tow truck driver. That's horror movie stuff. I can still picture that guy's toothless smile and that tattered ball cap.

I heard the truck's tires begin to roll over gravel, and my eyes widened in fear. It appeared that I wasn't the only one paralyzed by the situation: next to me, the faces of Frazier and Andrew showed total terror as well.

Then out of the windshield, a light appeared about a hundred yards ahead. The tow truck continued to roll down the gravel road, making its way toward the dull glow that emerged from the blackness. Slowly, the light made itself out to be a faintly illuminated yellow sign.

GAS

No fuel type, no prices, just three capital letters. Beside the sign was a small house—*shack* may be a more appropriate way to describe it—that, we now saw, had a few lights on within it as well. The truck came to a halt.

"Stay'n 'ere," the driver said, not waiting for an answer as he opened the driver's door, slipped out, and shut it again. About five seconds of silence passed.

"What the—" Andrew said, breathing heavily. "Where are we?"

"No clue," Michael replied from up front.

"This is how we die," Frazier said, his eyes intently scanning the scene and trying to see where the truck driver had disappeared to. "This is the part when he returns with a gun and—"

Michael cut him off. "Frazier. Shut up." I could tell that even he was uneasy with the scene too. How could he not be? We were totally defenseless in that tow truck cabin. Even if we had decided to run, where would we go? I couldn't have told you which direction was back to the freeway, let alone how long it would take to get there. The next noises I heard were a couple of clunks, followed by a long whir.

"What was that?" I asked with a jump. Michael responded almost instantly.

"Gas, genius."

The whirring noise, I then realized, was indeed the sound of a car being filled up with fuel. I had heard that noise hundreds of times before—but when my mind was preoccupied with the plot of *Texas Chainsaw Massacre,* the sound of a fill-up seemed completely foreign to me.

"God, he actually *is* filling up here?"

"Guess so."

"Why did we have to drive all the way out here?"

"No clue."

As the truck continued to fill with gas, the driver's door sprang open again and our dear friend popped his head in. He didn't say anything, nor did he acknowledge the four wide-eyed boys sitting in his cabin. Instead, he reached toward the cupholder, grabbed the fifty bucks we had paid him earlier, and withdrew back to the shack, closing the door behind him. The gas clicked off, signaling its completion—but the driver did not return. Three minutes passed. It was just as tensions were beginning to rise again that he emerged from the shack and wandered to the back of the truck. We could discern him unhooking the nozzle from the gas tank and screwing the lid back on. Then we heard the crunch of his shoes on the gravel as he approached the truck's cabin one more time. The door opened.

"OK!" the man said in a voice louder than we had heard yet. "Tampa, right?" He hoisted himself back up and into the driver's seat and threw two items into the cupholder. The first was his old ball cap, which he then promptly picked back up and used to dry the sweat off his forehead. The second was a small paper bag. After finishing wiping his brow, the driver grabbed the bag and shuffled it awkwardly to his left side, reaching down and placing it in the compartment attached to the door, where it was out of sight. He jammed the hat back onto his head.

"What do they say in Italian?" he asked of nobody in particular.

"Huh?"

"Ah! *Andiamo!*" We stared back at him.

And with that, he gunned the engine and pulled the tow truck out of the "gas station" with vigor, whipping The Van behind him. Fifteen minutes later, the lights of the freeway returned to our vision. The driver turned right onto the interstate and began to drum his fingers on the wheel while humming "Casey Jones" by the Grateful Dead. Every once in a while, he'd halt his tune to return to muttering: "Tampa . . . Tampa . . . frickin' *Tampa.*" Again, I felt Andrew's hand clench into a nervous fist as we plunged deeper into the Florida night.

BOTTOM OF THE SEVENTH
Tropicana Field

AN INVESTMENT

7:45 a.m. | Tuesday, July 19

Near the beginning of this recounting, I mentioned that we awoke twice on that trip to a tapping on The Van's window. The first was the woman in the pink jumpsuit with the urinating poodle in Beverly Hills. The second was that morning in northern Tampa.

Tap, tap, tap.

Opening my eyes, I recognized the friendly beams of daylight shining into the car. Night had passed; morning had come.

I banged my head on the tire before propping my body up from the folded-down bench seat. A figure was standing outside of The Van's sliding door. At first, I feared it was the tow truck driver from the night before—but no, this man wore a gray jumpsuit and held a clipboard in his hand. I swung my legs onto the floor and reached for my glasses while Michael opened the door.

"Yes?" he asked. "Can we help you?"

The man outside appeared genuinely confused by Michael's inquiry. "I feel like I should be asking that question," he said, releasing an uneasy laugh. "Uh . . . what are you guys doing here?" I put on my glasses and turned my head around, looking out the back window of the camper. As the rest of the scene came into focus, the remainder of the previous evening's events did as well.

The tow truck driver had, miraculously, made it to Tampa around one forty-five a.m. After briefly consulting one of his many maps to find a mechanic near the freeway exit, he eventually located one and backed the truck into its driveway, unlatched The Van, and ushered us out of his car. With an impersonal tip of his crooked ball cap, the man took off before we could blink, leaving our vehicle immobilized in an awkward diagonal position across the driveway that led up to the mechanic's garage.

"That guy may have been the strangest person to enter my life yet," Frazier said, watching as the red taillights of the tow truck disappeared down the poorly lit street. "My god, I'm amazed that we're here—and not dead." The rest of us muttered in agreement.

"Well, there's nothing else we can do right now," Michael replied, taking a step toward The Van, which looked helpless in its improper, unmovable position. "Might as well get some sleep." I could not have agreed with this statement more. The four of us climbed into the broken vehicle, popped the top open, and crashed immediately, not caring about anything else. Andrew used two baseball gloves as a makeshift pillow; I slept with my head propped against the tire.

As these memories returned to me, I realized that we were now speaking with the mechanic whose driveway we were surely blocking. I could hear Andrew and Frazier shuffling upstairs as Michael uttered a couple of apologies to the man while simultaneously attempting to describe exactly *why* we were there. The mechanic, tapping his clipboard the entire time, listened to his tale with a calm smile on his face. He even laughed when Michael told him of the tow truck driver and his "gas stop" somewhere deep in the Florida boonies.

"My," the man said, now sliding the clipboard beneath his armpit and folding his arms. "You guys have had one hell of a night."

"We've had one hell of a month, man."

"I'll bet."

Taking a breath, Michael then posed the pendulum-swinging question: "So . . . do you think you might be able to help us?"

Running his eyes over The Van's variegated design, the mechanic pursed his lips. He waited a good fifteen seconds as he pondered Michael's question, stopping the breath of each of us with his pause. Eventually, he shrugged his shoulders nonchalantly.

"Shit. I've got nothing to do today."

Never before have I been so delighted to hear an unnecessary swear word in a semiprofessional setting. I felt a collective sigh of relief emit from the others and a small surge of optimism whip through The Van. We definitely weren't out of the woods yet, but there was still hope.

We each stepped outside and watched as the mechanic opened up his garage and used a small machine to tow The Van into his shop. The four of us sauntered after him, not saying a word as we entered the lobby and peered through the windows. Andrew still held the mitts he had slept on in his left hand while he lightly tossed a baseball up and down with his right. The soft smack of the ball hitting his palm is all I can remember accompanying the scene as I watched the mechanic raise our dear vehicle onto the car lift to see if it was savable.

The hours that followed played out like an episode from a bad hospital drama. As Michael paced the floor in front of the windows that looked into the garage, I sat on an uncomfortable folding chair, sipping bad coffee from a Styrofoam cup that the machine in the corner had dispensed. The fluorescent-lit lobby had become an ER waiting room, as the four of us nervously waited for the doctor to return and inform us of the status of our severely ill relative. We didn't know what the diagnosis was, we didn't know if a cure would be possible—and even if one was, we didn't know what such a procedure would cost.

The most interesting dynamic to watch, however, was that of Andrew and Frazier. It was no secret that the two's relationship had been on the fringe for essentially the entire trip thus far, with hardly an hour elapsing since we set out from Seattle in which one of them didn't give lip of some sort to the other. Brandon's presence had provided a brief hiatus, but the underlying arguments never truly faded. Yet here, in the cool, air-conditioned lobby of a random mechanic's shop in northern Tampa, I watched as all their past disagreements were washed away in mutual anxiety for The Van. The two were like brothers once long divided after a falling-out and now reunited over collective concern for the health of a beloved relative, or the family dog.

"Think it'll be OK?" Frazier muttered to Andrew, who sat next to him.

"Absolutely," he said, patting Frazier on the back. "Don't worry. We'll get through this. Everything will be OK—I promise."

I kid you not, this nostalgic vernacular was actually being used. Above the soft buzz released by the room's industrial lighting, the rest of us each picked up on Andrew's optimistic remarks and began adding some of our own to comfort Frazier. In doing so, we comforted ourselves.

"The Van's a warrior, man. It'll heal."

"This is just a test of its—and our—ya know . . . spirit and resilience."

"Everything will be OK soon. I know it."

As I said: emergency room scene from a bad hospital TV drama. Frazier smiled in appreciation of our efforts, putting his head down as Andrew continued to pat his back. I couldn't tell if he was crying. He definitely wasn't crying; crying would have been *too* much for the scene. But he might have been crying. After a minute, Andrew lifted his hand from his back and opened his mouth again.

"Frazh. Wanna have a catch?"

Even the simple utterance of this question had an uplifting effect on Frazier. Nodding his head, Andrew reached for the gloves he had been holding earlier and slipped one onto his wrist. The other he plopped into the lap of his friend.

"Let's go."

Neither Michael nor I spoke as we watched the two of them stand up from the lobby folding chairs and approach the exit. The Florida heat crept in as Andrew opened the glass door, holding it for Frazier to walk through. They then headed outside and peeled apart from each other, with Andrew walking to the left and Frazier to the right until about fifty feet stood between them. I wished I had grabbed my red lawn chair.

Wsssh-pop!

As the familiar rhythmic pattern of ball and glove began, my mind flashed back to Milwaukee and the similar scene I had observed outside Miller Park. There, as they had done in numerous other places along the journey, Andrew and Frazier had used the medium of having a catch to sew up various tears in their friendship. What was once an anger-infused tussle was easily repaired by the simple action of throwing a baseball to the person who, only minutes before, they had vehemently disagreed with.

But this catch was different. Andrew hadn't suggested it as a remedy; he had suggested it as an activity—something to do to pass the time with a person he enjoyed. It was the type of action that he and Frazier had built their relationship on oh so many years ago, and it was what they returned to in effort to *re*build.

And this catch didn't just repair the bond between two of my best friends, this one *built* it further. It made their friendship stronger. Here in the parking lot of that random Florida auto shop (I still forget the name), Andrew and Frazier patched up their recent spat and then moved beyond *all* the disagreements that had emerged between them during our life on the road, which resulted in them becoming even better friends than before we had departed Seattle. I physically watched it happen. Andrew stood in almost the exact same location where The Van had been paralyzed just hours before.

It was at this moment that I knew that everything with our camper would be OK. I was sure of it. Something about my realization that Andrew and Frazier would be OK moving forward triggered a similar feeling toward The Van—and our trip in general. It was as if the two were somehow connected; if my friends could move beyond their combustible past relationship and work to build a new, positive one, then our car could too. It was therefore not much of a surprise to me when the mechanic-doctor-veterinarian poked his head into the lobby and announced that an operation was definitely doable.

"Oh my *god* yes," Michael replied immediately, openly showing his immense pleasure and relief at this statement. "Wow, man, you have no idea what what you just said means." I reiterated Michael's statement through fairly inarticulate expressions of gratitude before sticking my head out the door to call Andrew and Frazier back into the lobby.

"No worries, brother," the mechanic replied. "I've seen it before. Axle issue—nothing I can't fix. I can have it done by tomorrow too." Music to our ears. "But I should warn you," he said after a pause, "it's something that's probably going to cost you about twenty-five hundred dollars."

Now we had of course been expecting a high price. The basic fact that our car had broken down made it clear that a severe mechanical operation was going to be necessary, and we knew that such a fix wouldn't be cheap—if a fix was even possible at all. Seeing that the latter part of that statement was now indeed true, we then faced a decision point of whether we were up for paying it.

"Can you give us a minute to discuss things over?" Michael asked the man, who politely nodded his head and retreated into a back room.

. . .

If you owned a severely misbehaving dog that came down with a terrible illness, would you pay thousands of dollars to cure it?

This was the type of question we faced as we sat in the mechanic's lobby. The Van had been nothing but a problem since that very first drive from Seattle to Los Angeles. With the clicking, the shaking, no brake lights, and no cruise control, that old Volkswagen was our Marley, prone to causing nothing but trouble yet beloved by its owner(s) nevertheless. Was it insane to save something that had caused us only stress?

From somewhere beyond the ether, however, The Van made me realize that it hadn't *only* caused stress, though. Even with all its issues, The Van had been incredibly useful as well. Its ability to act as a home on the road was imperative to the success of our trip, forcing us to voice a collective recognition that we could have never functioned without it. The number of nights we had spent in freeway rest stops, and the times we had pulled over to rest between long drives (or even resting *during* long drives, with the bench seat folded down as the vehicle continued moving), was all thanks to The Van—clicks, shakes, and all. Yes, we each tacitly agreed, even with its agitating tendencies, The Van was of course worth saving.

But superseding the question of emotion was the question of money. And more importantly, where that money was coming from. The four of us had poured all our savings into this trip, and we simply had no excess funds for a twenty-five-hundred-dollar operation. If we were going to go through with this procedure, we would have to pay with the money we were raising for the Martinez Foundation.

"I hate that idea," Michael said. "That money isn't for us." I nodded in agreement. We had no business taking from this account.

"But what about saving our trip?" Frazier asked.

"I know, man," Michael replied, "but I'm very uneasy doing it that way."

I thought the point would be dropped here. We pretty much never argued with Michael—the dude corrected the teacher once, for god's sake—and it seemed to me that nobody felt good arguing to use the money raised for charity to pay for The Van's operation anyway. And yet I was wrong.

"I'm not sure, though," Andrew said. "I think there's still more left in this trip. It feels . . . it feels incomplete to abandon it right here, ya know?" It was curious to hear this come from Andrew, who had been the most critical of purchasing The Van in the first place. But although what he said made me slightly nervous, I also liked seeing him take Frazier's side. He turned again to Michael. "I mean, how much do we have in the account for the Martinez Foundation right now?"

"Roughly seventy-five hundred dollars."

"And how many days into the trip are we?"

"Thirty-eight."

"Right. And how many does our schedule say we're going to be gone for?"

"Fifty-three."

"So we have sixteen days lef—"

"Fifteen."

"So we have *fifteen* days left in this thing. That's over two weeks. If we pay this twenty-five hundred dollars right now, that sets us back to five thousand dollars. Still not a bad donation, not going to lie."

"Right, but—"

"I'm not finished yet." This moment of assertion pivoted the conversation, giving Andrew the rare role of leader, as opposed to Michael. "If we pay to fix The Van, we drop back to five thousand dollars, yeah, but we also have over two weeks to try to make up that gap. I think we can do that, man." He was gaining steam. "I think we can double our efforts at the ballgames, hit social media extra hard, and even use The Van's salvation as a hook, ya know? People would love the redemption story—like: *the trip continues!* And hell, if we don't make up our difference by the end of the trip, I say that we make it up ourselves. I'll pay half, man." He paused, then added: "Once I start making money, that is."

"Yeah," Frazier said, nodding his head. Cheesy, inspirational music should have been playing somewhere in the background. "I honestly think we could cover the deficit. And if we go over—like, if we make *more* than seventy-five hundred dollars by the time we make it back home—well, then it will have been *beneficial* to pay up to revive The Van! Right?"

"I don't follow," Michael said.

"Here," Frazier continued, holding out his hands out as if he were weighing different amounts of money. "If we call it quits right now, we would donate seventy-five hundred dollars. But if we pay the twenty-five hundred dollars to keep going and wind up making *more* than twenty-five hundred during our final two weeks, we would be donating over seventy-five hundred dollars, which means that saving The Van would actually bring more money to Edgar."

"Totally agree," Andrew answered. He and Frazier were both nodding their heads vigorously now, their arguments climbing atop one another and building in confidence and justification. I was starting to hear the logic in their stance as well. If we paid up right now, it set us back. But if that setback proved to be only temporary—if indeed we could raise *more* for the Martinez Foundation by the end of the trip—we would have actually *helped* by spending $2,500 for the operation.

"So," Frazier said, "this payment wouldn't be spending those funds so much as using some of them to raise even more. It wouldn't be a cost, it'd be more like a . . . a . . ."

"Like an investment." It was Michael who said it.

Investment. That was the word Frazier was looking for. That was the word *I* was looking for. Yes, paying for The Van would be an investment. It would be an investment in the Martinez Foundation, the organization we wanted to assist in any way we could. Using these funds to pay for the revival of The Van would place an even higher incentive on us to work to promote the organization: we would redouble our efforts outside of ballparks, send press releases to news agencies in cities we would soon be visiting, and alert those who were following us on social media of our current scenario. As these thoughts were tossed around that mechanic's lobby, I could feel the group's attitude collectively begin to lean down this path of investment—a path led by Andrew and Frazier, of all people.

But paying for The Van was not just an investment in the Martinez Foundation. Paying to revive The Van was also an investment in our trip in general. Our kitchen table dream had been to see *every* stadium, not just most of them. To pass up the opportunity to complete the final leg of the trip was to pass up the opportunity to complete what we had set out to do, in the vehicle we had set out to do it in.

And yet above all, paying for The Van was an investment in us. A new perspective had risen; the fall of The Van's strength had cued the rise of our own strength. What had been strained relationships created by the stresses of life on the road had flipped into a surge of unity on witnessing the breakdown of our lovable/detestable vehicle. Andrew and Frazier's newfound (or perhaps *re*-found) friendship mirrored the bonds among all of us. The past thirty-eight days had unraveled what we once thought were unbreakable ties—but when it all hit rock bottom, those knots retightened. We weren't fighting one another anymore; we were fighting to keep the trip alive. Opting not to revive The Van was to let the lows of travel claim victory over the four of us. Such a decision would have surely resulted in us packing up our baseball dream right there in Tampa, heading back to Seattle, and proceeding to college and beyond with the last memories of our childhood friendships being ones of argument, anger, and breakdown. On the other hand, opting *to* revive The Van gave us an opportunity to move beyond such memories, to recognize our genuine relationships, and to return to the happiness on which those connections had been founded. Not many words were needed after this. All four of us were in agreement with the reasoning behind this investment. The way forward with the Martinez Foundation, the trip, and our friendships was the way forward with The Van.

"Let's do it," Michael said. "All in favor?"

"Yep."

"Yep."

"Yep."

As he stood up to search for the mechanic and give him the go-ahead, the remaining three of us discussed what would happen next. We would find a way to get to Tropicana Field that evening—but then how would we get to Miami? The Van was to be fixed by tomorrow, and we had to continue on to Houston after that if we were to keep pace with our schedule. The easy choice was to scratch off Miami in total.

"No," Andrew said defiantly. "No way, man. We aren't investing this money to see twenty-nine. Let's see all thirty. We have to at least try."

"What do you propose?" I asked.

Andrew took a few seconds as he thought about it. "I propose we fly. If I remember right, we have a few days in Texas after the Rangers' game. I say we go to the airport then and see if we can't get a standby flight. Two of us—the other two stay with The Van. That way we don't spend too much money, and our odds are better of getting seats on the plane. There's gotta be flights heading down there every day. Business people must take them all the time."

"Go on."

"If we can get one, we'll be in Miami before first pitch and can then return either on a red-eye or the following morning."

"Where would they sleep?"

"Who cares? Look, as long as someone sees the game, it'll feel like *we* as a unit saw the game. Does that make sense?" It totally did. It also made sense that Andrew and Frazier should be the ones to try to accomplish this feat, as the trip was becoming their Cinderella story in a way. When Michael returned, the plan was presented and unanimously agreed on. To kick it off, we soon hopped in a cab and headed to Tropicana Field for that evening's game.

7:30 p.m.

Standing proud as the last remaining indoor-only stadium, Tropicana Field is the quirkiest of all the major league ballparks. *But no!* you say. *What about Fenway Park, with the Green Monster—*

or Wrigley Field, with the ivy? These are understandable replies, and I would agree with you that those stadiums carry a lot of character in their unique attributes. But you must understand that when I describe Tropicana as *quirky,* I don't exactly mean it as a compliment.

While places like Fenway and Wrigley are proud of these elements that separate them from the majority of other baseball stadiums, the actual gameplay of baseball can continue in these stadiums as it would in all others. Fenway's Green Monster alters play only in its positioning and size, and Wrigley's ivy doesn't really get in the way that much; sure, if a ball gets stuck in it, the hit is automatically ruled a ground-rule double—but that's the same in any stadium if a ball gets jammed beneath the fence, lodges itself under a chair in the bullpen, or bounces fair and into the stands. The ivy is indeed a quirk, but it doesn't get in the way of *baseball.*

This isn't the case in Tampa Bay. Instead of a large wall in left field or a sheet of foliage covering its fences, "the Trop" has rings of catwalks that hang from its domed ceiling. These walkways, unfortunately, do in fact get in the way of *baseball:* if the ball hits the catwalk, nothing special happens. The play is *not* called dead; a predetermined outcome (like a ground-rule double) is *not* declared. Essentially, the players on the field must adhere to the golf rule of *play it as it lies* and react accordingly. This means that the ball can carom off the catwalk at any angle, sending fielders racing after it and the batter racing around the bases. Tropicana Field has the regrettable tendency of turning the laziest fly ball into an inside-the-park home run and turning a would-be home run into an unlucky fly out. It's a mess that they still haven't figured out how to solve yet—other than by (accurately) declaring that the Rays need a new stadium.

The game we saw further painted the picture of the Trop's quirkiness. In the top of the second, a ball indeed hit one of the catwalks, completely diverting it from its normal path and instead sending it toward the seats down the first base line, directly at Andrew. We each watched, stunned, as the ball landed perfectly in his cupped hands.

"That's . . . that's the first ball I've ever caught at a game," he said, looking at it incredulously.

"Did it hurt?" I asked. I had never caught one before, either, but always thought the barehanded grab would sting.

"Nah," he said confidently.

Then, one out into the top of the fourth inning, the stadium's power went out completely. The lights shut down, and for about two seconds, there was total darkness before emergency floodlights began to shine from the catwalks. It took a good ten minutes of wandering around beneath this dim lighting for us to learn that the dome had been struck by lightning, and the game would resume—once the power returned.

"It happens," a local Rays fan informed us, shrugging his shoulders in a casual manner. We continued to stare at the silhouettes of ballplayers running across the dark field and into their respective dugouts while this man went back to sipping his beer as if nothing extraordinary had just occurred.

11:15 p.m.

The next thirty-six hours passed in a total blur. We returned from the game to the mechanic and spent the night in The Van while it was still parked inside the auto shop's garage. It was certainly an odd feeling to pop the top of the old camper while inside—let alone with the vehicle still perched on the grounded car lift. I slept the entire night fearful that somebody was going to hit a button and we all would slowly ascend toward the ceiling.

But at roughly 2:00 p.m. the following day, The Van was presented to us as ready to go. We paid up and thanked the mechanic as best as we could.

"Hang on," Andrew said, reaching into his backpack. He removed the baseball he had caught the night before.

"What's that?" the mechanic asked.

"It's a ball from last night's game. I caught it after it caromed off one of those catwalks."

"You're kidding."

"Not at all." Andrew looked at the ball for a second. He hesitated only slightly before extending his hand, offering the ball to the man. "Here. Take it."

"No, no, no," he replied, taking a step back. "I couldn't."

"No, I'm serious! You literally saved our trip. It's the least we can do."

"I fix cars for a living, man. Catching a baseball at a game never happens."

"I've caught a bunch before! Seriously, please." He tossed the ball at the mechanic, forcing him to catch it. The man held it in his hand, looking at the seams as if he was reading a book.

"You a baseball fan?" I asked. He took a few seconds to respond, continuing to slowly twist the ball in his hands. Eventually, he looked up at us with a grin.

"I am now."

Fifteen minutes later, we climbed into The Van and tried the engine. It turned over immediately, good as new. Honking twice as we pulled out of the mechanic's driveway, we then set off westbound toward Texas. No clicks, no wobbles, no arguments. In the rearview mirror, I saw The Van smile—finally, a real, genuine smile.

TOP OF THE EIGHTH
Minute Maid Park

Two Parking Lots in Houston

Wednesday, July 20 | 7:57 a.m.

We woke up that morning in a Walmart parking lot swimming in pools of our own sweat. This was not the first time where that disgusting sensation had greeted us to the day, but it was definitely the worst incident all trip: four guys and a tire baking in the Texas heat that was already at 101 before 8:00 a.m. I had slept in the top section of The Van, where the beige canvasing had created a greenhouse effect, trapping the sun perfectly onto my back and turning the cushion I slept on into a slimy bog.

"Screw. This." Frazier summarized my thoughts exactly as he rose next to me. Swinging his feet over the edge of the upper level, he hopped down to the floor of The Van, where Michael and Andrew still slept. They both began to stir when Frazier loudly opened the sliding door and then were both wide awake when he stepped out onto the pavement.

"Ah! God! Hot!" Frazier hopped like a man on coals back to The Van and stumbled into the car, banging his shin on the door as he fell atop Michael and Andrew.

"Pavement too spicy for ya?" Andrew asked, tossing Frazier off him.

"Spicy?"

"Hot."

"Oh. Yeah. It's burning out there, man."

"Put some shoes on then. What were you doing?"

"I was going to wander into the Walmart to take a piss."

"Walmart?"

"Yeah. We slept in their parking lot last night."

"Oh."

Fun fact: many Walmarts abide by an unwritten rule where they open up their parking lots to vagabond car dwellers to come in and park overnight.

Not fun fact: anything that has to do with sleeping in a Walmart parking lot.

Frazier slipped a pair of sneakers on and made it about ten yards from The Van before turning around, remembering that he needed to be wearing a shirt if he was to enter a public store. He paused on his way back, his eyes staring at something on the side of the vehicle.

"Did someone siphon our gas?" he asked.

"Frazier . . ." Andrew replied, putting his head back down on a pillow. "What?" His tone was one of bored dismissiveness with a hint of incredulousness.

"I think someone siphoned our gas!"

"What on earth are you talking about?"

"There's no gas cap on the canister!"

This was enough to pique the interest of at least Michael, who slipped into flip-flops and walked around to where Frazier stood. Sure enough, our gas tank had no lid on it anymore. In its place was just an empty hole, leading into the depths of The Van's underbelly.

"See?" Frazier said.

"You're right," Michael replied.

"I told you—someone siphoned it!"

"I think *siphoned* might be going a little far. We probably left it at a gas station somewhere last night."

This reasoning was enough to calm Frazier down. "Oh," he said. "That makes sense."

"But dang, I'm not sure what we're gonna do now."

"I dunno either. Rag?"

"What?"

"Use a rag."

"A rag for a gas cap?"

"I feel like that's a line from an Adam Sandler song."

"I think you're right."

"Which one was it?"

"'Piece of Shit Car,' yeah?" The two began to hum the tune. I apologized to The Van on behalf of the others.

"Yo, songbirds." Andrew stuck his head out of the driver's side window, craning his neck to look at the side of The Van. "There's an auto shop as a part of this mall." He nodded his head in the direction of the entrance to the parking lot, next to which stood a tall pole that advertised every shop in the complex, including Walmart, Jack in the Box, RadioShack—and sure enough, AutoZone.

"Well now, for once the world is with us," Michael replied, shading his eyes to look at the sign and then squinting as he tried to locate the AutoZone down the road. "It looks like it's a block or two away."

"Shall we go?" Andrew asked.

"Sure."

Within three minutes, the four of us had exited The Van and approached the mall. Michael and Andrew peeled off and headed in the direction of the AutoZone while Frazier and I wandered into the Walmart in search of breakfast. We were inappropriately upset when we discovered that the in-house McDonald's did not open until 10:00 a.m.—greasy burgers and nuggets had once again sounded great to start the day—and settled instead on prepackaged Caesar salads and a gallon of blue Hawaiian Punch. We passed the drink between the two of us and made our way to the electronics section, where *Ice Age 2* played on the many TVs that were being sold. It was the second time during the trip where I found myself sitting in a department store and watching something snowy on TV to cool down.

Andrew and Michael's anecdote was far more bizarre. The two of them continued walking down the Houston boulevard toward the AutoZone that, in the heavy heat, felt like walking toward a mountain. They finally arrived after about ten minutes, only to discover that the shop, like the McDonald's, *also* did not open until 10:00 a.m. A clock above the door showed that it was 8:35.

"An hour and a half," Michael said.

"Jesus," Andrew replied. "That's gonna take forever in this heat."

"You wanna go back?"

"No way. I don't want to do that walk again." He turned around and placed his back against the glass door, slowly sliding his body down to the concrete. "Honestly, it's not too bad here," he said, referencing the little bit of shade provided by the door's overhang. "I'm tired, man."

"Me too."

The two of them promptly fell asleep propped against the door of that Houston AutoZone. A couple of minutes before ten, they awoke to the store manager prodding them with his foot.

"Hey," he said in a gruff tone, "get out 'o here." The next few minutes were incredibly awkward, as Michael and Andrew attempted to pick themselves up from of the man's doormat and convince him that they were not actually teenage bums but instead were honestly there to shop in his store.

"Where's y'alls car?" the bearded manager asked, his eyes scanning the AutoZone parking lot, which was vacant apart from his black pickup truck.

"It's down the road . . ." Michael said, vaguely pointing his finger in a direction while trying to shake off the cobwebs of sleep that had set in during his slumber. "It's a . . . van . . ."

"What is it that you guys need, exactly?"

"A gas cap."

The man opened the glass door with a key and nodded for Michael and Andrew to follow him in. He walked over to a counter in the middle of the shop and booted up a computer, tapping the monitor as he waited for it to spring to life. When it did, he began asking questions.

"What brand?"

"Volkswagen."

"Model?"

"Eurovan."

The man let out a low whistle and shook his head slightly. "I don't mean to be bleak here, boys, but I highly doubt I've got anything that will work for y'all." Michael pursed his lips and remained silent. The rag for a gas cap was starting to look more and more likely.

"Year?"

"Ninety-nine."

"Christ, man. This thing is twelve years old?"

"Yeah."

"I'll bet your best bet is ordering something online."

"Ah darn . . . that ain't gonna work."

The shop manager ignored Michael's reply and continued entering information into the computer. "Manual or automatic?"

"That matters with a gas cap?"

"Manual or automatic?" he asked again.

"Automatic."

The manager typed a few more keys and then hit the *Enter* button with zeal, stepping back for effect while the computer processed everything. Michael and Andrew waited patiently but cynically. The odds of a gas cap as archaic as what they were looking for randomly popping up at this Houston AutoZone were slim—and even if miraculously there was one, surely it would cost a decent sum. Whatever; we were ready to pay for it.

The computer emitted a light ding, and the owner's eyebrows raised in surprise. "Well fuck my old brown boots," he said crudely. "Looks like I got one left."

"You do?" Andrew replied incredulously.

"Yep. Volkswagen Eurovan, 1999 automatic."

"That's us!" Michael said, excited. "I won't have sex with your boots, though." He meant it as a joke, but judging from the man's reaction, it came off weird. Michael tried to recover. "Er . . . How much?"

"Six ninety-nine."

"Six dollars and ninety-nine cents?" they both said loudly, amazed at the cheap price. "Um . . . yeah . . . yeah, we'll take it."

12:30 p.m.

If you found yourself standing at the corner of Crawford Street and Texas Avenue in Houston and did not know otherwise, you would have no idea that you're actually right in front of a baseball stadium. Minute Maid Park blends in that well, as the brick-lined left field entrance looks like any old business building from the outside. Once upon a time, this was Old Union Station, the city's main train depot. When ground broke on Minute Maid in 1997, it was actually going to be named "the Ballpark at Union Station"—which, had it survived, would certainly have been a good candidate for coolest name of all MLB stadiums. But no, the agreement for that name lasted only two years (during which the stadium was still being built), and by the time the ballpark opened in 2000, Enron had taken over the naming rights. Yet as this company slowly slipped into disarray and international shame, the Astros understandably wanted to part with the name "Enron Field," thus opening the door for the Minute Maid juice company to jump in at the last second and sign a gigantic contract. Although "Minute Maid Park" is here to stay until (at least) 2030,[28] the field still pays tribute to its railroad origins in two ways. The first is the aforementioned Old Union Station entrance on Crawford and Texas. The second is within the ballpark, where an arched concourse in left field supports a large, old-style ornamental train. Whenever an Astro hits a home run, it chugs its way down eight hundred feet of track at a whirring 2.5 miles per hour.

The thermometer on the dashboard cruelly read 107 as we pulled into the parking lot and piled onto the pavement. Andrew immediately removed his shirt, stripped down to his boxer shorts, and began digging through the cooler.

"What on earth are you doing?" I asked.

"I'm hot."

"I get that—but why're you almost naked? And what are you looking for?"

"The Jelly."

"We still have that thing?" I hadn't seen the flimsy water jug in weeks.

"I think so."

"Why do you want it?" I asked. "The water's not gonna be cold."

"Doesn't matter—I gotta shower, man. I feel disgusting." Sure enough, he found the plastic water jug at the base of the cooler. "Can you hold this up in the air?" he asked, handing it to me. I obliged, raising it up and twisting the cap so that the water slowly dripped out onto Andrew.

It had reached the point where we were now showering in the parking lot outside of a ballpark—but to be honest, we were perfectly fine with it. Life on the road had combined with the constant stream of days with triple-digit heat, and the last wash we had taken was at a rest stop outside of Cincinnati. Within a minute, Michael and Frazier had removed their clothing as well and were taking turns hopping into the Jelly's lazy stream. Fans making their way to the game were, needless to say, more than surprised when they walked by this strange scene of nearly nude teenagers dancing around a hippie van, cooling themselves beneath a trickle of lukewarm water. But it was that hot. After everybody had rotated through—including me—Andrew once again asked for me to hold the Jelly out so that he could shower.

"You already did!" I replied.

"Yeah, but it's been almost five minutes, and I already feel gross again."

MIDDLE OF THE EIGHTH

Rangers Ballpark and Sun Life Stadium

Friday, July 22 | 7:45 p.m.

In any coming-of-age story, there inevitably comes a moment when teenage boy meets teenage girl. These encounters are often as awkward as you can imagine, cued by the actions of the boy (who knows nothing whatsoever) screwing up in attempt to impress the girl (who knows everything in the world). Our moment came on the evening of Friday, July 22.

It all started as we stood in line to get food at Rangers Ballpark in Arlington (now called Globe Life Park), a stadium surrounded by red brick capped by white lining that wraps around in continuous Romanesque arches. Were it not for the light fixtures peering over the top, a person visiting the area might think they had stumbled onto a large, majestic cattle ranch sunk into the Texas countryside when they spot the structure. Yet despite this grandiose appearance, the interior of the ballpark actually feels fairly compressed, with three levels of seating towering over the field from all sides, including a large office building in center.

Everything in Texas has to contribute to the state's stereotype of being *big,* correct? Rangers Ballpark certainly thinks so. When we visited, a food stand on one of the main concourses proudly sold a two-foot-long hot dog called "the Boomstick." Two feet! We of course hopped in line to buy one.

"That's a loooong wiener," Frazier said, looking at the gigantic sticks of meat that were glistening on the grill behind the counter. We each laughed at the comment, entertained as teenage boys ever are by dick jokes.

"Is it?" came a voice laden with mockery from behind us. "I've seen better." We turned and came face-to-face with three simply stunning girls, each of whom looked to be roughly our age, if not a year or two older. Shoot, they had heard us laughing at that stupid phallic joke.

"Uh—yeah . . ." Frazier said, balking completely and not knowing how to respond at all.

"Y'all are from Seattle, it looks like?" she asked, reaching out and brushing the logo of his Mariners T-shirt—an action that immediately gave her complete and utter control of the situation.

"Uh—yeah . . ." Same answer. I think Frazier's internal systems might have actually stopped working for a minute or two there. The girls each sported a piece of Rangers apparel that was accompanied by something plaid, all draped over jean shorts and cowboy boots. They fit the southern girl image that the television had always told us to expect. It was straight out of a cheap teenage movie.

For some reason we couldn't understand, the girls continued to engage us in conversation as we proceeded to order two feet of wiener. (They claimed to be in line for lemonade.) Finding our voices, we talked to them about the nature of our trip, the places we had been, and the tough times we had had, making everything sound as rough as possible in an attempt to make us seem more appealing.

"Wow," the girl who had touched Frazier's chest said. Her hair was tied with a bow that was, of course, plaid in design. "We'd love to hear some more about that." Still in charge of everything, she nodded to her friends before turning back to us. "Maybe after the game? Would y'all like that?"

Again, it was Frazier who replied. "Uh—yeah . . ." This third iteration of the phrase forced Andrew to nudge him in the back and whisper, *"Shut up, man,"* into his ear. The girls seemed not to notice.

"Tell you what," the girl with the bow continued, reaching into her purse and removing what looked to be tickets. "Since y'all are new here, why don't you come and join us for a bit 'o Texas? It's Friday, and there's a big honkytonk just a few miles away." It was as if she had preplanned the whole thing. "We've got some free entries—here!"

She handed the wad of tickets to Frazier, who reached out his hand and received them in a dumbfounded way. The girl must have noticed that his body wasn't working anymore, for she tilted her head and looked him directly in the eye.

"Ever been to a honkytonk before?" she asked.

"Uh—yeah . . ." After feeling another nudge from Andrew, however, he added, "All the time." The girls giggled.

"Oh yeah?" the girl answered. "Well all right then. See you there! Bring yer dancin' shoes!" And they left without buying their lemonade. We still bought that two-foot hot dog, though.

"Damn it, Frazier." Andrew said.

"What?"

"We go to honkytonks all the time."

"Oh. Sorry. Yeah, I think I blacked out there for a second."

"They *were* super hot."

"Uh—yeah . . ."

The Rangers game seemed to pass with suspicious speed after that encounter: we were out of the stadium as soon as the final out was recorded and into The Van before the players were even off the field. We then drove straight to the honkytonk that was listed on the tickets. It was some place called Billy Bob's.

9:35 p.m.

Advertised as the "World's Largest Honkytonk," Billy Bob's prides itself on having over 127,000 square feet that's open nightly for dancing, singing, and drinking. It was once a venue for professional wrestling but has since shifted to a popular country nightclub with an obscure history. The acts Billy Bob's has hosted range from Bob Hope to B. B. King—and, until 2016, it held a Guinness World Record for the largest round of drinks ever purchased at a bar (Merle Haggard: forty gallons of Canadian Club Whiskey).[29] It can get really crowded on weekends, and oh my god were we out of place.

Our rainbow car pulled into the dirt parking lot and drove slowly past an endless stream of pickup trucks and motorcycles. They were all either red or black in color, and they all glared at The Van in the way one does when spotting someone who is so, so lost. Behind every vehicle, it seemed, stood at least four people who held a minimum of one beer in each hand. The Van nestled itself apologetically next to a pile of old tires that marked the end of the parking lot. We got out and made the long walk to the entrance of Billy Bob's, forced to retrace our way through the entire scene. Everybody and everything glared at us, wondering what the hell we were doing there.

The bouncer at the door was completely baffled when we handed him four free-entry tickets. "IDs, please," he said after a pause. *Damn it.* We flashed our Washington State driver's licenses and received neon wristbands in return, which loudly broadcasted our underage status to the entire state of Texas.

The four of us then entered, fearing that we were about to plunge into a large crowd similar to what we had seen in the lot.

But the worst thing about Billy Bob's was that the place *wasn't* crowded. The regulars must have been those drinking out in the lot because only fifty or so people were actually in the place when we walked in a little after 9:30 p.m. A big crowd would have been better, as that way we could have hid behind the masses if things got awkward. Instead, we were immediately visible to everyone and quickly *made* things awkward. The girls from earlier were nowhere to be seen.

Take four teenage boys from the Pacific Northwest and plop them into the middle of a place like this. While everybody else was wearing jeans, boots, and cowboy hats, we were strutting in Nike athletic shorts, flip-flops, and baseball caps. While everybody else ordered a beer at the bar, we were rejected and told to order soda. While everybody else tapped their feet along to the beat of some country song, we didn't even know what country songs were.

A line dance began, and somehow we wound up in the middle of it. It felt like a ritual had commenced; at the strike of a few vague notes, every single one of the fifty other people in that place got up obediently, headed to the dance floor, placed their hands on their hips, and proceeded to do the exact same leg-swinging, body-turning, tap-dancing thing.

"How do they all know exactly what to do?" Frazier asked, just as he bumped into a man wearing a leather jacket. "Sorry," he grumbled, backing away—an action that only made him bump into another guy. "Sorry." I tried to hide myself, but it was impossible.

It was here that the girls from the game found us. Right here, at the peak point of us standing out in the crowd and the deepest moment of our own self-loathing. My dignity is still rolling around that dance floor. The girls still wore some form of plaid paraphernalia, but they had swapped their Rangers gear for Billy Bob's apparel. They also now held small straw baskets, from which they handed out beer koozies, bracelets, and cheap sunglasses—all branded with the Billy Bob's logo. I quickly realized that they worked as promoters for the honkytonk, and it was their job to hook unsuspecting out-of-towners like us and then easily reel us in. No wonder they had free tickets.

"But I thought you said you went to honkytonks all the time?" the one with the bow asked, shooting a knowing glance toward Frazier and his clumsy dance moves as she handed me a koozie, which I embarrassingly slipped over my can of Pepsi.

Within three minutes, they were gone. The four of us soon followed suit, realizing that there was no happiness for us to be found in that place. We exited and again made the trek back across the parking lot, fighting our way against the throngs of pregamers from earlier. (They each were now making their way toward the entrance, having somehow unanimously decided it was time for everyone to enter the honkytonk.) By the time we reached the pile of tires and opened the sliding door of The Van, the dirt lot was vacated, save for a couple of stragglers turning the radios off in their trucks and locking up their motorcycles.

For about two minutes, The Van didn't move. The four of us just sat there in silence, trying not to make eye contact with one another and trying not to admit the horrible defeat we had just suffered at the hands of Billy Bob's Honkytonk and its extremely attractive promoters. It was Andrew who broke the silence.

"Welp, I'm gonna do something that should've been done weeks ago," he said, getting up from the jump seat and opening the sliding door. Twisting back around, he grabbed the white sack that encased the bulky tire and dragged it off the bench seat, forcing it to fall to the floor of the car with a loud thud.

Bending over, Andrew peeled off the bag and hoisted the tire up onto its side. He then pushed it out the open sliding door, giving it a kick to propel it forward. We each watched as that intrusive thing slowly rolled fifteen feet before coming to a stop and falling down at the base of the pile of other discarded tires. I hope it's still there.

12:15 p.m. | Two Days Later

"Turn right onto Interstate 20 and continue for nine hundred and ninety-seven miles as it merges with Interstate 10."

Even The Van laughed when Tina said this. We had just picked up Andrew and Frazier at Dallas Forth Worth International Airport, and now apparently we would not be budging from I-20/I-10 until near Phoenix, when we would take a slight left and divert onto I-8 for another 340 miles.

As had been the plan, Michael and I had dropped Andrew and Frazier at the airport the morning before. After four and a half hours of trying to snag a standby flight to Miami, they were finally admitted onto a plane and given a return trip for a red-eye later that night. The two never slept at all, save for a few hours on a bench in North Miami Beach. They saw a game at Sun Life Stadium, which is no longer where the Marlins baseball team plays. The team has since shifted from being the Florida Marlins to the *Miami* Marlins and now plays in Marlins Park, which is an awkwardly massive building that has bits of Miami sprinkled all around. Just beyond the left field fence is a night-club that bumps loud music around a swimming pool, emulating the popular South Beach nightlife scene. An aquarium behind the walls of home plate contains actual live fish, offering a glimpse into the waters surrounding the city. The exterior of the ballpark is primarily made up of white, blocky patterns that mirror the popular art deco adopted by many Miami buildings. And the odd starfish/palm tree sculpture in center field—well, to be honest, I still have no idea what that's doing there. It looks like something out of *Candy Land*.

We picked them up early the next morning and pointed The Van west again. Four hours of nonchanging I-10 scenery later (Texas is boring), a lunch break was declared. We spotted a handmade sign for tacos stuck into the ground about a hundred yards before a freeway exit and convinced ourselves that it would probably lead us to some classic homemade Mexican food. We were close to the border—surely this would be the real stuff. The Van took the exit and then followed another scribbled sign that directed us to a gas station. Still confident that we were onto something legitimate, we walked in. The place looked apocalyptic, with dirty aisles and shelves that were primarily empty save for a few stashes of canned food and beef jerky. Food from here was clearly a dangerous choice, but we were the type of people who ignored such warning signs. Our stomachs growled.

"There," Frazier said. He pointed to the back of the store, where someone had painted HAND-ROLLED TACOS! onto the white slab of wall next to the bathroom, with an arrow pointing out the back door. Of all things, it was the exclamation mark that made me slightly leery of the situation. Nevertheless, we followed the sign, which led to a small back lot where an overweight guy in a cowboy hat sat next to a rollaway grill. He looked to be dozing off, but the sound of our footsteps woke him up.

"Tacos?" he grumbled, opening the grill's cover to reveal a handful of wrapped tacos sizzling on the grate. They looked to have just been removed from the freezer.

"Yes."

"How many?"

"How many ya got?"

We ate thirty-five of those things between us. I threw up for the next three hours of dull Texas countryside, until falling asleep somewhere near Midland.

11:45 p.m.

When I awoke, it was approaching midnight. My shift was not to start for another couple of hours, but something had yanked me out of sleep and demanded that I stay awake. Life has a cool way of doing that. It knows when you should be experiencing something, and it somehow finds a way to make you realize it as well. Thank god for this, because for me, what happened next became the most vivid memory I have of that entire summer.

"Someone needs to document this," Andrew said from behind the wheel.

At first, the flashes came sporadically—about once every minute or so—and we never thought we would actually catch up to it. But as The Van continued west and rolled deeper and deeper into the Texas midnight, the lightning began to pick up in both frequency and brightness. It was violent; it was fantastic.

Flash.

From my perch in the back, I was able to take in the entire scene through the car's large side windows. Michael slept in front of me, sprawled out on the impromptu mattress created by the folded-down bench seat. My legs rested next to his back while my eyes remained glued to the sky.

Flash.

Just as the shimmering lights of El Paso appeared somewhere out there on the horizon, we plunged headlong into the electric storm. Headlights became pointless; nature lit our way, its electric fingers stretching down from the sky every two or three seconds.

Flash.

In western Texas there lies a sixty-seven-mile stretch of Interstate 10 that trapezes the southernmost edge of America, dancing perilously along the banks of the trickling Rio Grande. Traversing this section is a lot like trying to cross a border on a balance beam; a slip to the left drops you in Mexico while a slip to the right lands you in America. It was on this stretch that we now drove, The Van teetering along in the right lane, its bulky frame easily swayed by the strength of the rising wind. The lightning flashes now seemed to match our rpm rate. It was like driving through a cultural photo booth: every flare of light exposed us to the reality of our current position in fleeting snippets of illumination.

Flash. A glimpse to the right showed the rooftops of large department stores, gas stations, and fast-food joints standing immediately on the side of the road. America. *Flash.* A quick look to the left saw the lightning catch the silhouettes of small houses and barren streets across the river, only fifty or so yards away. Mexico. *Flash.*

"Someone needs to document this," Andrew said again, craning his neck to try to catch as much of the wondrous scene as he could.

"I'm trying!" Frazier said next to him, staring through the lens of his camera. Yet his efforts were quickly proving to be in vain; no matter how many times he clicked, the lightning evaded his capture. No matter how many different angles he tried, he could not catch both sides of the road—both countries—at once. The Nikon could do no justice to the scene, and the lightning flirted with the frame, taunting Frazier's efforts. As each image showed up dark on the digital screen, he began cursing the unfortunate results. "Damn!"

For me, this was the moment. This was the moment when I realized that what Andrew was saying was as true as it gets: somebody *needed* to document this. Yet it went far beyond the awesome lightning storm. This was the moment when I realized that somebody needed to document our *entire* story, for it was worth telling. It wasn't all flashes of light, it wasn't all epic travel anecdotes, and it certainly wasn't a canonical coming-of-age story—but what we were doing deserved to be told nonetheless.

But perhaps above all, this was the moment when I came to understand the true potential of the written word. As I watched Frazier continue to fail to capture the fleeting scene, I realized it wasn't his fault at all; even if he did manage to snap a picture of a bolt of lightning, a camera simply can't reproduce everything that goes into a scene like that. An image perfectly encapsulates visuals, but it often misses emotions and sensations. It was at that exact moment when I developed my own mantra as a writer: If a picture is worth a thousand words, then I shall write a thousand and one. I think I actually said it out loud right then and there.

Flash. I leaned forward and picked up the navy notebook I had purchased back in Phoenix. I hadn't written in it for a while, but a pen was still stuck into its spiral binding. I removed it quickly. Now tucking my legs up near my chest, I flipped to a blank page somewhere in the middle of the notebook, clicked the pen open, and wrote every word you just read.

"Somebody needs to document this," Andrew voiced once more.

"I'm on it."

Flash.

1:50 a.m.

Two hours later found Frazier and me up front, him now driving and me in the passenger seat. It was the first time since we
had approached New York City where we were the only ones
awake for a drive; the other two slept soundly in the back. The
windows were of course down, allowing the steamy southern
night to whip through The Van with a loud whir that surely
woke Michael and Andrew periodically. The lack of air-
conditioning was a real bummer. A few minutes passed, however, before I started to realize that the whipping was getting
louder and more intense than normal. I glanced at the speedometer and noticed that we were going eighty. A 70 mph speed
limit sign then whizzed by, and I opened my mouth to note it to
Frazier—but something held me back.

As the speed increased to eighty-five, the howling of the
wind continued to grow louder and my eyes darted up into the
central rearview mirror to make sure that Michael and Andrew
were still able to sleep. Neither stirred, so I shifted my gaze
back to the road.

Ninety. There were no lights in front of us that showed cars
that might be coming up ahead. The road, too, showed no sign
of anything but pure straightaway. I now turned my head to
Frazier, wondering if he was noticing the increasing speed.
Nope, he seemed to be in a different world completely. His
head bobbed along to some song that was stuck in his mind, as
The Van continued to accelerate down the pavement.

Ninety-three. A slight whistle began to sound as the wind
lashed violently through the windows and open vents. Michael
began to shuffle in his sleep, no doubt subconsciously disturbed
by the rising sound.

Ninety-seven. Papers began flying. The front section of The
Van now looked like a sports parade, as a confetti of discarded

notes and baseball tickets flew up into the air, encircling Frazier and me. As I swatted a few away, I turned my eyes once again to Frazier. Surely he must be noticing our speed by now? But no, the draw of his own world appeared to prevail, as he now drummed the steering wheel to the rhythm of whatever song he was humming. I looked again at the speedometer as it ticked to ninety-eight . . . ninety-nine . . .

One hundred. I smiled, enjoying the 2:00 a.m. sensation of bulleting through nowhere Texas in a rickety old Volkswagen at triple-digit tempo. The Van screamed in glee, its voice stretching endlessly across the flat planes that surrounded it on all sides and extended forever. For about ten seconds, we maintained that pace, free with speed.

"Whoa!" Frazier then said, removing his foot from the gas pedal and bringing The Van to a coast, easing the vehicle back to a smooth seventy-five miles per hour. "Whoa, my bad."

"What happened?" Michael asked, raising his head lazily from the back after hearing Frazier's exclamation.

"Nothing," I replied. Nothing at all.

2:56 a.m.

We had just crossed into New Mexico when Frazier mentioned that he was getting tired and wanted to change drivers. Eager to begin my traditional graveyard shift, I encouraged him to take the next exit he saw so that we could switch positions. The Van began moving right, leaving the freeway on an unmarked exit that plopped us onto a small one-lane road. About one hundred yards later, Frazier pulled off to the side of the skinny strip of pavement and threw the hazards on—an action that at first I found funny, as there were clearly no other cars in this area. All we could see out of the windows was darkness. The only thing we could hear was the crunch of gravel beneath us as The Van turned slightly, its headlamps illuminating the immediate foreground as the car began to roll toward a stop.

Then, about fifty feet in front of us, a large black gate appeared. It was made of wrought iron and decorated with Baroque-looking swirls and skeletal faces, which loomed out of the abyss in intimidating existence. I then realized that this wasn't a patch of gravel—we were on a driveway.

"What the . . ." was all Frazier managed to get out as he threw on the brakes, not wanting to get any closer to the freaky-looking gate. Through the iron bars, we could see a well-paved strip of road leading farther into god knows what. None of us wanted to find out.

"Where are we?" Michael asked from the back. I twisted in my seat to find that both he and Andrew were both now upright and wide eyed, staring forward at the black gate with a similar fright to what I felt. But as I looked back, however, my fear only increased.

Through the rear window of The Van, a new light appeared. It seemed to come from a ways away, not from the exit we had just taken but farther down the one-lane road we had ended up on. I squinted, trying to make out its shape in the penetrating darkness. It appeared to be headlamps, but it wasn't a normal set of headlamps. There were three of them, and one looked to be higher than the others. Weird. As the odd collection of lights grew closer, however, I soon discerned that they were the front lights of a pickup truck with a small police beacon atop the car's roof. The beacon rotated slowly in an off-red and off-yellow glow. It did not look official at all.

"Are we doing anything wrong?" Frazier asked, seeing what I was seeing.

"I don't think so."

Michael and Andrew turned and watched as the truck drove closer, eventually pulling up about forty feet behind The Van. Our hearts pounded as the driver's side door opened slowly and a tall figure emerged.

"That's no cop car," Michael said, voicing what we all were thinking. It was indeed not a cop car, nor was it a police officer. The figure, a man, wore dark jeans and a large beige trench coat with a cowboy hat atop his head. Slowly, he began walking toward The Van. My heart pounded with every step he took, as the sound of his gravely footsteps matched the booming of my pulse. All at once, what had been an eerily quiet scene now seemed chaotically loud.

"Yer in the middle of the road," the man said once he was about fifteen feet before The Van. He held his left palm out in a questioning gesture but kept his right hand inside his trench-coat pocket. It looked like it was holding something. He walked up to the open driver's window of The Van and leaned down slightly, making direct eye contact with Frazier. The man looked to be about fifty years old, with wrinkles cutting into his face, the skin of which seemed to have been significantly worn down by something other than aging. His eyes were beady and dark brown, and they rarely blinked. He had no facial hair, and for some reason that made him scarier.

"Er," Frazier said, gulping and trying to appease the man. "I'm sorry. We just wanted to make a quick driver chan—"

"I don't think you heard me," the man interrupted. His voice was unnaturally calm. "Yer in the middle of the road."

Fear cemented me to the passenger seat as I continued watching the man stare at Frazier. The brim of his cowboy hat brushed the top of the driver's side door as he placed his left hand onto the ledge of the rolled-down window. His right hand had not budged from the trench-coat pocket.

"We'll leave," Michael said from the back. "We'll leave now."

The man's head slowly turned to the sound of his voice. His eyebrows squinted as he tried to see through the darkness and into the interior of The Van. The only source of light was coming from the dull beams of the pickup's headlights and the lazy rotations of the beacon atop it. "How many of you are in here?" he asked.

"Four."

"All boys?"

That was not a question we were expecting. "Yes," Michael replied after a few uneasy seconds. The man moved his head back a bit, apparently dissatisfied with that answer. He removed his hand from the door and stepped back a couple of feet.

"Yer in the middle of the road," he said once more. It's a phrase that still haunts me to this day. "And I recommend you get out of here now."

The Van took off by itself and drove out of the gravel lot with unprecedented motivation. It returned to the paved one-lane road and continued into the middle of the night, heading nowhere in particular other than away from wherever the hell we had been, whatever the hell that gate had been, and whoever the hell that man had been. After making it a hundred or so yards down the road, I turned in my seat and looked back at the scene to make sure he wasn't following us. No, he was still standing there, having barely moved. His left hand now rested on his hip. His right was still in his trench-coat pocket.

I don't remember how we got back onto Interstate 10, but when we did, the feeling that spread through us was the same one we had experienced in Missouri after the encounter with the black dog. It was a feeling of relief to escape what we had just seen and a feeling of relief at being welcomed back by the boring-but-friendly glow of the interstate. Frazier continued driving, now claiming that he was wide awake and did not want a change of driver for a little while longer.

"When we do, though, let's stop at a gas station," he said. "A brightly lit gas station."

About fifteen minutes later, we pulled off the freeway yet again, this time onto an exit that was well signed with options for food and fuel. It was now 3:40 a.m. and definitely my time to drive. We opted to reload on gas, paying $4.99 per gallon in what was the most expensive fill-up of the trip. But this was the only fueling spot we had seen in the past hundred or so miles— and might be for the next hundred or so as well. That gas station could have charged whatever it wanted, and people would still pay.

I took over the wheel as The Van moved farther west, breathing slightly easier now. After the lightning storm, the triple-digit speed, and the encounter with the trench-coated man, Interstate 10 had brought us more excitement than any stretch of freeway to date. The rest of the journey to San Diego, however, was peaceful. Andrew sat up front with me as we passed into Arizona, and the early-morning hours trickled slowly by. I sipped a cup of gas station coffee as the two of us dipped in and out of conversation, debating everything from the best flavor of sunflower seeds to whether we believed in heaven. A soft song played in the background, and the world was good. Everything was. It all had been since the resurrection of The Van.

Another hour slipped by as we continued. Then far, far behind us, the sun began to rise in the east, dawning the desert with the new day's first rays of light and illuminating the two-armed cacti on the side of the road. It made them look like humans, stretching as they got out of bed.

BOTTOM OF THE EIGHTH

Petco Park

JACK KEROUAC

5:05 p.m. | Tuesday, July 26

The ability to watch baseball from a beach makes me wonder how anyone could ever find issue with Petco Park. In center field of the San Diego Padres' stadium is a small sandy area that is open before games for anyone to come on down, kick off their shoes, and watch batting practice while sitting on warm, golden sand. After first pitch is thrown, however, the beach becomes closed to all except those who hold a ticket for the bleachers just above it, making Petco one of the only parks in Major League Baseball where an outfield ticket can be more expensive than an infield ticket.

Like Miami in Marlins Park, the city of San Diego is well represented in the Padres' stadium. When Petco was under construction, the contractors wanted to try to find a way to place various bits of the hometown into its new baseball field. They started with the beach, obviously. But a large park also sits just above the center field complex, showing off the city's copious green space with trees, statues, walkways, and open patches of grass. There's even a miniature baseball field up there, where kids can organize their own games of Wiffle Ball while looking out over the big-league diamond they dream of one day playing on.

The ballpark gives a nod to San Diego's strong US Navy presence as well. One of the largest naval bases in the country is located just south of the stadium, and Petco at times feels like a continuation of it. Multiple miniature models of aircraft carriers and various naval vessels both modern and antique stand in the middle of the ballpark walkways for visitors to examine. When a Padre hits a home run, a ship's whistle sounds, ringing around the stadium and into the nearby harbor. And to cap it all, the Padres players even sport camouflage uniforms on occasion. Although the effort here is valiant, it's also horrifying; the brown-on-brown splotched jerseys are easily the ugliest in all of baseball.

The final element of San Diego that Petco proudly boasts is the incorporation of the area that surrounds the ballpark. The stadium is nestled into the Gaslamp Quarter, a once down-and-out section of the city that is now hip and expanding at a rapid rate, thanks to the ballpark (remember Nationals Park and DC's Navy Yard?). The Gaslamp Quarter bleeds into Petco via its many brand-new apartment buildings, which stare down onto the ballpark if not open directly *into* the stadium's confines. One apartment advertisement we saw read: "Live Here and Skip the Lines!"

But easily the most recognizable incorporation of the Gaslamp Quarter is the large brick warehouse that stands in left field. Just like Camden's old B&O Warehouse, this Western Metal Supply Co. building is the defining feature of Petco Park. The building has stood here since 1909[30] and was welcomed by the ballpark's design team, who wanted to mimic Camden in working *with* the city as opposed to clearing it out. Therefore, the warehouse still stands proudly, with three sets of bleachers protruding at different floors and a rooftop terrace that offers stellar vistas into the ballpark and out over the surrounding city.

Petco Park was perfect. It was a perfect reminder of some of our favorite ballparks we had seen thus far, nearly all of which had a similar feel of urban and trendy. Meanwhile, the relaxed environment offered a perfect moment for the four of us to catch our breath, as we were now finally able to just sit back, relax, and enjoy baseball—without worrying about travel—for the first time in a while, having hit a calm three-day break in our schedule before preparing to turn north and beginning our ascent back toward Seattle.

1:44 p.m. | Two Days Later

We soaked up those three days by spending two near Torrey Pines, using the Pacific Ocean as our shower. The final day we spent at Mission Beach, playing catch with our feet in the water. Later that afternoon, Andrew and I broke off from Michael and Frazier for a while to wander the Mission boardwalk. As we strolled through the various beach shops and taco stands, I made a brief mention of the new state of his friendship with Frazier.

"You guys were once practically incompatible, and now you're almost inseparable," I remarked. "How . . . what happened?"

Andrew just smiled in return. "I don't know," he said, "but I also don't care."

I opened my mouth to pry further—but a voice from my left cut me off.

"Sorry," it said. "Can you help me?"

Andrew and I turned and came face-to-face with a girl who stood with her back propped against the wall of a sunglass stand that marked the entrance to a small alley, which led away from the crowd toward a lesser occupied section of the beach. She wore fake yellow aviators that reflected her light-brown hair, which was woven into thin braids that frayed slightly at the ends. A blue-and-white sundress cascaded from her shoulders, billowing out just below her knees, and a medium-size brown-and-white dog lay panting at her feet, which were slid into ratty Birkenstock sandals.

"Yes?" Andrew replied. I noticed a change in his voice from how we had been talking only a second before. I couldn't blame him; I knew that if I had spoken, mine would surely have sounded different as well. It probably would have been a lot higher.

"Do either of you know how to fix a bike chain?" the girl asked.

"Of course," I immediately replied. I didn't really know how to fix a bike chain. I had dabbled with them once or twice but was by no means a master. Yet at that moment in my life, I *made* bike chains.

"Can you try to help fix mine, maybe?"

"Of course," I said again, now trying to make my voice deeper than normal.

The girl spun on her heel and began walking down the alley, her dress waving lazily behind her. The dog hopped up and followed as well, and Andrew and I soon did the same. After about fifty yards, the alley opened into a wide dirt lot encircled by a short cement wall, with one small opening that led down to the beach. At the far end was a blue bicycle that lay on its side. It was an older model, with larger spokes in the wheels and handlebars that curved slightly inward. Above the rear tire was a thin black rack that supported a small wooden box, now upended. On the dirt next to the bike lay the box's former contents: a notebook, a light sweater, and a can of Pacifico beer.

"It popped off when I was riding down Mission," the girl said, pointing at the chain that hung loosely from the gear cassette. "And I wheeled it in here because I don't have a lock."

"How come you don't have a lock?" Andrew asked.

The girl smiled back. "I never need one."

As I bent down to look at the broken chain, the girl walked over to the wall and hoisted herself up onto it. Her feet swung freely beneath her as she twisted her toes to loosen them from the Birkenstocks, which fell to the ground. The dog wandered over and flopped against the wall, locating the only bit of shade it could find.

"What's the dog's name?" Andrew asked, bending down to pet it.

"Jack," the girl replied. Even the way she spoke was breezy and casual. Andrew wanted to hear more of it, so he searched for conversation.

"Are . . . are you guys from this area?"

The girl paused a second before answering this question. "Kind of. I suppose we are now."

"What's that mean?" Andrew responded with a slight laugh, standing up from petting the dog and propping himself against the wall, near to where the girl sat. He shifted a few times, struggling to find the ideal position that would make him look casual without having to crane his neck to stare up at the girl. "Are you not from San Diego originally?"

"Nope."

"Where are you from, then?"

"Well, *originally* I suppose I'm from Utah." She raised her head a bit to look up at the sky. As her fake yellow aviators continued to reflect the sunlight, I realized that I had not seen her actual eyes yet.

"Utah!" Andrew replied. "Wow. Beautiful place out there. What brought you here?"

"The Mormon life wasn't for me."

"Ah . . . er, I see. What . . . what about it wasn't for you?"

"Missions," the girl said, forming a story with two syllables. "Seclusion from the rest of society. No alcohol, no drugs, no sex . . ." She held this last word longer than the others. It drifted up from her mouth and floated lightly to the ground like a feather that I never wanted to land. "I have nothing against that life, but it just wasn't for me. I was born in the wrong place, to the wrong family."

Positioned slightly below the girl, it looked like Andrew was groveling beneath her. He practically was. I mean, I was too.

"When . . . uh, when did you realize all this?" Andrew asked.

"When I started reading books of my own choice."

"Oh yeah?"

"Yeah."

"They wouldn't let you read regular books?" His slight grimace told me that he regretted using the word *regular* in this sentence. But the girl didn't seem to care.

"It wasn't that they didn't *let* us," she replied, her bare feet continuing to swing, "it was just that they didn't *encourage* it. My teachers and school had a clear agenda. Read this, believe that, do this, preach that. Books were one way that they could control their influence. It was like a Ray Bradbury novel."

"So you started reading other books?" Andrew asked, still trying with all his might. Meanwhile, I was getting nowhere with the bike chain.

"Well, my high school didn't exactly have much . . . *variation* in terms of selection of books at their library. But for my fourteenth birthday, my aunt got me a library card." Recounting this memory brought a smile to her face. "I still can't thank her enough for that because that library opened the world to me. I could read anything I wanted, learn about anything I desired, and believe whatever I thought sounded right."

"So you left then?"

The girl shook her head. "No, I was still too young. But the next few years were hard because I knew I didn't belong where I was. With every book I read, I found myself drifting farther and farther away from the world I had been born into." The way she spoke was flawless—as if she was reading a well-written script. "By the time I read *On The Road*, I knew I had to leave. I waited until I graduated high school, but the very next day I packed up my old Toyota, said something mean to my parents, and drove away, vowing never to return again." She then nodded her head in the direction of the dog. "I stopped by the pound and picked up the dog on the way out of town that day. I named him Jack immediately."

"Why Jack?"

"Kerouac," she said simply. As if on cue, the dog perked its head up slightly and looked in the direction of the girl.

"Got it," Andrew said. He didn't get it at all.

"I still don't know what type he is, exactly," she continued, "but he was the symbol of my leaving Utah. So I turned left on a freeway and came out here to California to begin again."

"Did you come straight to San Diego?"

"Nope. I went to Los Angeles first. But it was too noisy, too dirty . . . so I drifted farther south a couple of years ago." She smiled and shrugged. "And I've been here ever since."

"Have you spoken to your family at all?" I asked from behind the bike. It was the first time I had talked since starting to fumble with the chain, but the girl did not seem surprised by the new voice in the conversation. Her head slowly turned in my direction. Again, the bright reflection of the fake yellow aviators obstructed my view of her eyes.

"No," she said, a soft smile reappearing on her face. "I don't want anything to do with my past. I found me here, and I'm not looking to lose me again."

At that exact instant, the chain locked onto the gears and the back wheel began to turn in coordination with the pedals again. "Oh!" I said, surprise in my voice. "I guess I've fixed it!"

"Yay!" the girl responded, clapping lightly as she pushed herself from the wall and dropped back down to Earth. After sliding her feet back into the Birkenstocks, she wandered over to the bike. Andrew gathered the notebook, sweater, and beer for her off the ground and placed them back into the wooden box above the back tire.

"Thank you both," she said with yet another beautiful smile. "I feel bad . . . I never got to know either of you. Maybe one day—who knows?" And with that, she swung her leg over her bike and began to ride away. Seeing the girl leave, Jack hopped up from his shaded perch and began trotting after her yet again. The two of them went out of the alley, turned left onto the main drag, and disappeared.

Neither Andrew nor I spoke for a little while. I had no idea how long we had been in that alley speaking with the girl. It could have been five minutes; it could have been fifty. Apart from the obvious attraction the two of us had toward her, we both had seen a bit of ourselves in her person as well. The desire for travel and a strong yearning to see what else was out there in this country was obviously shared—and yet the reasons that pushed us to want this could not have been more different. Whereas the girl had despised her childhood and everything that went with it, we had loved ours. It had formed our friendships and communal desire for the road. We were lucky to have met her and also lucky to have been different from her.

"I never got her name," Andrew said, staring at the end of the alley where the girl had last been visible. I smiled at my friend, sharing his sentiment in wishing that she had stayed longer. Yet something about her casual tone and wanderlust past made the lack of knowing anything else about her seem appropriate. I would have loved to have seen her eyes and I would loved to have learned her name, but it seemed fitting that even these basic things had evaded me. I opened my mouth and replied to Andrew's statement.

"To be honest, man, it almost feels right that you didn't."

TOP OF THE NINTH
Oakland Coliseum

LOMBARD STREET

7:10 p.m. | Friday, July 29

The Oakland-Alameda County Coliseum is a warehouse pretending to be a sports stadium. Its impersonal gray walls hold a strong sense of brutalism, caring not for aesthetics but only for function. Small crowds often force the staff to close off nosebleed sections, if not vacate entire levels, the result of which can make you feel like you are wandering through an abandoned airplane hangar. Occasionally, a faded Athletics or Raiders mural on the wall reminds you that no, you are actually still in a venue for sports.

Concrete is everywhere here. It dominates the outer facade of the ballpark, covers the interior hallways, and spreads forever across the floors of the endless, drafty concourses. It actually feels as if the designers chose to place *more* concrete in areas where it wasn't really necessary at all; rarely is a color other than gray visible in the Oakland Coliseum.

Those who take public transit to see the Athletics play are required to enter the stadium by walking across a long, skinny bridge that leads from the ballpark's BART stop into the center field entrance. Lined with chain-link fences that are topped with prickly barbed wire, the bridge trapezes a series of old railroad tracks, a junkyard, and a dirty pond that is easily mistaken for a moat. A season ticket holder told me that he used to take BART to reach the ballpark, but this bridge made him feel like an inmate returning to prison every time he went to watch his baseball team play. He drives to the stadium now.

The A's as a franchise have been able to overcome their horrible stadium by conquering the reason they're forced to play in it: minimal finances. Currently, Oakland's total payroll checks in at just over $83 million—far behind the leading Boston Red Sox, who can afford over $221 million.[31] And yet, fueled by baseball brainiac Billy Beane and his addiction to sabermetrics, the A's have somehow found ways to produce consistently good ball clubs. Sure they have their down years, but Oakland has made the playoffs an astounding seven times since the Mariners last did, in 2001.

The A's as a fan base, meanwhile, have also found ways to overcome their horrible stadium. As previously mentioned, small crowds are a reality in Oakland; it's not abnormal to see only seven thousand fans in attendance for weeknight games. Yet while this would seem depressing for many, the game-goers in Oakland use it as a positive: fewer fans means fewer obstacles for being heard. In right field, for example, a group of crazies takes advantage of this by constantly pounding on the metal bannisters, creating a jingling tone throughout the game that slowly turns into the monotonous soundtrack of the Coliseum.

The game that evening seemed to fly by. We pretended that it was the draftiness of the ballpark and the drone of the constant banging from right field that distracted our minds from baseball—but in reality, the game's suspicious speed was due to the fact that the trip was almost over. And although we were growing more confident that the four of us would in fact stay in touch after returning to Seattle and entering the next phase of our life, we each knew that The Van would have to be left behind.

We had to sell the thing. We had taken out a loan to purchase it, and keeping such a vehicle entering freshman year of college was ludicrous. Yet despite our regular proclamations of disappointment with the old camper in the past, the four of us had at this point grown completely attached to it. Relationships unfortunately work like that, don't they? No matter the trials and tribulations that frayed them, just as they're coming to an end, you start to feel a flame again. Maybe it's the once-great connection making its final stand; maybe it's you getting cold feet at the prospect of going through with what you know is best, but suddenly you experience feelings that you haven't felt for a while. Feelings you wished had resurfaced earlier. Maybe feelings that could have kept the relationship alive.

Had you reminded us about selling The Van when the camper's clicks and shakes were omnipresent, we probably would not have defended it one bit. But now that we were facing the end of our tenure with the car, those old feelings of attachment were flaring up again. Sure, it had broken down in Florida and caused us to sacrifice $2,500 to fix it. Yeah, its many malfunctions along the way had expedited the appearance of gray hairs on my head. And all right, the majority of our rhetoric directed toward the vehicle had been severely laden with animosity, as anger at The Van's unpredictable, head-scratching ways had at times been the only thing the four of us could agree on.

But fixing that frustrating car had in the end actually proven to be fruitful. Spending the $2,500 back in Tampa had resulted in a temporary decrease in Martinez Foundation funds, but—as Andrew and Frazier had projected—it had indeed proven only temporary. Our goal of intensifying our efforts to increase fund-raising had worked: having raised almost $5,000 for the organization since Florida, our donation total now approached $10,000. And although The Van's issues had regularly been the origin of arguments among us, the communal decision to invest in that car had restitched the many tears it had caused in the fabric of our childhood friendships; behind us were the trivial disputes we had experienced in places like Milwaukee and the far more intense ones like New York. Fixing The Van had been worth it. The Van itself had been worth it. And the following morning, we stumbled on the perfect way to celebrate the imminent end of our time with that old camper.

11:40 a.m. | The Following Day

In the northern part of the hilly city of San Francisco stands a twisting chunk of road called Lombard Street. With eight tight switchbacks crammed into a steep one-block stretch, Bay Area locals proudly promote the iconic lane as "the most crooked street in the world." At the top of the hill, a large sign advises drivers to use extreme caution if they attempt to descend the windy road. In large, impossible-to-miss block letters, the sign reads:

COMMERCIAL VEHICLES
TOUR BUSSES
VANS & CAMPERS
PROHIBITED

But of course we wanted to take our camper down the hill. Lombard Street loomed as a rite of passage for The Van—that last obstacle to clear, if you will. It wasn't *necessary* by any means, but to us, those postcard images of hairpin turns on a steep, urban street were symbolic in a way. If The Van could successfully navigate them, all lingering doubts would be wiped away; Lombard Street was to be the car's ceremonial sendoff into the sunset. We drove right up to the top of that hill as noon approached and tourists looked on, confused as to what a tie-dye shirt on wheels was doing on the street, let alone at the edge of the most crooked street in the world.

"Commercial vehicles, tour busses, vans, and campers prohibited," Michael voiced from the back as we passed the warning sign. "Well, a few of *those* sound familiar."

"Are we . . . are we *each* of those?" asked Frazier, who sat in the passenger seat.

"I think so. We're obviously a van—a camper van too—and we're on a tour, part of the point of which is to raise money for Edgar, as the wrap says, which makes us commercial."

"Four for four."

"I'm tuning you guys out," Andrew said from behind the wheel. "We're going down this thing, whether the sign wants us to or not." He patted the dashboard as if to give the car extra encouragement before whispering to it, "I got you."

And so The Van approached the tip of Lombard Street, pointed its nose down, and began its descent. From my vantage point in the back, I can still distinctly remember every single one of the eight switchbacks on that windy little road, each bringing back a memory about the camper that now attempted to navigate them.

Switchback 1: that first drive to Los Angeles, when we discovered that we knew simply nothing about the car we had purchased only thirteen days prior. After departing at 4:00 a.m., our ignorance of the vehicle's tendencies and dilapidated state became quickly apparent through the door popping open and the reception of a speeding ticket—both of which were soon compounded by the recognition of a malfunctioning cruise control, brake lights that never shut off, and a total lack of air-conditioning.

Switchback 2: the slow meander out from Los Angeles, which was the first moment when we experienced just how hot it could get in The Van. As the triple-digit heat of Southern California trickled into the car's air-condition-less confines, the sweat we rapidly accumulated forced us to pull off Interstate 10 to cool down in a Target of all places. With this stop also came a warning sign of many insufferable moments of heat to come. No matter where we decided to sleep—campgrounds, city street corners, freeway rest stops—and no matter the climate we found ourselves in—brisk mountains, loud cities, boiling southern deserts—it was *always* hot in The Van. Four (at times five) testosterone-filled boys crammed into two sleeping areas that together formed a space equal to a queen mattress didn't help.

Switchback 3: the drive through New Mexico, when we first heard that clicking sound—a noise that surely accompanies the other cacophonies one would find in the deepest circle of hell. The clicks were never too intrusive in their volume, but that's what made them deadly. Like Chinese drip torture, their subtle pervasiveness eventually worked its way into our own psyches and caused us to go stark-raving mad.

Switchback 4: the first time we attempted to fix those clicks. Cued by the luck of sitting next to an auto dealer in Saint Louis, we drove The Van to the outskirts of town, only to receive a new member of the group in the form of a gigantic spare tire that somehow stayed with us for thirty days in that small, cramped vehicle.

Switchback 5: the *second* time we attempted to fix the issue. The Van click, click, clicked all the way to the Toronto mechanic, pretended to be perfectly fine after Walt hopped in, and then click, click, clicked as soon as we departed. Oh, the profanity we discovered we were capable of releasing that afternoon.

Switchback 6: when those clicks finally got the best of us, as our attention to them had become overshadowed by our own rising arguments. That loud bang in Florida and the miserable hours that followed were both the low point of the trip and the climax of our summer's narrative arc.

Switchback 7: the decision we made to fix the car—a decision that was certainly questionable on all fronts, given our monetary status and The Van's fragility and uncertain future. But even with the vehicle's old age and decrepit condition, it was this decision that kept the trip—and, truly, our friendships—alive. We never fought after Tampa.

Switchback 8: the unfortunate reality that soon we would have to sell the car. Yet although it would not physically accompany us into the next section of our lives, it would still be there nonetheless—for I knew that every memory that Michael, Andrew, Frazier, and I would ever recount from that summer baseball journey would in one way or another incorporate The Van. A horror scene in the heart of Missouri, lit only by the car's headlamps and fireflies that clung to our windshield. A mid-drive driver change somewhere in Massachusetts in the middle of a torrential downpour. Darting across the Texas desert with the windows down, music loud, and the world suddenly feeling wide, wide open. And then, perhaps best of all, those countless midnight discussions over gas station cups of coffee, sunflower seeds, and what seemed to be endless road ahead. As I stated way back in the beginning of this book: our trip was the best of times, and it was the worst of times . . . but all those times involved The Van.

· · ·

I barely noticed when Andrew completed the final hairpin turn. My mind was so lost in our car's past that it failed to recognize its accomplishment in the present. But indeed, the old Volkswagen had now officially done it all. It had survived rainstorms, it had survived 108-degree heat, it had made it through

rush-hour Manhattan traffic, and it had now successfully ma-
neuvered the most crooked street in the world. The car bounded off Lombard Street like a happy dog, its tail wagging in pride
at what it had just completed—not over the past two minutes
but over the past two months.

MIDDLE OF THE NINTH
AT&T Park

ESPN

8:45 p.m. | Monday, August 1

A cold wind whipped up from the San Francisco Bay, stinging the upper levels of the ballpark and nosebleed seats where we, of course, were sitting. After attending games in the heat of Arizona, Texas, Florida, and Southern California, the upper-fifties Bay Area weather was a nasty shock to our systems. As we watched local Giant fans button up Tim Lincecum jerseys over hooded sweatshirts, we shivered, cursing the shorts and flip-flops we had unfortunately decided to wear.

AT&T Park sits on the edge of McCovey Cove, a small inlet that's part of the greater San Francisco Bay. The ballpark's proximity to the water gives it a unique feel—beyond the biting cold—for those lucky enough to enjoy a game there. And when you can't get *inside* the stadium, well, you can still enjoy it from just *outside* the stadium; at AT&T there exists an extremely niche fan club that chooses to experience Giants baseball from the bay itself, piling into kayaks and floating out into McCovey Cove just beyond the park's right field wall. They cannot see the field from here—but that's not their objective. With a radio in tow that broadcasts the game, these fans sit in their little boats and wait for one thing: a left-handed hitter to pull a home run. When this occurs, there's a good chance that the ball will sail completely out of the ballpark and plop into the water, where the kayakers wait like bloodthirsty sharks. This tradition peaked during the iconic years of Barry Bonds, who made McCovey Cove his own personal driving range with the number of dingers he slapped into it.

Within the stadium, a sign above the right field wall notes how many balls have been such "splash hits." This number has significantly declined since the golden age of the juiced-up power hitters of the mid-2000s: it showed fifty-seven splash hits when we visited the park, thirty-five of which had been hit by Bonds between 2000 and 2007. Only two had been hit thus far in 2011. Shoutout to steroids.

But although this kayaking element is certainly one of AT&T's defining characteristics, it is perhaps eclipsed by the park's investment in cuisine. Remember back in Los Angeles, when I described Dodger Stadium's "traditional" approach to food at the ballpark? Well, for everything they have opted to exclude from their vending stands, AT&T has made up for. From sourdough bread bowls holding local clam chowder to Caribbean barbecue sandwiches with pineapple salsa, Chinese food, Mexican food, and everything in between, you can find it all at AT&T Park. To combat my freezing state, I devoured a plate of hot crab cakes while I listened to Renel Brooks-Moon, the only female PA broadcaster in Major League Baseball, announce the starting lineups.

As had been the case in Oakland, that evening's game also passed at an alarming rate. I blinked, and suddenly the notes from the stadium's preprogrammed organ were being pumped through the speakers, signaling that it was time for fans to depart. We exited AT&T, walked past the kayakers disembarking from their float in McCovey Cove, and got back into The Van. With a touch of extra attention, I sat down in the driver's seat and gunned the engine. I then pulled out of the parking lot and pointed The Van's nose north to commence the final leg of its greatest adventure.

3:02 a.m.

We spent that evening at a rest stop somewhere across the state border, just on the other side of Oregon. I didn't fall asleep until 3:00 a.m. or so, preferring instead to lie on a picnic table near the parking spots. Staring at the stars, I wondered where I would be at this time next year. In a dormitory in Milwaukee, I guess. But that was physically.

6:25 a.m.

I awoke a few hours later on that picnic table to an unpleasant dew that had settled on my clothes and an even more unpleasant sound emerging from my left. Rolling over, I lifted my head and squinted to see a figure squatted about fifteen feet away from me, puking into a trash can. It was Michael.

"Wow," I said, sitting up straight. "Are you good?"

"Yeah," Frazier replied from The Van. He was leaning his head out of the rolled-down passenger window, watching to make sure Michael was OK through his guttural heaves. In the most casual of manners, he spoke again. "He's been doing that for an hour or so now. Something he ate." I turned to look again at Michael, who raised his hand just above the top of the trash can and gave a loose thumbs-up as he continued to vomit.

"Wow," I said again.

I got up from my damp wood bed and walked back toward The Van, rubbing my eyes to get rid of the little sleep that had gathered in them. I had left my contacts in that night and plucked them out in disgust. Michael then came back a couple of minutes later and grabbed a towel, wandering off toward the bathrooms in search of a shower. He mumbled something about seeing his mother the following day, and I chuckled. A glance at the dashboard clock showed that it was nearly 6:30 a.m. The first rays of the Oregon sun were just beginning to stretch across the lot, which was completely vacant apart from us.

Fifteen minutes passed before another car pulled into the rest stop. It was a modern red station wagon that looked to be in pristine condition, with Connecticut plates and one of those Thule storage compartments strapped to its upper racks. I watched as the car paused near the entrance to the lot before pulling into the spot directly next to The Van. This felt weird, seeing as there were easily fifty other places they could have chosen. The driver's door opened and a young man got out. Through my cloudy vision, he looked to be just a few years older than us, twenty-two or so, maybe.

"No way," he said, leaning against the hood of the car. "You guys are doing this too?"

"Sorry?" I replied, trying to find my glasses while simultaneously attempting to pat down the cowlicks that ravaged my early-morning hair.

"The ballparks," the guy responded, nodding his head at the side of The Van and referencing its design. "You're doing this too?"

"Yep." It took me a couple of seconds to grasp exactly what he had said. "Wait . . . *you* guys are as well?"

"Yep!"

Andrew jumped into the conversation, swinging down from the top platform in The Van. "What!" he said. "We're actually almost done—on our way back home to Seattle now!"

"Nice. We were just there. Heading down to San Francisco."

"Trading places! I love it."

"Sure thing."

"What's been your favorite park thus far?"

The man shrugged his shoulders, as if indifferent to the ones they had seen. "Not sure," he said, casually. "Who you working for?"

"Sorry?"

"This trip—the ballparks. Who are you doing it for?"

"Uh . . ." Andrew struggled for words as I continued to look for my glasses. "I mean, for us? I guess, well, we've been raising awareness and donations for the Martinez Foundation along the way, so . . ." He reached into the glove box and removed a few of the pamphlets we handed out before games.

"Are they paying you?"

"No? Uh, I mean, we're raising money . . . yeah . . . but we're donating it when we get back." A few seconds passed as he put two and two together. "Are . . . are you guys working for someone?"

It was then that I found my glasses and put them on. Looking through the window of The Van, I immediately got a better feel for the station wagon and the man who was leaning so casually against its hood. Even at 6:45 a.m., his hair was well combed and perfect, and he looked to have gotten good sleep the night before. Meanwhile, the trunk of the car was packed with technical equipment: laptops, camera bags, tripods, and three or four microphones of different shapes and sizes. Two other guys in their early twenties sat in the car as well. They also had perfect hair and seemed well rested, which annoyed me, as it all felt far too cleaned up for life on the road. It was certainly a stark contrast to how we surely appeared or at least felt: Michael had just been puking and was now using a truck stop facility to shower while I had just slept on a picnic table and looked like Sid Vicious in my current state of bedhead.

"Yeah," the asshole said. He then dropped a bomb on us. "We're doing ours for ESPN."

. . .

Up until that moment, we had thought that our trip, our summer baseball odyssey, was completely unique. We had grown proud of our accomplishment in its planning and execution; sure, people had done this before (we had read a few brief recounts of similar journeys from years past), but nobody had completed it in such a short amount of time—let alone at such a young age. Our journey had seemed so unparalleled that America's ballparks had begun to feel like *ours*. Ours to string together in a chaotically organized way, ours to experience every other night, ours from which to create memories that would certainly last forever. We had cherished the distinctive place we held in those couple of months on the road; the individuality of the trip was part of what glued it together. We thought we were the only ones doing this—we *knew* we were the only ones doing this.

But in a split second and the mention of four letters, that all came crashing down to a well-produced reality. As you are surely well aware, ESPN is the mecca of all television stations devoted to covering sports. Even with rivals NBC and Fox now developing their own twenty-four-hour sports channels, the Entertainment and Sports Programming Network has always been the leader of the pack. It has six main stations (ESPN, ESPN2, ESPN Classic, ESPNews, ESPN Deportes, and ESPNU), along with numerous other affiliates (SEC Network, Longhorn Network, and so on), and therefore has its hand in every single athletic pie imaginable. Reporters from ESPN are normally the first on the scene for any big game, or they are the ones breaking any story that has to do with sports. And there we were, thinking that our own story was surely one of the few that would slip by them this year, keeping it reserved for *us*. But no. Others were doing the exact same thing, with ESPN—and thus the rest of the world—watching them do it.

After muttering some form of good-bye, the handsome young man with the well-combed hair got back into the nice station wagon and drove away, leaving the four of us and our patchwork car in a small cloud of exhaust behind them. They hadn't even used the bathrooms in the rest stop; they had just pulled in, said a few words, and pulled out. Poof, gone.

A wind picked up and ripped a Martinez Foundation pamphlet out of Andrew's hand. It fluttered across the parking lot, bouncing along the cracked pavement like a tumbleweed. Michael, who had popped out from the restroom a few minutes earlier and watched the final bits of the conversation from afar, returned to The Van.

"Who were those guys?" he asked. Nobody answered.

BOTTOM OF THE NINTH
Safeco Field

HOME

12:30 p.m. | Wednesday, August 3

Simply put, no happiness was to be found for the rest of that day. The ESPN guys had completely wiped out our confidence and pride, and the remainder of August 2—the penultimate day of our trip—was unfortunately stained as an awful one. Yet as the sun rose the following morning, the four of us pledged to temporarily forget about our ballpark counterparts. They would surely continue to irk us, but not today. Today we were going home.

Home is a word that carries a special meaning when referenced in sports. The team that plays in its own stadium is the *home* team; the locals who support this team give them a *home* field advantage; high schools and colleges gather for the biggest games of the year at their *home*comings.

But in baseball, *home* carries even more weight than a simple location advantage and support system. *Home* is the goal of the game, the objective that the two sides are trying to accomplish more than the other one. The team that crosses home the most in a baseball game wins. Hitting a *home*run, rounding third and heading *home,* root-root-root for the *home* team—the word is littered across the vernacular of America's pastime.

Safeco Field was our home stadium, and we felt as if we had just rounded the bases of the United States and safely crossed home as we sat in the left field bleachers, soaking up the

Wednesday afternoon sun while watching a matinee game against the Oakland Athletics. It felt right to use a possessive tone when referencing the ballpark. As fans, Safeco Field was as much ours as it was the Mariners', in my opinion. And despite now being called T-Mobile Park, it still is.

Our ballpark sits in the southern part of downtown Seattle, about three blocks inland from the water. Its dark-green seats are the shade of the classic Pacific Northwest evergreen trees that shroud the city's many hills and fill the state's many forests. Sitting on the first-base side of the stadium, fans are treated to views of Seattle's skyscrapers that tower above the ballpark's retractable roof on days when the rain holds out. Meanwhile, those seated in right field or wandering the upper-deck concourse can pause to take in the stunning vistas of Emerald Bay, watching as the ferries reflect the blue water during afternoon games and shimmer in the final rays of daylight during night games, as the sun sets behind the Olympic Mountains off in the distance.

A special moment had occurred just before that game began. Roughly three days prior, we had made contact with a person at the Martinez Foundation, notifying them that we would be wrapping up our journey on August 3 and that we would like to present them with a check for the donations we had accumulated. They told us a representative would gladly meet us before the game to accept the check and to thank us for our efforts.

That "representative" wound up being none other than Edgar Martinez himself. Our childish mouths fell open as we came face-to-face with the man who all Seattleites know best as either "Papi" or "Gar." He opened his massive arms to give us a hug and to thank us for the work we had done for his organization—as well as simply promoting baseball.

"Whether you know it or not," Martinez said, speaking slowly through his thick accent, "you four have advertised not only for the Martinez Foundation but for the sport of baseball itself." I don't know if I've ever blushed more.

If you are a Mariners fan, Edgar Martinez automatically holds a large place in the baseball-loving portion of your heart—not because he is a recent Hall of Fame inductee (although that certainly helps), but because he is a key reason why baseball still exists in the city of Seattle. ESPN senior writer David Schoenfield puts it best: "To understand the love and affection longtime Mariners fans have for Martinez . . . You must understand 1995 and what happened after."[32] For those unfamiliar, I'll do my best to give you an idea.

As the 1995 season turned into August and began its final stretch of play, the Mariners as a team were two games below .500. As a franchise, they were facing potential termination. After nineteen years of existence, Seattle had put together only one winning season and was yet to even come close to making the playoffs. The team's consistently bad performance resulted in few wanting to travel to the ugly Kingdome to watch a game—the stadium was so bad, tiles fell from the ceiling at one point[33]—which in turn meant that revenue was down and the Mariners were up for relocation. With cities like Tampa waiting eagerly in the wings for a team, the future of baseball in Seattle essentially came down to whether or not it could agree on funding for a new ballpark. A public vote was held, but it failed. Suddenly, it was announced that the city had thirty days to agree on a new package, or the M's would more than likely be moved to Florida.[34] Just three weeks prior, the team had been a dozen games out of the playoffs, and support was nowhere to be seen.

Then out of nowhere, a comeback occurred. Led by the trio of Ken Griffey Jr., Randy Johnson, and Edgar, the Seattle ball club began to string together winning streaks and, to everyone's disbelief, made the playoffs for the first time in franchise history. In the shadow of the failed public vote, the fans began to flock to the ballpark once again—and a week later, the M's were locked in extra innings against the New York Yankees in the rubber match of the Divisional Series. With Seattle down 5–4 entering the bottom of the eleventh, every person in the (now sold-out) creaky old Kingdome knew what was at stake: the team had done a lot to rekindle interest in committing to a new ballpark, but taking this game (and thus winning the ALDS) would surely solidify this commitment and save baseball in Seattle.

It was then that Edgar Martinez delivered the most memorable moment in Mariners history. The calm designated hitter stepped up to the plate with runners on first and third and, with the eyes of the entire city watching and the fate of its baseball team in his hands, lined a shot down the left field line. The hit, unanimously referenced in the Pacific Northwest as just "The Double," scored both runners, advancing the Mariners into the Championship Series and preserving them as *Seattle's* team. The late Dave Niehaus's call of the play still triggers chills down the spine of anybody who watches it: *"It just continues—my oh my."*

I was three years old when this happened. It was the spark that ignited my love of baseball and eternal investment in the local team. And even though we had not yet met at that early age, I know that The Double had the same effect on Michael, Andrew, and Frazier. So with Papi being the reason that the four of us even had a team to unite around in the first place, it was needless to say a strange and incredible feeling to have our Mariners idol thank *us* for our performance. I'll never forget it.

2:55 p.m.

As the sun began to drift beyond the third-base bleachers and the afternoon moved on, the game extended into the late innings and our summer of nomadic baseball bliss drew to a close. The Mariners pulled out a win against Oakland that day, topping the A's 7–4 and wrapping up our thirtieth ballpark in victorious nature. Yet even when the game ended and the majority of the fans began to file out of the stadium, not one of us budged. To stand up was to leave, and to leave was to declare the trip over. The next steps would be cleaning The Van, selling The Van, and then moving away from Seattle. It was something that clearly had to be done—but we were not ready for it. Not quite yet.

"We'll see each other," Michael said. I turned to look at him. His head was facing forward, looking not at us but at the green ball field, which was now vacant save for a few groundskeepers raking the dirt of the basepaths. Feeling my gaze, he then twisted his head and made eye contact with each of us. "After this," he continued, nodding slowly, "we'll still see each other. I know it."

"I know it too," Andrew chimed in, supporting the point Michael was trying to make. "There's no way we can't." He looked at me. "I know what's coming is intimidating, with us going our separate ways and all. But too much happened this summer for us to just drift apart as friends." He then turned his face back in the direction of home plate, and I watched as his eyes read the white letters of *Welcome to Safeco Field* that stared back at us from the press box. "Yeah, those ESPN guys were a total downer, but they were sponsored, man. They had money helping them at all times, nice equipment, and a nice car. I know we said we wouldn't talk about them today, but the point I'm trying to make is, well . . . they really didn't do what we did. Because people don't just *do* what we did." He paused again before continuing. "We've shared too many memories these past couple of months to simply have the four of us fade away as friends 'cause we're moving to different places. We've shared too many stories with The Van, too many miles in super hot weather, too many sleepless nights at freeway rest stops, and too many—"

"Too many ballparks."

It was Frazier who said it. Andrew's eyes didn't move from their position. Instead, they remained locked on the press box, glazing over the white letters that welcomed us back to our home. Then slowly, his head nodded and a smile—very small but definite nonetheless—crept into the corners of his mouth.

"Yeah," he said. "We've shared too many ballparks."

Eight Years Later

Despite this declaration, our friendships did indeed fade. Not completely but significantly. It has now been eight years since we returned to Seattle and sold The Van, and I regret to inform you that I rarely speak with Michael, Frazier, or Andrew these days. The cause of this is not out of any sort of antipathy or falling-out—no, our dispersion has simply been a product of life being what it is. After departing for college and beyond, we were each drawn in different directions and pursued various paths, with each of us following what was right for himself. And although we always assumed they would, unfortunately none of our paths ended up paralleling each other. I moved to Washington, DC, after graduating, and now live 2,748 miles from the entrance to Safeco Field—which isn't even called Safeco Field anymore. Andrew remained in Oregon while Frazier spent that year in Peru and then attended undergrad in Illinois before departing yet again for distant shores—this time in India. Michael returned from college in California and took a job in Seattle. He's married now.

About three weeks after we sold the old camper, I was watching *Sunday Night Baseball* on ESPN when an advertisement came on that featured the young men in the red station wagon who had spoken to us in that Oregon rest stop. The ad was professionally produced and showed those guys changing the numbers of the scoreboard at Fenway and swimming in the pool at Chase Field and interviewing players and eating ballpark hot dogs and playing catch in front of different stadiums. Between these moments, it showed them having fun—all the fun we had, but without any of the stress. To any who saw their piece, it probably looked as if those guys in the red station wagon had just experienced the summer that baseball lovers dream of. The summer I thought I was going to have.

At the end, however, a brief messaged popped on the screen: "This was brought to you by Holiday Inn, the official hotel of baseball road trips." I smiled slightly, amused at the thought that those guys slept in comfortable hotels for the entirety of their cross-country journey. What would that have been like?

No, our summer had *not* been the dream summer I had initially thought it would be, the one portrayed by that ninety-second advertisement on ESPN. Not at all. But I wouldn't have traded it for anything. Over the course of those stressful, unglamorous, and at times awful 14,171 miles, I experienced very few moments of comfort or relaxation—but I also learned something. However, as an eighteen-year-old, I wasn't quite sure what that *something* was yet. As many feel after concluding a long journey, I believed that what I had experienced on the road had been educational and *meaningful*—but what it had taught me and what it had meant didn't set in right away. Eight years later, I think I've finally it pieced together.

That fifty-three-day journey taught me the value of childhood friendships, and *re*telling it has taught me that they, like everything else, do not last forever. At least, not in the same facet that you grow up thinking they will. Life is brief, and personal connections are even briefer. What matters is what you do with the people who are close to you here and now. And the four of us did that.

Often my mind clicks back to the first time I saw New York City as it emerged from the early-morning darkness and the thoughts that were going through my head at that moment. Are friendships indeed a thing of geographic convenience? Through writing this collection of memories from our 2011 baseball trip, I have come to decide that yes, they are—and at the same time, no, they aren't.

The fact that I now speak only two or three times a year with the others who joined me on that journey shows that geographic proximity is indeed needed to maintain strong friendships. Since I moved away from Seattle, the people I became closest with were the ones who were physically closest to *me*. The people in your life shift as the location of your life shifts. Michael Gonzalez, Frazier Moore, and Andrew Clement drifted slowly into states of sporadic communication, turning what was once every day into what is now every few months. As I stated in the introduction, the four of us still bemoan the Mariners' many losing streaks—but it's not something we do together anymore. And that's fine. Because at the same time, those guys will forever occupy a spot in my life that's reserved for my best of friends. They're not the only ones there; others have since filled in as the closest and most prominent people in my life. But they're there. And that's what matters, for it shows that a lack of regular contact cannot take away from childhood memories or the miles we rolled and the things we experienced together in that summer of baseball. I can call up any of them at anytime, and we can pick up a conversation as if we were eighteen—if not eight—years old again. Andrew's words at Safeco

Field, although slightly altered from their original meaning, still ring true: we saw too many ballparks for any sort of distance to get in the way of our *true* connections. Those friendships are still some of the most meaningful ones I will ever know, and although we are now each doing our proverbial "own thing," we will always have those memories in our collective bank of reference and experience. We're in different places now, but we'll always have Joshua Tree, Benton City, and El Paso. We spend time with different people now, but we'll always have Walt, Max, and Brandon. And we'll always have The Van.

But this story was not just about us. Although I learned a lot traveling it—and perhaps even more writing it—telling the story of our peregrination through America and its pastime was also about showing that such a feat is indeed *possible*. Thus, the final word of this recounting turns to you, reader. If you consider yourself a baseball fan, then I'll bet you have an itch to see a few other ballparks—if not all other ballparks. But what you might not realize is that you're also itching for the incredible journey that accompanies such an endeavor.

So go find that journey. Go find the bits of this country that you don't even know exist. Go find stories that you will tell for the rest of your life. Grab a friend (or three) and go find how strong and meaningful those relationships are, both in the present and moving into the future. Go find yourself.

Go find baseball.

BOX SCORE

Ballpark	Date	Opponent	Result	Miles	Odometer
Angel Stadium	June 12	Royals	L 0–9	1,215	1,215
Dodger Stadium	June 13	Reds	L 4–6	52	1,267
Chase Field	June 15	Giants	L 2–5	416	1,683
Coors Field	June 17	Tigers	W 13–6	861	2,544
Target Field	June 18	Padres	W 1–0	941	3,485
Wrigley Field	June 19	Yankees	L 4–10	415	3,900
Miller Park	June 20	Rays	L 4–8	91	3,991
US Cellular Field	June 21	Cubs	W 3–2	104	4,095
Busch Stadium	June 22	Phillies	L 0–4	327	4,422
Kauffman Stadium	June 23	D-Backs	L 3–5	245	4,667
Comerica Park	June 24	D-Backs	L 6–7	878	5,545
PNC Park	June 25	Red Sox	W 6–4	324	5,869
Rogers Centre	June 27	Pirates	L 6–7	374	6,243
Yankee Stadium	June 29	Brewers	W 5–3	558	6,801
Citizens Bank Park	June 30	Red Sox	L 2–5	130	6,931
Citi Field	July 1	Yankees	L 1–5	131	7,062
Fenway Park	July 4	Blue Jays	L 7–9	257	7,319
Nationals Park	July 6	Cubs	W 5–4	471	7,790
Progressive Field	July 7	Blue Jays	W 5–4	403	8,193
Camden Yards	July 14	Indians	L 4–8	416	8,609
Great American	July 15	Cardinals	W 6–5	539	9,148
Turner Field	July 16	Nationals	L 2–5	498	9,646
Tropicana Field	July 18	Yankees	L 0–4	448	10,094
Minute Maid Park	July 20	Nationals	W 3–2	1,043	11,137
Rangers Ballpark	July 22	Blue Jays	W 12–2	273	11,410
Sun Life Stadium	July 23	Mets	W 8–5	0	11,410
Petco Park	July 26	D-Backs	L 1–6	1,398	12,808
Oakland Coliseum	July 29	Twins	L 5–9	517	13,325
AT&T Park	August 1	D-Backs	L 2–5	18	13,343
Safeco Field	August 3	Athletics	W 7–4	828	14,171

POST-GAME INTERVIEW

As the dedication states, this book is based on a true story. In the summer of 2011, my three best friends from childhood—Kellan Larson, Kendal Young, Jack Wilson—and I indeed took off in a colorful, rickety old 1999 Volkswagen Eurovan to try and see a game in every Major League ballpark. Giving ourselves the cheesy title of the "Seattle Ballpark Boys," we created and followed a demanding itinerary based on that year's MLB schedule—the exact same itinerary that Andrew, Michael, Frazier, and I attempt to keep up with in *Touch 'em All.*

In reality, the four of us spent significantly more time interacting with media than our characters do in the text. The story of four high school graduates capping off their teenage years with a trip through America's Pastime was one that sparked the interest of not just sponsors but numerous news outlets and sports stations across the country, and we were regularly asked to pop into studios or broadcasting booths to chat about what we were trying to accomplish. While at first we were hesitant about this publicity—this trip was supposed to be about us, not about advertising—we soon recognized that these interviews were monumental in helping our fundraising efforts for the Martinez Foundation, and therefore continued. (Hearing journalists commend our trip also increased our confidence that what we were doing was completely unique . . . which in turn made the clash with the ESPN crew even more devastating).

TOP: *The Van.* MIDDLE: *Frazier and me at Miller Park; at Joshua Tree.* BOTTOM: *Andrew (Kellan), Frazier (Jack—his hair was actually shorter back then; it has since grown), myself, and Michael (Kendal) at Wrigley Field.*

TOP: *Brandon (Ruben), Frazier, Michael, and Andrew in Cincinnati.*
MIDDLE: *sleeping inside The Van; standing outside The Van.*
BOTTOM: *The Van makes its way down Lombard Street.*

Meanwhile, this exposure also created a grapevine of communication that wove its way through our extended networks and alerted relatives, friends, friends-of-friends, and friends-of-friends-of-friends of what we were up to. Occasionally, these people would reach out and offer us beds to sleep in, showers to take, and even home cooked meals to eat along the way. If you believe humans are inherently evil, take a trip like this: we had never met the majority of these people, and yet they opened their doors to us as if we were long-time friends. Despite accepting these invitations gratefully when they were extended, we still spent far too many uncomfortable nights in The Van, sleeping in places like freeway rest stops and Walmart parking lots . . . and our showers remained way too few and far between.

As is the case in almost any memoir, there are a few instances in *Touch 'em All* where a character's relationship to us was slightly altered, or an event was moved to a location other than where it originally took place. However, every person that appears or incident that occurs in this book is rooted in fact. Walt, for instance, was not our Toronto mechanic, but instead a distant connection of Kellan's mother (her old friend's college roommate, I believe)—but he indeed led us to a mechanic, joined us for the Blue Jays game, and taught us the tricks of hosting underground poker parties. Similarly, the scene with the pizza shop owner and her daughter actually happened in the small town of Ashley, Indiana (not Rutland, Ohio)—but we were indeed encouraged to "choose optimism" from this warm and smiling duo.

As stated in the introduction, this book shouldn't be taken as a guidebook to America's ballparks. Some stadiums have obviously gone through changes since we saw them in 2011, and I'm sure a few of our observations don't carry the same weight today as they did eight years ago. But that doesn't mean that the atmosphere in each isn't still fascinating—heck, the respective uniqueness of each ballpark has probably only increased since we were there.

There are three moments in *Touch 'em All* that differ significantly from our 2011 trip. First, the late night excursion Andrew (Kellan) and I took in Detroit actually led us past a decaying hospital building that we popped our heads into; Michigan Central Station was much further down the road, inaccessible at that moment but still there for us to gaze upon and ponder over. Second, my respite from the trip lasted longer than the handful of days my character is absent in the text. The stresses of travel, weight of homesickness, fear of the future, and irritation I felt at the others pushed me into taking a ten-day break, and I consequentially missed a few more ballparks than just Progressive Field. But the biggest difference is the character of Brandon. The free-flowing, agenda-lacking college student was actually Ruben Palmer, another friend of ours growing up who, upon hearing of our many disputes and my resulting hiatus, hopped a flight to Baltimore and joined us all the way to San Diego. (There were actually five of us who made that trek on Interstate 10—oh, how cramped it was in The Van). However, like the impact Detroit offered and the reasons for my departure, Brandon, too, is based in fact: Ruben supplied the exact same breath of fresh air and dose of hard perspective that his character provides in the text. And I maintain that his temporary addition was the best thing that happened to the trip.

At every ballpark, we purchased two things. The first was an item unique to the stadium we were at—something that could not be found at another team store. (An example: we could buy an Orioles hat or T-shirt almost anywhere, but only at Camden Yards could we buy a mini Orioles construction helmet). After purchase, these items were then placed on our dashboard, creating a mosaic of MLB trinkets that slowly grew as our mileage ticked upward. The second was a mini baseball bat with every team's logo on the barrel. This souvenir is popular, small, and fairly cheap—but one that we knew each ballpark would offer. The collection of mini-bats (below) remains intact today, a small symbol of the passion we hold for America's baseball teams and baseball stadiums.

And yet despite this passion, Kendal, Kellan, Ruben, Jack, and I grew up baseball fans in a world where the sport is slipping in popularity. It's no secret that today's America favors hard-hitting, fast-paced competitions above its cerebral, methodic pastime. The NFL dominates the headlines (for both sport and scandal) and more and more high schoolers prefer to swing lacrosse sticks than Louisville Sluggers these days. Those who question baseball say it's boring, and that there are too many games in a season—to which I respond by saying it isn't a boring sport, it's a thinking sport, and grinding through 162+ games a year make baseball fans the most committed of any out there. Perhaps it's foolish for me to think that the current and future generations will recognize this and soon flock back to baseball . . . but I'd like to think that our 2011 trip—and this book—have helped. It's a beautiful sport.

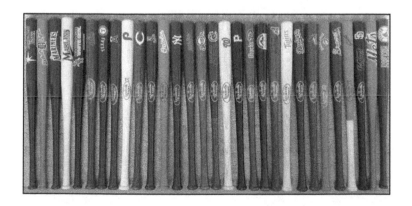

GAME NOTES

[1] Landers, Chris. "15 Years Ago, the Angels' Rally Monkey Was Born

[2] "MLB Fans Predicted to Eat More Than 19 Million Hot Dogs in 2018." National Hot Dog and Sausage Council. March 28, 2018. http://hot-dog.org/press/MLB-Fans-Predicted-to-Eat-More-than-19-Million-Hot-Dogs-in-2018.

[3] Shaw, Wilder. "The 22 Best Things to Eat at Dodger Stadium." *Thrillist: Los Angeles.* April 17, 2017. www.thrillist.com/eat/los-angeles/best-dodger-stadium-food#.

[4] Barber, Glen. "Dinger, the Rockies' Purple Prehistoric Mascot." *Denver Post.* June 30, 2016. www.denverpost.com/2016/06/30/dinger-the-rockies-purple-prehistoric-mascot-photos.

[5] Ibid.

[6] "Best Unique Things at Target Field." CBS Minnesota. November 6, 2010. https://minnesota.cbslocal.com/top-lists/unique-things-at-target-field.

[7] "Professional-NBA Basketball Court Dimensions." Sportsknowhow.com. 2018. www.sportsknowhow.com/basketball/dimensions/nba-basketball-court-dimensions.html.

[8] Gelman, Joey. "Cubs World Series Celebration Ranks as 7th Largest Gathering in Human History." WGN Radio. November 5, 2016. https://wgnradio.com/2016/11/05/cubs-worlds-series-celebration-ranks-as-7th-largest-gathering-in-human-history.

[9] "Wrigley Field History." MLB.com. 2018. www.mlb.com/cubs/ballpark/information/history.

[10] Vettel, Phil. "The Cubs Get Lights at Wrigley Field." *Chicago Tribune.* January 3, 2008. www.chicagotribune.com/news/nationworld/politics/chi-chicagodays-wrigleylights-story-story.html.

[11] Sullivan, Paul. "Wrigley Field Video Board Ready for its Close-Up." *Chicago Tribune.* April 3, 2015. https://www.chicagotribune.com/sports/baseball/cubs/chi-wrigley-field-videoboard-ready-for-its-closeup-20150403-story.html

12 "The Bears at Wrigley Field." *Chicago Tribune*. November 18, 2010. www.chicagotribune.com/sports/chi-101118-bears-at-wrigley-field-pictures-photogallery.html.

13 Kot, Greg. "Shows That Shook Wrigley All Night Long." *Chicago Tribune*. April 1, 2014. www.chicagotribune.com/entertainment/ct-xpm-2014-04-01-ct-ent-0402-wrigley-concerts-20140401-story.html.

14 Ibid.

15 Zorn, Eric. "Steve Goodman Rests in Little Pieces at Wrigley Field. Why Not Other Fans?" *Chicago Tribune*. October 2, 2007. http://blogs.chicagotribune.com/news_columnists_ezorn/2007/10/steve-goodman-r.html.

16 Kot. "Shows That Shook Wrigley All Night Long."

17 Epplin, Luke. "The Problem with Remembering Stan Musial as Baseball's 'Perfect Knight.'" *The Atlantic*. January 24, 2013. www.theatlantic.com/entertainment/archive/2013/01/the-problem-with-remembering-stan-musial-as-baseballs-perfect-knight/272489.

18 Binelli, Mark. "How Detroit Became the World Capital of Staring at Abandoned Old Buildings." *New York Times*. November 9, 2012. www.nytimes.com/2012/11/11/magazine/how-detroit-became-the-world-capital-of-staring-at-abandoned-old-buildings.html.

19 "Ballpark and Stadium Comparisons." Ballparksofbaseball.com. 2018. www.ballparksofbaseball.com/comparisons.

20 "NFL Attendance—2018." ESPN. 2018. http://www.espn.com/nfl/attendance.

21 "Premier League 2017/2018 Attendance." Worldfootball.net. 2018. https://www.worldfootball.net/attendance/eng-premier-league-2017-2018/1/.

22 Howard, Johnette. "Why Beloved, Quirky Home Run Apple Is a Perfect Symbol for Mets." ESPN. October 29, 2015. www.espn.com/mlb/playoffs2015/story/_/id/13992952/why-beloved-quirky-home-run-apple-perfect-symbol-new-york-mets.

23 Eskenazi, Gerald. "Baseball Statistics: How Much Is Enough?" *New York Times*. April 30, 1990. www.nytimes.com/1990/04/30/sports/baseball-statistics-how-much-is-enough.html.

24 Berka, T. J. "When Fandom Goes Bad: Most Miserable Fanbases in Pro Sports." ESPN. December 21, 2018.

www.espn.com.au/nfl/story/_/id/24367000/the-top-25-most-miserable-fan-bases-professional-sports.

[25] Forgrave, Reid. "MLB's Most Important Stadium Turns 20." Fox Sports. April 10, 2012. www.foxsports.com/mlb/story/camden-yards-baltimore-orioles-ballpark-changed-baseball-fan-experience-turns-20-end-of-multipurpose-stadiums-041012.

[26] Eggener, Keith. "The Demolition and Afterlife of Baltimore Memorial Stadium." *Places Journal*. October 2012. https://placesjournal.org/article/the-demolition-and-afterlife-of-baltimore-memorial-stadium/?cn-reloaded=1.

[27] Encina, Eduardo A. "So Near and Yet so Far: Camden Yards Warehouse an Inviting Target, Just Not Within Striking Distance." *Baltimore Sun*. July 10, 2017. www.baltimoresun.com/sports/orioles/blog/bs-sp-orioles-camden-yards-warehouse-0711-story.html.

[28] Reuters. "Baseball; Astros' Park Is Minute Maid." *New York Times*. June 6, 2002. www.nytimes.com/2002/06/06/sports/baseball-astros-park-is-minute-maid.html.

[29] Felton, Priscilla. "Merle Haggard's Record for Buying the Largest Round Busted." *Wine and Spirits*. June 16, 2016. www.wineandspirits.com/2016/06/16/merle-haggards-record-for-buying-the-largest-round-busted.

[30] Newcomb, Tim. "Ballpark Quirks: Petco Park's Historic Western Metal Supply Co. Building." *Sports Illustrated*. July 21, 2014. www.si.com/mlb/2014/07/21/ballpark-quirks-san-diego-petco-park-western-metal-supply-company.

[31] "MLB Team Payroll Tracker." Spotrac. 2018. www.spotrac.com/mlb/payroll.

[32] Schoenfield, David. "Edgar's Hall of Fame moment is Seattle's Hall of Fame moment." *ESPN*. January 23, 2019. http://www.espn.com/mlb/story/_/id/25770826/mlb-edgar-martinez-hall-fame-moment-seattle-hall-fame-moment.

[33] Condotta, Bob. "Ten years after the Kingdome tiles fell." *Seattle Times*. July 19, 2004. http://old.seattletimes.com/html/sports/2001982925_tile19x.html.

[34] Schoenfield. "Edgar's Hall of Fame moment."

ABOUT THE AUTHOR

Travis Parker Smith is a twenty-something millennial living, working, and writing in Washington, DC. While his primary work points him in the direction of European travel, culture, politics, and diplomacy, his passion beyond the office walls is baseball: Travis remains and shall forever remain a die-hard fan of the Seattle Mariners . . . which, as stated in the beginning of this book, means he dies a lot.

9 781733 583701